Simulation Validation
A Confidence
Assessment Methodology

Simulation Validation
A Confidence
Assessment Methodology

Peter L. Knepell
Deborah C. Arangno

IEEE Computer Society Press
Los Alamitos, California

Washington • Brussels • Tokyo

IEEE COMPUTER SOCIETY PRESS MONOGRAPH

Library of Congress Cataloging-in-Publication Data

Knepell, Peter L.
    Simulation validation: a confidence assessment methodology /
Peter L. Knepell and Deborah C. Arangno.
        p.   cm. — (IEEE Computer Society Press monograph)
    Includes bibliographical references and index.
    ISBN 0-8186-3512-6.
        1. Computer simulation.   I. Arangno, Deborah C.   II. Title.   III. Series.
QA76.9.C65K63   1993
003 ' .3—dc20   92-36123
                                                                                        CIP

Published by the
IEEE Computer Society Press
10662 Los Vaqueros Circle
P.O. Box 3014
Los Alamitos, CA 90720-1264

IEEE Computer Society Press Order Number 3512
Library of Congress Number 92-36123
ISBN 0-8186-3512-6

Additional copies can be ordered from

IEEE Computer Society Press	IEEE Service Center	IEEE Computer Society	IEEE Computer Society
Customer Service Center	445 Hoes Lane	13, avenue de l'Aquilon	Ooshima Building
10662 Los Vaqueros Circle	P.O. Box 1331	B-1200 Brussels	2-19-1 Minami-Aoyama
P.O. Box 3014	Piscataway, NJ 08855-1331	BELGIUM	Minato-ku, Tokyo 107
Los Alamitos, CA 90720-1264	Tel: (908) 981-1393	Tel: +32-2-770-2198	JAPAN
Tel: (714) 821-8380	Fax: (908) 981-9667	Fax: +32-2-770-8505	Tel: +81-3-3408-3118
Fax: (714) 821-4641	mis.custserv@computer.org	euro.ofc@computer.org	Fax: +81-3-3408-3553
Email: cs.books@computer.org			tokyo.ofc@computer.org

Technical Editor: Uma Gupta
Production Editor: Robert Werner
Copy Editor: David Sims
Original cover artwork by Louis Arangno
Cover production: Joe Daigle

99 98 97 96   5   4   3   2

The Institute of Electrical and Electronics Engineers, Inc.

Dedication

To my wife Roz and my children Joe and Ruth,
for their love, humor, and inspiration.

Peter L. Knepell

To Lorraine, Pamela, Andrea, Allen, and Amanda,
but especially to our parents, Louis and Maria,
who inspire us in all our endeavors.

Deborah C. Arangno

Preface

This book is concerned with assuring that simulations are appropriate representations of the real-world systems being studied. After following the *methodology* provided in this book, one can determine the degree of *confidence* that can be placed in the behavior and outputs of the simulation. The words methodology and confidence are italicized to stress their importance in the design of this book. This is a guide that can be applied to a variety of simulations. It is systematic, procedural, and practical. We will differentiate between the assessment of a simulation tool and the verification and validation of general software products. Accordingly, we break from the strict V&V terminology and will refer to the confidence assessment of a simulation.

While we are concerned about good software development and quality assurance practices, we do not explicitly cover these topics. There are many excellent references on these subjects. In general, we also do not explicitly cover the design, development, or application of simulations. However, cognizance of the assessment methodology will mitigate risks involved with these areas.

Who can use this book?

This book is written for several audiences, including technicians and managers engaged in industry or government. It should also appeal to computer science, operations research, and operations management students and educators. The methods addressed here are presented primarily with large-scale simulation models in mind, but can be useful for the validation of smaller-scale models as well. We tried to bridge the gap between academic and pragmatic concepts on simulation assessment. Thus, this book is written to be used in three ways.

- *A guide for practicing professionals who are concerned with the credibility of their simulation models.* They can establish methodologies and procedures to perform confidence assessments that will suit their needs.

- *A reference book and road map for software developers and quality assurance experts.* Our thorough listing of assessment procedures is a handy guide to aid in the unit, integration, and system testing of new or revised software. An understanding of our process will provide a vision of how to continuously assess the simulation tools throughout the software development life cycle.

- *A reference for simulation methodology and software engineering courses offered at the undergraduate or graduate levels.* Students should benefit from the structured approach provided in this monograph. Some experience with statistics will provide useful insights to the assessment methodology.

This book is divided into three blocks: concepts, methodologies, and special topics. We annotated each chapter heading with a box that notes the block for that chapter, a capsule comment on the content, and a recommendation on the audience that would be most interested in the contents.

Practical experience

The practical aspects of this book are based on our experience assessing large-scale simulations. The models we examined in the past had a variety of applications including discrete-event simulations of complex systems; specialized tool sets to generate data for other simulations; and simulations that supported interactive gaming involving human players. Some models had hundreds of modules, simulating the interaction of thousands of entities. Obviously, these assessments required a team effort and considerable planning, which is reflected in the content and organization of this book. The numerous procedures and phases may seem overwhelming to apply; however, we took care to provide ways to tailor our methodology for particular situations and objectives. We also tried to provide numerous assessment aids along the way. One such aid, a road map of the phases and activities of a complete assessment, can be found at the back of the book.

We also understand the need for close coordination between the technical team assessing the simulation, the model developers, and managers. In fact, managers are very interested parties in the assessment of a simulation. They must have full confidence in a simulation before it can be used as an analysis tool or decision aid. They also must decide on the resources that they can afford to devote to a confidence assessment. Our methodology prescribes the active involvement of both managers and model developers in a simulation assessment during each phase.

Finally, we observed that the work of a simulation model developer is never done. As long as there are time, money, and personnel, there are more details and features to build into the simulation. Thus, an assessment can be a continuous activity over the life cycle of the software. Improvements in software engineering, such as structured coding, graphical modeling tools, animation, object-oriented design, module reusability, use of automated code analysis tools, and computer aided software engineering (CASE) tools are making it easier to maintain confidence in a tool as it grows in complexity and sophistication. However, without a methodology that supports ongoing model assessment, an initial assessment could be doomed to obsolescence as a one-shot effort. Accordingly, this book addresses a full range of assessment activities over the life cycle of the model.

Acknowledgments

The inspiration for writing this book came from a working group created to advise the managers and technicians working at the National Test Bed. The NTB was established by the Strategic Defense Initiative Organization to provide hardware and software to support simulations and experiments conducted on strategic defense concepts. The Simulation Evaluation Methodology Technical Group (SEMTG) was conceived by Nelson Pacheco of MITRE Corporation in 1988 to advise the NTB on how to systematically evaluate simulation models and how to wisely apply them. He and Mort Metersky, from the Naval Air Development Center, cochaired this unique group of experts in the field. The foremost technical advisor was Robert G. Sargent whose framework provides the structure underlying the confidence assessment methodology. Ronald Gados, also of MITRE, wrote a summary of the activities and recommendations of the SEMTG.[1]

The SEMTG recommended creation of the *Confidence Methodology Guide*.[2] This document came to fruition after the arduous efforts of an NTB team, whose most notable members were Wayne Graybeal and Pat Sandoz, both from Geodynamics Corporation and Curt Frankenfeld, from Logicon Corporation. The *Confidence Methodology Guide*[3] and its ultimate application to the assessment of more than 10 simulation tools at the NTB form the foundation of this book. We would like to thank our supervisors and colleagues, Ray Kolibaba, Ron Jacobsen, Dick Matsi, Jim Hardy, and Don Brand, for their support, patience, and assistance in the production of this book.

Peter L. Knepell
Logicon R & D Associates

Deborah C. Arangno
Geodynamics Corporation

March 1993

Simulation Validation
A Confidence Assessment Methodology

Table of Contents

Table of Contents
(continued)

Figures and Tables

Chapter 1

Introduction

```
┌─────────────────────────────────────────────────┐
│       CONCEPTS - Background and Rudiments.        │
│           Recommended for all readers.            │
└─────────────────────────────────────────────────┘
```

The problem of simulation validation came to a head in early 1988. The General Accounting Office had just issued a report to Congress, titled "DOD Simulations - Improved Assessment Procedures Would Increase the Credibility of Results."[4] The report stated that "while DOD [Department of Defense] officials agree that credibility is important, DOD generally has not in fact established the credibility of its simulations systematically and uniformly." In the Department of Defense, simulations are a multibillion dollar business. Later that spring, the Computer Professionals for Social Responsibility (CPSR) expressed a major concern of the technical community. They issued a report criticizing a one billion dollar investment in a Strategic Defense Initiative project that involved a vast network of computer facilities and simulation centers which, if ever completed, "will be the world's largest simulation network."[5] The objective of the Strategic Defense Initiative is to build a trustworthy defense against ballistic missiles. The CPSR group's major statement was that "we cannot realistically simulate the conditions of such a conflict" thus invalidating any decisions based on simulation results.[5]

These concerns are not limited to the government sector. Simulations in private industry help managers and engineers design or operate complex systems. In his book, *The Day the Phones Stopped*, Leonard Lee provides graphic illustrations on how software failures can and have affected segments of our society.[6] His examples include the 1990 failure of AT&T's entire long-distance network and crashes of fly-by-wire aircraft. These sophisticated fly-by-wire aircraft include the Air Force's F-16, Boeing's 767, Airbus' A320, the Navy's F/A-18, and Sweden's Gripen jet fighter. The latter two experienced catastrophic failures due to software design problems. The design and test of the fly-by-wire systems are highly dependent on simulations. After the crash of the Gripen, the developer's program manager said, "We never encountered that situation in the simulation."[6]

If the risks and costs are high, why do we continue to build and use simulations? Perhaps the primary reason is that simulations allow us to investigate and understand systems that either do not exist or cannot be used for experimentation. The simulation of a system that does not exist will provide information on the system's probable performance under a variety of conditions. This will support decisions on basic concepts, system design, and feasibility of operation without going to the expense of developing prototypes or test models. This is especially important if testing a system may result in its destruction. It may be prudent to simulate the operation of existing systems because of the costs of running experiments, the inability to create or apply realistic test conditions, the difficulties in accessing the system, the lack of adequate testing equipment, or concerns about safety.

On the other hand, it is important to understand the risks involved with simulation. A simulation may not adequately represent the real-world system. The data used to drive it may be inaccurate. It may be too difficult to model the operational environment or all the interactions that affect the real system. Output data may be flawed or subject to misinterpretation. Despite all their potential for saving money, simulations can be costly in terms of human effort and computer resource requirements. And of course, there are always questions about the credibility of the simulation tool and its output.

Objectives

This book provides a systematic, procedural, and practical approach toward the evaluation of simulations. The process describes tools and techniques that should lead to an efficient, credible assessment of a simulation model. As such, the specific goals are to
- highlight key points concerned with establishing a model's credibility,

- provide a practical, systematic process and not a philosophical treatise on simulation issues and pitfalls,
- make the assessment less a matter of faith and more the result of the methodology, and
- establish the credibility of simulations used to support decisions, thus increasing confidence in those decisions.

Simulations are attempts to model the real world. They must be used carefully within their domain of application. Typically, models are developed for specific uses and have limitations on their application. When used for experimentation, variation of simulation parameters must be done wisely to prevent misinterpretation of output data or, consequently, of the system being modeled. In general, we will not explicitly cover the design, development, or application of simulations. However, cognizance of the assessment methodology will mitigate risks involved with these areas.

Definition of terms

The difficulty in establishing clear terminology in this field is legendary. A comprehensive bibliography search reported by Balci and Sargent encountered the following 16 common terms: acceptability, accuracy, analysis, assessment, calibration, certification, confidence, credibility, evaluation, performance, qualification, quality assurance, reliability, testing, validation, and verification.[7] One can even argue about the correctness of the title of this book since there are certain situations where simulations can never be validated given a strict definition of the term. Regardless, careful consideration of terminology is helpful in understanding the tasks at hand in the confidence assessment process. Implicit in the terminology are the limitations on simulation assessment as well. For example, if a simulation models a real-world system that does not yet exist, then we technically cannot validate the simulation. In their text on simulation modeling, Law and Kelton compares real-world data and simulation output. They state: "If there is reasonable agreement, we have increased confidence in the 'validity' of the model."[8] This statement shows the authors' preference for using levels of confidence to express model validity. It illustrates the difficulty in applying strict terminology in the field of simulation assessment.

In 1979, the Society for Computer Simulation Technical Committee on Model Credibility provided a framework for assessing simulations, as illustrated in Figure 1-1.[9] The definitions provided later are in the context of this illustration.

This figure illustrates a convenient decomposition of a simulation into three basic elements. The inner triangle shows the interrelationship of these elements. The outer arrows in the cycle refer to the procedures employed to establish credibility of a simulation. The scheme was further expanded by Robert Sargent and his model (described in Chapter 2) is the cornerstone of the confidence assessment methodology.

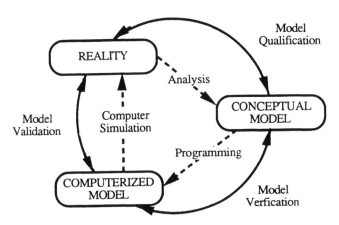

Copyright © 1979 Society for Computer Simulation.

Figure 1-1. Simulation model.

The committee gave a set of definitions that describe the basic elements and their interrelationships.[9] This book is written in the context of these definitions, although for variety, alternative terminology is occasionally substituted. (These and other definitions are summarized in the Glossary in Appendix A.)

- *Simulation.* Modeling of systems and their operations using various means of representation. (Occasionally referred to as a model, tool, simulation model, or toolset.)
- *Reality.* An entity, situation, or system selected for analysis. (Also referred to as real-world system or real-world entity.)
- *Domain of applicability.* Prescribed conditions for which the computerized model has been tested, compared against reality to the extent possible, and judged suitable for use.
- *Range of accuracy.* Demonstrated agreement between the computerized model and reality within a stipulated domain of applicability.
- *Verification.* Substantiation that the computer program implementation of a conceptual model is correct and performs as intended.
- *Validation.* Substantiation that a computer model, within its domain of applicability, possesses a satisfactory range of accuracy consistent with the intended application of the model.
- *Confidence assessment.* The process of assessing the credibility of a simulation by means of the methodology as described in this book. (Occasionally referred to as assessment, simulation evaluation, or model evaluation.)

The terms model, tool, simulation model, and toolset are often substituted for the word simulation, as noted in the definition above. In the strictest sense, these terms have different meanings. In fact, a simulation may refer to the application of a simulator to an input data set and the collection of the output data. In the field, this is sometimes called a simulation run. A model is defined as a physical or mathematical abstraction of a real world process, device, or concept. A simulation model can be defined as the representation of a model in computer code. Simulators are tools to support analyses. A simulation toolset can be thought of as a simulator and the entire toolkit that makes it work (that is, host computer, input data preprocessor, output data post-processors, and so on). In this book, these terms are most often used correctly in context. From time to time, the words are interchanged for variety.

Historical background

The literature on simulations and simulation validation is rich and fascinating due to the breadth of application. Credit is given to Conway, Johnson, and Maxwell for the earliest discussion of simulation methodology in their 1959 paper.[10] Conway continued his vanguard work by providing the earliest documented listing of simulation assessment techniques in his 1963 article.[11] Naylor and Finger provided a very comprehensive article on the subject in 1967.[12] Yet Naylor, in his 1971 text on simulation lamented on the difficulty in establishing universally acceptable criteria for accepting a simulation model as a valid representation.[13]

In 1978, the Society for Computer Simulation formed a Technical Committee on Model Credibility. Their 1979 report to the general membership provided the first framework for simulation assessment.[9] In 1984, Balci and Sargent compiled over 300 references on the credibility assessment and validation of simulation models.[7] Sargent codified much of the previous literature in his landmark work.[14-18] Gass made a number of contributions to the field[19-23] and most recently coauthored a case study based on an assessment procedure.[24] Two other leaders in the field, Averill Law and David Kelton, provided guidance on building valid simulation models by devoting an entire chapter of their text to the subject.[8] Law and Kelton's list of techniques and three-step approach provide a practical methodology for evaluating simulations. This book contains all their techniques.

Simulation validation was a major concern for managers and users of the National Test Bed (NTB). The NTB was established by the Strategic Defense Initiative Organization to provide hardware and software to support simulations and experiments conducted on strategic defense concepts. In recognition of the GAO report mentioned earlier, the NTB formed a group of experts to advise their managers on how to systematically evaluate simulation models. The Simulation Evaluation Methodology Technical Group recommended creation of a confidence methodology guide.[1] The NTB commissioned the production of this guide,[3] which was subsequently applied to the assessment of many large-scale simulations. This guide provided much of the inspiration and material in this book.

Applying the confidence methodology guide

This book provides a complete methodology. It will apply for the worst-case scenario of assessing a fully developed tool where no previous assessment was performed. It gives procedures to take advantage of testing, verification, or validation previously performed on the model. Guidance is also provided on applying the methodology to evolving models. The methodology given in this book may appear overwhelming to apply; it can be tailored for particular situations and objectives. Numerous assessment aids and tools are provided. In fact, an entire chapter is devoted to providing an extensive example of aids for a formal assessment.

Figure 1-2 describes the flow of this guide. It illustrates that after this introduction, the basic concepts of simulation assessment are covered in depth in Chapters 2 and 3. Given the practical advice and tools provided in these chapters, the practitioner must decide on the type of assessment to perform, either a formal or limited assessment. This is illustrated by the branch point on the flow chart for Chapters 4 and 5. There are two special topics areas in this guide to help assess simulations that involve man-in-the-loop or hardware-in-the-loop. For example, a simulation that supports an interactive tool for training operators of a power generation plant may need to apply both special procedures. Finally, Chapter 8 goes through a mock formal assessment to further familiarize the practitioner with all of the planning and organizing aids given in this guide.

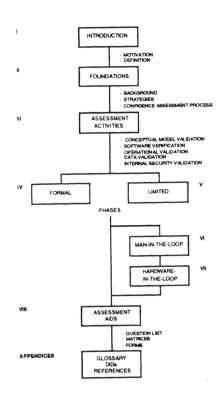

Figure 1-2. Confidence methodology guide flow chart.

This book is organized into three parts, as shown in the table below.

Part I - Concepts	Part II - Methodologies	Part III - Special Topics
Chap. 1 - Introduction	Chap. 4 - Formal Assessments	Chap. 6 - Man-in-the-Loop Models
Chap. 2 - Foundations	Chap. 5 - Limited/Maintenance Assessments	Chap. 7 - Hardware-in-the-Loop Models
Chap. 3 - Assessment Activities		Chap. 8 - Assessment Aids

Table 1-1. Organization.

Part I, *Concepts*, introduces the fundamentals of confidence assessments at a survey level. This part should be of special interest to managers who want to know the rudiments of confidence assessment without too much detail on programmatic issues.

- Chapter 1, *Introduction*, motivates this subject from a pragmatic point of view. After defining some common terminology, the subject is put into perspective with an anecdotal example. A brief recount of historical background is provided for researchers in the field.

- Chapter 2, *Foundations*, lays out the practical issues involved with implementing the confidence assessment methodology. It introduces the team concept, developer involvement, user involvement, and general approach. A structure is described for viewing simulations which accordingly provides a natural basis for prescribing assessment activities. We also present issues governing model certification and recommend some alternatives.

- Chapter 3, *Assessment Activities*, is the guts of confidence assessment. Assessment processes and their associated activities are explicitly discussed. The processes provide five different perspectives on the model being assessed. This is a very thorough set of processes – probably the most complete listing in the industry – which can be disorienting to the practitioner. For easy reference, a comprehensive listing of the assessment processes is provided at the end of the book.

Part II, *Methodologies*, provides structured schema for the confidence assessment of simulations. It is addressed to the members of the confidence assessment team that should be comprised of technical experts, software engineers, software quality assurance personnel, and a team director. The director will use the information in Part II and, possibly, Part III to plan, organize, and monitor the assessment effort.

- Chapter 4, *Formal Assessment*, is a guide for the complete assessment of a simulation model. The methodology provided involves the greatest depth and scope, and should be applied when the intended use of the simulation is very well defined. It will result in assurances that the development of the model was thoroughly investigated, that it was rigorously tested, and that the risks involved in using the simulation are exposed.

- Chapter 5, *Limited/Maintenance Assessment*, describes a lower level of confidence assessment that provides an indication of model credibility when a formal assessment cannot be undertaken because of time or resource constraints, or when a quick look is adequate. This methodology can be applied during model development, while model discrepancies can easily be corrected. Maintenance assessments are performed on previously assessed models which were either modified or applied to significantly different conditions.

Part III, *Special Topics*, examines aids for assessments. The first two chapters cover procedures for unique concerns. Here the assessment of the simulation will require different procedures and modifications to the assessment methodology.

- Chapter 6, *Man-in-the-Loop Models*, provides guidance for assessment of models that involve human interface in the simulation process. These simulations model man-machine interfaces and must include algorithms to provide information to humans, accept their responses, and generate actions based on the human response. These simulations pose unique evaluation criteria.

- Chapter 7, *Hardware-in-the-Loop Models*, discusses the special concerns when the simulation must interface with hardware. Specifically, these models may be linked to machine emulators, real hardware devices, or integrated portions of the system being modeled.

- Chapter 8, *Assessment Aids*, contains specialized tools to assist in planning, organizing, and conducting a systematic assessment. These include a question list for formal assessments, a model characterization matrix, cross-reference matrices, and a typical assessment schedule. An anecdotal example illustrates application of these tools.

Total Quality Management (TQM)

The TQM process is reinforced with the application of the confidence assessment methodology. A quality organization is concerned with the people and products that establish organizational values, forming a foundation for an organizational approach toward quality. Figure 1-3 illustrates the TQM pillars of quality, as defined by Organizational Dynamics, Inc.[25]

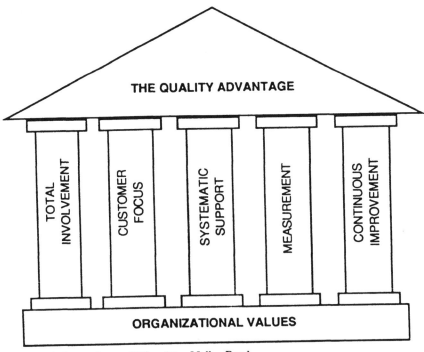

Reprinted, with permission, from ODI, 25 Mall Road, Burlington, MA 01803.

Figure 1-3. Five TQM pillars of quality.

The association between the confidence assessment methodology and these pillars is described below.

- *Total involvement* gets everyone in the organization involved in achieving quality. The team concept, described in the next chapter, includes the assessment team, management, developers, users, and a review group. Someone in this team also represents the sponsor of the assessment.

- *Customer focus* is the link between the organization and its customer. The customer can be the intended user of the simulation or the sponsor of the assessment. The team concept and periodic reviews of the assessment process always include the user or sponsor. This will ensure that customer expectations and requirements are satisfied.

- *Systematic support* is the support of all systems in the organization toward a quality effort. In an organization that either develops or uses a simulation, the entire support structure must work together. For example, operations personnel must allow for simulation operations by providing facilities, data, and equipment. It is also a by-product of the team approach.

- *Measurement monitors quality.* Assessment involves the characterization of the simulation tool and a set of procedures to evaluate selected technical areas. This decomposes the problem into measurable components.

- *Continuous improvement* requires constant vigilance to correct problems, prevent problems, and make improvements. The Confidence Assessment Methodology is built on this principle. Limited and Maintenance Assessments are made on simulations as they evolve. Discrepancies are noted and reported to the simulation developers. All assessments encourage good configuration control and correction of discrepancies. The final products of an assessment are a characterization of the simulation and identification of any risk areas. This is an organized effort to prevent problems with the ultimate application of the simulation.

Illustrative example

Several chapters introduce or mention examples of real-world systems that are excellent candidates for simulation studies. These examples illustrate the complexity involved in adequately representing these systems in a simulation and the corresponding challenge in assessing those models. As a means of introduction to this guide, consider the following power distribution problem.

The Goodbytes Company was contacted to perform a confidence assessment of Spark State Power Company's system simulation. Their model is 10 years old and was informally reviewed by an in-house team two years ago. Since then, the company hired Loosebits Company to create a mock-up control room and modify the simulation to drive the displays. The mock-up control room will be used for training employees. The system being simulated is a network of four power generation plants supplying a customer base in the Midwest. They are also linked to their neighbor, the Surge Power Company, in case of sudden changes in demand.

Given a broad problem statement like this, Goodbytes' assessment team may have difficulty defining their effort. Chapter 2 discusses the practical aspects of starting an assessment. In the early stages the team needs to ask the following questions.

What is the intended use of the simulation?

Here it seems fairly clear that the simulation will interact with human input in order to provide realistic training scenarios.

Who is the user and who are the model developers? Are there any other interested parties? Who is ultimately interested in the outcome of the assessment?

Here they can clearly determine that Spark State is the user of the simulation and Loosebits are the developers. But, will the public utilities commission or some other regulatory agency be interested in their assessment? If so, they must anticipate the political atmosphere.

How important are the decisions resulting from the use of this simulation model?

The decisions may significantly affect the revenues of the company. Public safety may be a factor. The potential impact of these decisions should influence the extent and cost of the confidence assessment effort.

How extensive is the simulation?

This will help them judge the scope of the assessment and decide on the expertise that they will need on their team. No doubt, the actual system is quite complex with the potential for several scenarios. The inputs, like changes in weather or power-generating capacity, are time varying. Is the simulation capable of integrating real-world data inputs?

What has been done in the past?

The previous review mentioned could be very helpful as a spring board into the assessment or it could be entirely worthless. The team can judge that by comparing the procedures used with those recommended in this guide, in Chapters 3, 4, and 5. If the previous review was credible, they may want to employ a limited/maintenance assessment as described in Chapter 5 instead of the more extensive formal assessment described in Chapter 4.

What are the users' expectations? What is their budget?

This could be a very complex question. For example, the assessment may be requested because of pressure from a regulatory agency. Then the user's expectations are that they will make the agency happy. Then they need to establish the agency's expectations and not the user's! The answers here will also help them determine if they should do a limited or formal sssessment.

Are there any special considerations in this assessment? (For example, are the developers done? Does the assessment team have access to the model? Are there man- or hardware-in-the-loop models?)

This is especially important because the answers will tell the team about the extent of and constraints on their assessment efforts and the work atmosphere that they will encounter. Clearly, this problem will involve "interactive gaming" which is another term for man-in-the-loop models. Chapter 6 will be their guide for that consideration. Does the simulation interact with power plants or distribution centers? If so, then this is a hardware-in-the-loop model and they will need to consult Chapter 7.

As you can see, the evaluation of a simulation can be almost as much fun as designing the simulation itself. Now that you are sufficiently prepared and motivated, dig into the guide and happy hunting!

Chapter 2

Foundations

This book describes procedures and techniques for determining the degree of confidence that can be attributed to the behavior and outputs of simulations. This can be accomplished by systematically evaluating the model's design, development, operation and results.

A model's assessment and development are certainly complementary activities; many assessment procedures can be incorporated into the development of a simulation, enhancing the quality of the finished model. However, it is not within the purview of this text to establish procedures for model development but rather to provide guidance and measures for the evaluation of the quality of such products.

We wrote this book in response to an urgent need for a validation tool that will help users and developers evaluate the reliability of a broad range of simulations. This tool must also help identify the potential risks inherent in their application. The need for such a tool is especially compelling because these simulations possess a wide variety of attributes, operate at different levels of detail and in different experimental modes, and address a broad range of key technical issues and system architectures.

Given the extraordinary level of complexity and detail in system-level simulations, as well as the intrinsic ambiguity of the physical phenomenon and strategies typically being represented, the creation of an authentically objective and rigorous methodology is a formidable challenge. The confidence assessment methodology provided in this text has proven to successfully address that challenge.

Limitations peculiar to the special environments of an industrial or defense model might include uncertainties in the data employed and absence of a universal or standard model against which comparisons can be made. In both cases, much reliance must be placed upon the technical guidance of the resident experts and experts in the outside community, as well as upon interaction with the developers themselves. Furthermore, in the absence of adequate documentation (which frequently occurs), vital information as to the intended use, content, development, or appropriate operation of the model may not available, and interaction with the developer is essential (to the extent feasible).

In response, the methodology described herein has been founded upon procedures that are intended to tackle a worst case of simulation quality assessment, to be applied even in the most uncertain operational environment, reflecting the most ambiguous developmental and experimental requirements.

The methodology is very flexible. It is convenient for users and developers alike, since they are both concerned with matters of simulation validation and verification. This chapter is concerned with the foundations of the confidence assessment methodology. These fundamentals include a discussion of the practical issues involved in performing a confidence assessment, a broad description of simulation model characteristics, and an introduction to a structure for simulation evaluation. Following this, a chapter is devoted to assessment activities, the tools for conducting an assessment.

Confidence assessment enables users and developers to consider a spectrum of requirements and a wide range of resources that can be committed to a confidence assessment, while being realistic about time and resource constraints. Chapters 4 and 5 provide formal and limited methodologies to accommodate this range of requirements and limitations. Chapters 6 and 7 extend these methodologies if the simulations involve man- or hardware-in-the-loop. The final chapter gives a practical guide for using the assessment aids covered in earlier chapters.

Practical issues

It is important to understand that performing an assessment and reporting the findings have organizational impacts. The most effective way to address personal and organizational concerns evoked by an assessment activity is to have a team concept for conducting the assessment. A team approach gives an opportunity to raise concerns and confront them directly. This can create a spirit of commitment and cooperation. From a manager's point of view, limitations on resources and time may dictate the scope on an assessment effort.

The team concept. A confidence assessment effort is inherently a team undertaking. This concept underlies the methodology's structure and drives the process. The confidence assessment team's composition is a function of 1) who is sponsoring the effort, 2) the origin of simulation under evaluation, 3) the relation of the simulation developer's organization to the assessment sponsor, 4) the nature of the model, and 5) the resource constraints governing the rigor of the assessment. The important players in an assessment effort include the following.

- *The assessment team.* The members of the assessment team should all be trained in the confidence assessment methodology. Members may be selected on the basis of their background in analytical methods, expertise in technologies pertinent to the model being assessed, familiarity with appropriate hardware systems or software/coding methods or techniques, access to the technical community or other relevant resources, and exposure to specialized operating or testing environments.

  Consider the special case, in which the organization that developed the simulation is sponsoring the assessment effort. In that instance, either the assessment is conducted by a third party (for example, an outside consulting firm), or is undertaken as an internal effort. In both instances, the members of the assessment team should strive to be objective in their application of the assessment methodology.

- *Management.* In general, the assessment team will be most effective when it is not unduly encumbered by the bureaucratic processes. Management involvement can provide support and the direction necessary for setting and meeting the goals of the assessment.

- *The developer.* The confidence assessment team will need to consult with the developers of the model. This includes members of the developer's organization and the actual developers. The developer's organization may establish and operate the infrastructure (including computer platforms, software engineering tools, and peripheral equipment) that supports simulation development. Leaders of this group may have been instrumental in establishing the requirements of the simulation model and formulating the concepts underlying the model. Developers are the individuals who generated prototypes, wrote the code, and were responsible for integration and testing activities.

- *The user.* Frequently it is the user of the simulation tool who sponsors an assessment, with the intention of determining the credibility or reliability of the simulation or to determine whether it will meet their special needs. The potential or actual user of a given simulation can be an important player in identifying the goals of an assessment. Their intentions for applying the simulation will help the analysts focus on important capabilities or risks inherent to that type of model.

- *Community experts.* Subject matter experts are valuable resources for evaluations of a simulation. If they are available for extended periods, they can assist in detailed, objective evaluations of the validity of the conceptual model and its implementation into software code. If the experts' availability is limited, then they can provide subjective, "face validity" analyses. Those experts can come from in-house or the external community.

- *The review team.* Depending on the desires of the assessment's sponsor and the level of the assessment effort, members of management, the confidence assessment team, representatives of the developer organization, potential users, and community experts can be assembled to conduct intermittent and final reviews.

Developer involvement. The importance of interaction between the confidence assessment analysts, the developer, and community experts has already been emphasized; however, an assessment should be performed independent of the developers. That is, the developers must not be placed in the position of assessing their own code. Discretion should be exercised in selecting the assessment team and in undertaking the effort impartially, so that the findings are not biased. While they will be involved with the assessment, they should not unduly exert influence over the direction, methods, or conclusions of the study. Developers should, however, be consulted concerning the intent, design, development, installation and execution of the model. In the event that the assessment is an internal validation effort conducted by the developing organization itself, absolute independence can often not be afforded. In such a case, there will be a trade-off between the efficacy of involving developers and the costs, resources and delays incurred by sponsoring a purely independent assessment team.

Lastly, the developers can be involved with the report of assessment findings without making the report appear biased. The developers should have the opportunity to review the findings before they are reported. Then they will not have the feeling that they must publicly defend their work against surprise criticism. Given the opportunity to respond beforehand, they can explore the findings, address technical details, clarify issues, propose model changes, and assess the extent of any revisions necessary. The overall result will be to enhance a team spirit of cooperation and, ultimately, produce a more complete assessment report.

User involvement. Equally critical to a simulation assessment is user involvement. Initially, it is vital that the user contribute in defining the scope and objectives of an assessment and have the opportunity to respond to the initial plan and schedule. Subsequently, the user should be kept abreast of progress through periodic reviews or interim status briefs. The user needs to be advised of updates or modification to the schedule, participate in decisions which may impact it, and remain well acquainted with refinements in the assessment's direction.

Since assessment results are intended to define the credibility of the simulation under consideration, the user may also serve as a subject matter expert. Users are often familiar with the technical and practical requirements of their particular application and with the needs and conventions of their special operational environment. As an example, consider a simulation that models the transport and shipping industry. A trucking firm, wanting to employ the simulation to study optimal utilization of its fleet, first undertakes an assessment of the model to ensure its credibility. If the confidence assessment team does not solicit the involvement of the firm administrators or employees, the assessment results could be significantly compromised by inappropriately defined scenarios, by the use of irrelevant or anomalous input data or units of measure, or by the invalid exercise of options or functions. The assessment could be designed on the basis of nonapplicable capabilities or limitations. For example, the assessment team might falsely presuppose that refrigerated produce is transported year-round from a given geographical region. Or, the study might neglect the seasonal variability of traffic volumes, revenues, fuel prices, supplies, taxes, road maintenance, truck maintenance, and shipping demands. Additionally, an unwary analyst might presuppose accessibility of storage facilities or goods and services. These are issues governing proper use of the model for which the trucking personnel themselves can be consulted as subject matter experts.

Moreover, it is valuable to stimulate user interest in assessment. The greater their involvement, at least at the level of exposure and availability, the more thorough will be the their ultimate understanding of the capabilities and risks of using the model. This will in turn provide the user with a degree of training in the correct use of the model as a tool to serve their needs.

For clearly practical reasons, therefore, user participation is meaningful if not altogether essential to the assessment of a simulation.

Management review. As will be described later, the assessment should be performed in four phases: preparation, planning, application, and evaluation. Each phase should involve management review of the assessment status. These incremental reviews provide an opportunity to present assessment findings and allow management direction of the assessment effort. The review team, chaired by management, should include some analysts from the confidence assessment team, representatives from the developer and user organizations, and community experts. It is also useful to include potential users, in addition to current users. If the assessment is being conducted by members of the developer organization, it is important that members of the review team are objective and impartial, to the extent feasible. To assure this, Management may want to employ the services of an independent consultant.

Hosting the model. One further practical issue concerns the availability of the model and supporting documentation to the assessment team. The model should be hosted and tested on the appropriate hardware prior to beginning the assessment. Problems encountered in loading, compiling, or linking the software detract from resources committed to the assessment effort (and constitute an area of risk, per se). This adversely impacts the assessment schedule and presents a technical risk to the validation process.

As will be noted later in discussions of assessment procedures and objectives, the simulation should be hosted, whenever possible, at the assessment site. If this is not possible, then an alternative, albeit less desirable, is to host the model at facilities accessible, if not dedicated, to the assessment effort. Priority access may be necessitated by the extensive testing, and frequency/rapid turn-around of simulation execution required to validate most simulations. This is especially true for large-scale, system-level simulations which are usually extensive in scope and level of functional detail.

Difficulties that arise when hosting the model present a particular problem in the absence of adequate documentation. Instructions and recommendations should accompany delivery of the model, to describe

- intended use,
- functional capabilities,
- configuration management standards and specific model version received, and
- recommendations for model loading and operating.

If that information is not provided with the model on delivery, or if it is inadequate, then the information should be gleaned directly from the developer.

In brief, upon identifying the need for an assessment, arrangements should be made to load, compile, link, and test drive the model before the actual assessment process begins.

Reporting results. One of the most sensitive aspects of conducting an assessment is the report of results. As discussed earlier, some of the concerns can be mitigated by the team approach. Developer involvement and management reviews should prevent surprises. Regardless, there are certain concerns and issues that should be identified and ironed out early in the assessment, including the following.

- Who will receive the final results? Who will have access to those results?
- Who is the final approving authority? Who determines the dissemination of results?
- What are the politics? What risks/stakes attend possible findings? Whose neck is on the line?
- What is the desired level of detail?
- How will the results and supporting data be archived? How will the information be secured?
- What degree of formality is required for presentation of findings?
- What format is preferred for presentation of the final results? Options include a formal report with fully documented substantiation, an executive briefing, an executive summary for the read file, or a memorandum for record.

Specifically, a confidence assessment report could be written to formally document the final results of an model assessment. Such a formal report would describe the steps taken in the assessment process, the assessment procedures applied, results of each step, description of how the model capabilities were derived, and any findings, or risk areas. The report of risk areas identifies open issues that could affect the credibility of the model. It is especially vital that these risk areas be explained to the potential model user. Additional assessment activities can provide a better understanding of any open issues that could affect the model's credibility.

Information concerning models assessed should be carefully archived. This retention of costly assessment results provides the basis for future reassessment of the models.

Occasionally, the assessment team and the user should formulate recommendations to the developer concerning model enhancements that the user may require prior to adopting the model or accepting its advertised capabilities. If the model is upgraded or considered for a vastly different intended use, it should be reassessed, examining the affected portions and how they interact with the remainder of the model. Based on this evaluation, a new recommendation will be formed.

In the event that a model does not appear to be valid in development, construction, theory, or implementation, it will need special treatment. The user and the developer will have to define an action plan to address the various concerns regarding the credibility of a model.

Approach

The confidence assessment methodology presented in this book can be described three different ways, depending on the view point of the observer. Assessment activities give procedures for systematically assessing a simulation. Assessment phases provide a practical approach toward organizing an assessment. Levels of assessment are designed to address the trade-offs between assessment objectives and the time and/or resources available to perform an assessment. Each of these are interrelated. How they are applied together will be described in much greater detail in Section 2.4, and Chapters 4 and 5.

Assessment activities. Assessment activities are derived from a framework representation of a simulation model. The fundamental building blocks of a simulation are the real-world problem entity being simulated, a conceptual model representation of that entity, and the computer model implementation of the conceptual model. Dr. Robert Sargent, from Syracuse University, created a pictorial representation of this framework, shown in Figure 2-1.[16] The outer circle (conceptual model validity, software verification, and operational validity) along with data validity are the technical processes that must be addressed to show that a model is credible. Assessment activities are spawned from each of these technical processes. For example, technical experts may be consulted to review the conceptual model to judge if it is valid. This activity, called face validity analysis, is performed to support the technical process of conceptual model validity.

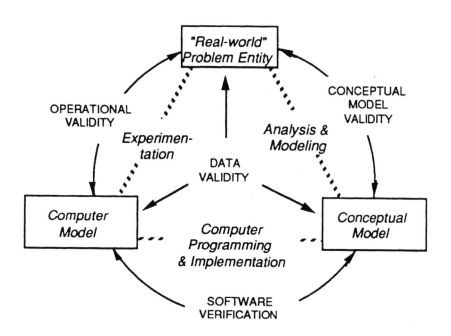

Figure 2-1. Sargent framework for model evaluation.

Assessment phases. The phase concept is an efficient approach to organizing an assessment. Each of the four assessment phases has a unique purpose in the overall assessment.

- *Preparation.* Gather the required information about the simulation and its intended use and confirm that the assessment can be reasonably accomplished with the information available.
- *Planning.* Review the simulation, its development, testing, and documentation, and the simulation's intended use to form an initial determination of whether the simulation can meet the intended use. Perform limited independent testing of the simulation to investigate apparent problem areas in its performance. Plan the remainder of the assessment based on open problem areas identified during this process.
- *Application.* Complete the simulation assessment by applying assessment procedures based on requirements identified in the planning phase.
- *Evaluation.* Evaluate information compiled from the previous phases to form a recommendation concerning use of the candidate simulation.

The specifics of each phase will be discussed as they apply to the various levels of assessment in Chapters 4 and 5.

Levels of the assessment process. The four phases of an assessment can be followed at the level of a formal assessment, which is a thorough evaluation of the model's development and testing. If the assessment activities are subject to time or resource constraints, then a limited assessment is recommended. A limited assessment has the same structure as the formal process but is more selectively applied. If a previously assessed model has been upgraded, or if the intended use has been modified, or if deficiencies have been corrected, a maintenance assessment can be performed, which may be tailored to evaluate the model within the scope of the modifications. In summary:

- *Formal assessment.* This process can result in the assurance that the development of a model has been thoroughly investigated, that it has been rigorously tested, and that the risks involved in using the model are known. A traditional independent verification and validation (IV&V) approach would involve continuous evaluation of the model throughout its development. A formal application of the confidence assessment methodology can be applied when the model development is completed. While this effort is less extensive than the IV&V approach, it is just as effective and can be accomplished in a shorter time period relative to the model's development.

- *Limited assessment.* This level of the confidence assessment process provides an indication of model credibility when a formal assessment cannot be undertaken because of time or resource constraints. Moreover, a limited application of the formal assessment methodology can be made during the model development, while modifications can easily be effected. This level of assessment is considered the minimum acceptable effort; the costs savings of any lesser effort will provide only marginal benefits, but may result in false confidence in the model or in a misconception of its capabilities and/or risks.

- *Maintenance assessment.* An assessment which is performed on a model that has been previously assessed. This is usually suggested in the event of significant modifications in code, the operational environment or performance requirements, or when a great length of time has passed since the last evaluation. Changes in the operational environment, in performance requirements, or in the policies driving the use or development of the simulation may also necessitate a maintenance assessment. A maintenance assessment is treated as a special application of the limited assessment process.

These levels and their respective technical processes will be discussed in further detail in the section on system evaluation, and chapters 4 and 5 will provide methodologies for performing formal and limited/maintenance assessments, respectively.

Simulation model characteristics

Breadth and depth. Two issues that impact the direction and extent of an assessment of a simulation are the *level of model detail* and the *scope of the intended use*. Depending on the specific application, a user may acquire a model of almost any level of detail in simulating the real world. Unfortunately, detailed models are not necessarily accurate. As models become more detailed, their faithfulness in representing truth may be much more difficult to evaluate. This combination of detail and accuracy is sometimes called the model's *level of fidelity*. The greater the detail, the more involved and time consuming the assessment will be, and the greater the level of technical knowledge required. The aspects of model fidelity which must be verified are

- whether the fidelity, as declared by the developer, was consistently implemented throughout the components and segments of the model and was appropriately managed throughout the code, and
- whether that level supports the intended use of the simulation. The scope of the intended use similarly affects the complexity, duration, and technical knowledge requirements of an assessment.

The same principles can be thought to govern simulation design as govern lens optics. That is, given a simple lens, the more refined the focus, generally the more restrictive the field of view. Maximum scope can be achieved at the expense of detail, whereas maximum fidelity compromises breadth. However, optical equipment designed for the dual capability of detail and scope, requires highly technical and complex systems of lens. In the same fashion, the focus of simulations also ranges from global to local. Those simulations which accommodate both a macro- as well as a micro-view are highly complex and time-consuming models. Among these high-end models are the system-level simulations.

Consequently, the assessment of such a system-level detailed model (reflecting a high level of detail and breadth of scope of intended use) requires the most extensive analysis. These larger models may be composed of many models or components, so they can be assessed through compilation of the component-wise assessments. At the other extreme, the simplistic and limited-focus models require the minimum time and resources for the conduct of an assessment, especially if the expected behavior and results have already been established.

Taxonomy of model types. There is a wide range of functional attributes and scope of use, which characterizes the following kinds of models: system-level, integrated system level, tier/segment level, component/element level, subsystem level, and technology level. Figure 2-2 illustrates these various levels in context of scope and detail.

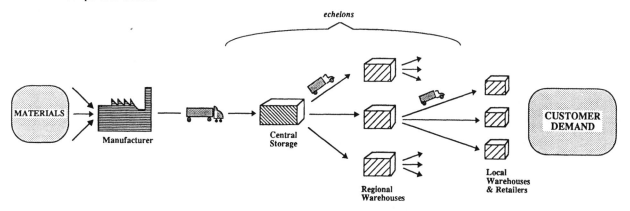

Figure 2-2. Product distribution problem.

- *System level.* These models address an entire system, operation, and environment. Scopes of use range from architecture studies such as relatively low-fidelity models, to medium-fidelity models, which are used to address detailed system performance and trade-off studies. System-level models are generally made to be as flexible as possible and are often composed of many system and component models tied into a simulation framework. [A robust model of the product distribution problem as presented in Figure 2-2 illustrates a system-level simulation. Such a model would necessarily involve numerous discrete and inter-related components and sub-systems, including demand (which is dependent on seasons/cycles, advertising/marketing, local/geographical zones) and supply (which incorporates raw materials, production rates, product inventories, transportation, and demand rates).]

- *Integrated system-level.* These models address a slightly smaller scope than system-level models in that they cover only one integrated system or interactions between the various systems. These models are constructed much like system-level models. [In the product distribution model, one interaction of interest might be the regional distribution problem, a model that focuses on the local distribution of goods, transport and storage, in meeting the demand of a given region.]

- *Tier/segment level.* Tier-level models are also similar to system-level models but only consider the systems contributing to a single tier or segment of a system. While these models can operate alone, they can also act as a module (subsystem model) for larger-scale models. [A segment-level derivative might extract from the multilevel storage system, only the regional transport model. This, for example, further refines the focus of the simulation to describe only the regional transport of the product from all regional warehouses to each of the local warehouses. This is also referred to as an *echelon* of the product distribution model. These product distribution echelons or tiers can be identified as the factory, central storage, regional and local shipping and storage, and local retailer.]

- *Component/element level.* Component/element models address the performance and activities of a particular component or element. These models are the primary building blocks used to create larger-scale models. Operating these models alone provides the component developer opportunities to explore component system designs. As part of a larger scale model, the developer and decision maker have the opportunity to study how the components interact, to perform system-level trade-offs, and to identify potential large-payoff system modifications. [The example of the transport simulation as was suggested in earlier, can be identified as a component of the product distribution system-level model. This component-level model would describe the features and attributes of, for example, a local transport problem from a specific regional warehouse to local retailers: routing/road networks, scheduling, personnel, materiel, facilities, regulations, administration, training, and maintenance. Whereas one component might involve only a single local trucking company (including parts, repair equipment, loading apparatus, and so on), another element might concentrate on a single local warehousing facility – docks, shipping/receiving yards, warehouses, refrigerated storage, maintenance facilities, administrative offices, and physical security.]

- *Subsystem level.* These models describe how parts of a component operate. While these can be stand-alone models during development, these models are usually contained in a component-level model. [To model, for example, the personnel component of the transport simulation, you would have to describe payroll, labor structure, job functions, management/employee relations, chain-of-command, working environments/conditions, training, job safety, and so on. Another subsystem might address the factory, another might describe a truck.]

- *Technology level.* This category of models includes many diverse types, such as 1) models associated with the interaction of a component – or subsystem of a component – with the physical environment, and 2) models which describe specific dynamic forces and physical phenomena of the environment within which the entire system is couched. These models have their own integrity, meaning they stand alone and provide information to other models as a discrete part of a large-scale simulation. [A simulation of the transport industry depends on accurate models reflecting correct vehicle/cargo tonnage limits; engine design; cab and trailer design and compatibility; fuel types and grades; quantity and variety of spare parts including tires, repair tools, and emergency roadside gear; interstate regulations regarding cargo restrictions, taxes, licensing, tonnage limits, and emissions requirements; accuracy in describing routes and road networks; weather conditions and diurnal effects influencing traffic patterns, route accessibility, driving conditions, cargo type, consumer demands, or scheduling. Another example, would be to model customer demand, to describe its time-varying nature, in that it does drive much of the supply problem.]

(Note that models may have hardware-in-the-loop or man-in-the-loop components, which we explore in Chapters 6 and 7.)

Model assessment generally concentrates on the component-level models and higher since the subsystem models are usually assessed as part of the component model. However, some of the physics and technology models are treated as component-level models because of their place in large-scale models.

Physical environments. Environments are especially important to special model subsystems or elements. For example, some space-borne optical equipment cannot observe objects against an earth or solar background; drying agents are influenced by barometric pressure and ambient temperature and moisture; workers respond to variations in season, air quality and noise levels; structures (such as bridges, buildings, and roads), as well as machinery, are undermined by stresses and forces; and vehicles are affected by wind velocities and propulsion dynamics.

Some simulations do not model backgrounds or environmental effects, but higher fidelity models usually include several different environments. These environments include chemical or nuclear effects, and seasonal/diurnal effects. Other natural backgrounds or environments can be modeled to include cloud heights, weather, geophysical phenomena, and celestial backgrounds. Manmade backgrounds might include spacing or sizing constraints such as capacities, pollutants, and communication noise.

Simulation attributes. Several attributes characteristic to a given simulation may affect a potential user's ability or desire to use a given simulation. Important attributes are fidelity, execution time, host computer, language, modeling approach, maintainability, ease of use, configuration management, code security, and postprocessor and preprocessor capabilities. These attributes are important to all simulations, and are therefore included as an integral part of the characterization of a simulation regardless of its intended use.

The *fidelity* of a simulation refers to the level of detail and accuracy of the simulation's algorithms, as discussed earlier. Higher model fidelity normally produces longer simulation execution times.

The *host computer* refers to the platform on which the simulation runs. Some simulations are specific to a single platform while others are portable across several platforms. Portability may be desirable for a user contending for computer time or having access to a single computer. Some simulations, especially those involving man- or hardware-in-the-loop, are distributed over several platforms.

The *language* of the simulation, that is the programming language used in writing the source code, will normally not be an issue to a general user as long as the language is capable of supporting the intended uses. Exceptions occur for a highly-specialized experiment, if the user plans to edit the code (without help from the developer), or if errors exist which require debugging and editing.

The *modeling approach* is usually not a direct concern, but three possible concerns are the consistency of the approach throughout the model elements, the appropriateness of the approach to the intended uses, and applicability to host platform.

The *maintainability* of the simulation is concerned with the development process. A model developed with good internal documentation (such as comment lines), current and thorough external documentation (manuals, guides, logs), and consistent code structure is generally considered to be more maintainable as well as easier to use. The ease of use of a simulation may be one of the most important attributes to a potential user. A user friendly, robust simulation will save valuable analyst time. A user-hostile simulation will not only consume valuable time, but may cause the unaware user to improperly apply or operate the model, or to make mistakes that produce inconsistent or incorrect results.

Configuration management, an important issue in development of the model, involves the tracking and control of revisions and new releases of the simulation model. If the simulation configuration is not properly managed, the credibility of that simulation can be jeopardized. In addition, improper configuration management may not allow an experiment to be repeated, affecting the verifiability and credibility of that experiment.

The *code security classification* is a specific aspect of configuration management. Rigor must be applied in proper identification of model version, and in tracking code modifications. This aspect of configuration management incorporates protecting code against computer viruses and unauthorized code-tampering and editing. (Note that this book will not address the specific issue of proprietary software or governmental security classification of the code.) Developers concerned with sensitive code must ensure the model meets the user's constraints. This has to do with "trusted code," especially relating to data and design security issues.

The inclusion of useful *pre- and post-processors* in the formal release of a model is important to a potential user. Pre-processors can be used to read in data files, set up files, size arrays, and so on. The execution of these pre-processors can reduce execution time of the simulation, as well as the effort required by the analyst. A model that does not provide post-processed output may produce valuable results which are not readily available or exist in a form impractical for the user.

Characterization of attributes. A set of functional attributes can be used to describe a system-level model. These attributes can be used to trace the required capabilities for a specific intended use. For other model types, a different set of attributes will be required. As a system evolves or a model requires a different set of attributes to meaningfully meet its intended use, the characterization of its capabilities will need to be modified as an integral part of the dynamic assessment process. Characterizations produced by an assessment address model capabilities. The functional attributes are the critical areas required to support the testing requirements of the program being represented. (For an example, see Table 4-1a.) Some general information may also be included to provide a high-level view of the model's implementation.

The confidence assessment methodology uses these attributes to characterize the model's designed capabilities and any problems identified with the derivation or implementation of those capabilities. A textual characterization of the model is developed and updated as additional information concerning the model capability is gained through review of documentation and test results or application of assessment procedures. Problems identified with the derivation or implementation of those capabilities are noted on a chart that references the technical areas of the assessment process (covered in Chapter 2) with respect to the characterization attributes. This creates a *characterization matrix,* which is an important product of an assessment. (See Table 4-1b.) In addition, a textual characterization of the intended use of the model is created based on these same attributes. The intended use of the model is the experiment or study for which the model is being assessed. Model capabilities required by the intended use indicate where the model must provide proven capability and provide the focus for the assessment effort.

Structure for simulation evaluation

The Sargent Framework provides a structure for discussing a simulation model. (A slight modification to Figure 2-1 is shown below.) The structure highlights the products and processes that describe a model. Each element on this figure should be considered in model development. The elements of the figure also define the technical areas and processes that should be addressed in model evaluation.

Figure 2-3 is extracted from "Guidelines for Evaluation of SDS Simulation Models Used at the National Test Bed" developed by the Simulation Evaluation Methodology Technical Group (SEMTG).[2] The group modified Dr. Sargent's original figure to include the internal security verification process. The inner triangle formed by the problem entity, conceptual model, and computer model blocks describes the model development process.

"The Problem entity is the system (real or proposed), idea, situation, policy or phenomena to be modeled; the conceptual model is the mathematical/logical/verbal representation (mimic) of the problem entity developed for a particular study; and the computerized model is the conceptual model implemented on a computer. The conceptual model is developed through an analysis and evaluation phase, the computerized model is developed through a computer programming and implementation phase, and inferences about the problem entity are obtained by conducting computer experiments on the computerized model in the experimentation phase."[16]

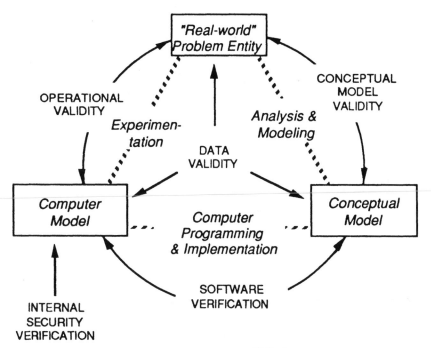

Figure 2-3. Structure for simulation evaluation.

The remainder of the figure shows the processes of assuring that the model and its implementation are correct and its integrity has been maintained during development and use. These processes are defined below.

- *Conceptual model validation.* Determination of the adequacy of the conceptual model to provide an acceptable level of agreement with the real world for the domain of intended application.

- *Software verification.* Substantiation that the implementation of the computer program of a model is correct and performs as intended.

- *Operational validation.* Substantiation that computer model, within its domain of applicability, possesses a satisfactory range of accuracy consistent with the intended application of the model.

- *Data validation.* Substantiation that the data used in model development and operation are adequate and correct.

- *Internal security.* Assurance that the model development and subsequent configuration control are adequate to minimize the possibility of external tampering.

The above concepts and definitions provide a structure for model evaluation. Each element of the structure is investigated during a formal assessment. Only a selected subset of the structure is examined during a limited assessment. In the next section, these procedures are described in much greater detail by giving some of the procedures applied to assess each area.

Technical processes for formal assessment. The preceding diagram and definitions help define a general structure for model assessment. Figure 2-4 shows the more specific technical assessment areas that are to be addressed during a formal assessment. Added to the Sargent Framework are the seeds of procedures that could be applied to the assessment of each area. Assessment procedures are covered in detail in Chapter 3. The methodology for performing a formal assessment is detailed in Chapter 4.

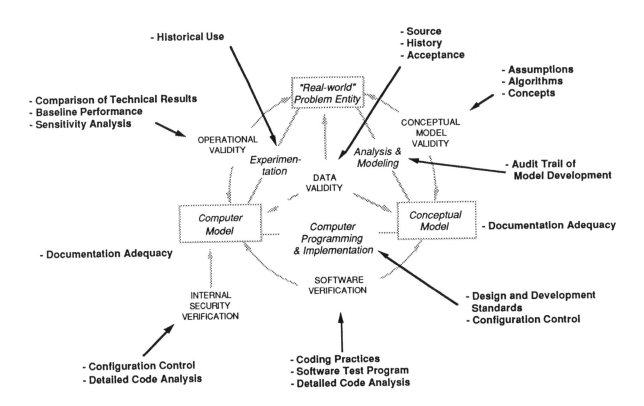

Figure 2-4. Formal assessment technical processes.

The following is a brief discussion of the technical processes associated with formal assessment.

- *Data validation.* Validation of the data used in the development and operation of the model is applied during each activity of the assessment process. It requires delving into the source, history, and past acceptance of the data. The source of the data includes its origin and any justification provided supporting its selection. The history of the data includes investigation of past studies that used the data. A key to the validity for data is community acceptance.

- *Conceptual model validation.* Validation of the conceptual model is divided into justification of the assumptions, algorithms, and modeling concepts used in development of the model. Assumptions can be explicit or implicit and may be related to application of an algorithm or embedded in the modeling construct used. Clear statement of the assumptions is a key to assuring that they were considered and their consequences weighed in model implementation. These assumptions may influence the domain of applicability of the model and will identify the bounds of model validity. Appropriateness of the algorithms and modeling techniques is also addressed.

- *Analysis and modeling.* Essential to assessing the development of the conceptual model are the documentation and organization of the analysis and modeling effort. This establishes an audit trail of the development from specification of the real-world problem to the testing required in the model's validation. The modeling specifications are also influenced by accuracy requirements. The degree of accuracy required is influenced by the intended use of the model and, to some extent, by the conceptual design.

- *Conceptual model.* The conceptual model should be completely described to clarify the purpose, function and development history of the model. Adequate documentation of this is a critical element in determining the model's functional utility.

- *Computer programming and implementation.* As the developer implements the conceptual model, there are many activities and methods that can be employed to support the model credibility. Examination must include whether good software design, coding, and testing practices, standards, and tools were imposed, as well as the effectiveness of configuration control during development.

- *Software verification.* Verifying that the software model is a faithful implementation of the conceptual model is essential to assuring potential users that the simulation results are credible. All procedures employed by the developer and/or independent evaluators to validate the model's implementation are assessed, and additional testing or analysis is accomplished as necessary. These procedures include validating the implementation of software design and coding standards and evaluating the thoroughness of the test program. This also involves detailed code analysis. The degree of accuracy required can be a factor in the depth of this effort.

- *Internal security verification.* Evaluation of the configuration management program and all detailed software verification efforts help establish whether the computerized model is currently free of any tampering devices that would affect its operation or results.

- *Computer model.* Adequate descriptions of the capabilities, limitations, use, maintenance, and so on are critical to the acceptance of the computer model. These must be described at a level that allows the users to understand how and when the model can be reasonably applied.

- *Operational validation.* The computer model must demonstrate consistency with the real-world problem it was intended to represent. Operational validation is the comparison of model performance with the real-world system, if possible. Otherwise, comparison is made either with a standard, with itself after variation of selected input parameters, or with other models. This can include both developer and independent testing efforts.

- *Experimentation.* Many of the models assessed will have been used in previous studies. How the models were used, acceptance of the results, and problems noted with the application are also contributors to the overall assessment of the model credibility. Adequacy of documentation is again essential here.

Technical processes for limited assessment. The key aspects of the confidence assessment methodology emphasized in a limited application are: conceptual model validation, model implementation verification, and operational testing. (These three areas constitute a subset of the many areas covered during a formal assessment.)

Figure 2-5 shows these technical areas to be addressed during a limited assessment. These areas are a subset of the areas addressed in formal assessment and need not be discussed further in this section because they only differ in depth and breadth. These areas were selected for a limited assessment effort because of their potential to provide the most added knowledge about the overall model, as well as its capabilities, limitations, and the risks in using it. The depth to which these areas are addressed may also be different from formal assessment. Again, the seeds of procedures that could be applied to the assessment of each limited assessment area are added. (Assessment procedures are covered in detail in Chapter 3.) A limited assessment is constrained by time and resources and it may not be possible to investigate all of the model in even these limited areas. The methodology for performing a limited assessment is detailed in Chapter 5.

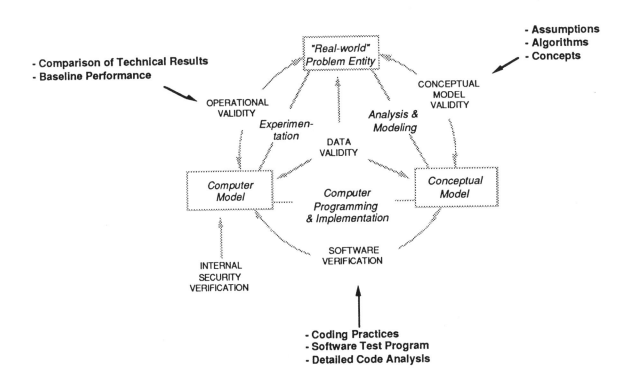

Figure 2-5. Limited assessment technical processes.

Iterative application of assessment methodology. Frequently, the software under consideration is transitional. Code is often evolving with respect to modifications in requirements, application or intended use, operational environment, and user or hardware interface. Over time, the model may also reflect improvements in the algorithms or in the code design.

Each cycle of development during the evolutionary process will require validation and an evaluation of risk, at the level of a maintenance assessment. As discussed earlier in this chapter, a maintenance assessment is a specific application of the limited type.

The problem of maintaining adaptive code has been very effectively addressed by the *spiral model*, which constitutes an improvement over the code-and-fix, stage-wise, waterfall, and transform models that were previously adopted as conventions in code development. Barry W. Boehm provides the spiral model in "A Spiral Model of Software Development and Enhancement."[26] He presents the process as shown in Figure 2-6. The spiral model approach to this type of evolutionary software development incorporates requirements, implementation, and evaluation at each level of prototyping. This process will be difficult to accomplish without adequate documentation and rigorously applied configuration control.

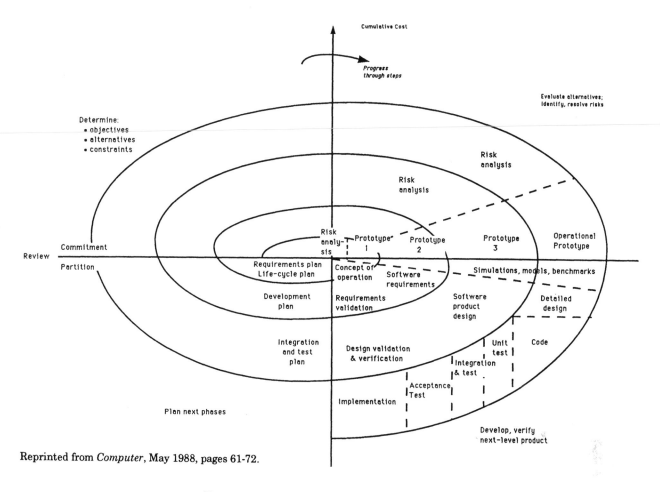

Reprinted from *Computer*, May 1988, pages 61-72.

Figure 2-6. Spiral model of evolutionary code development.

Boehm recommends that in a prototype environment, the requirements and design specifications of the model development be risk-driven. This mandates the kind of methodological approach to validation as provided by the maintenance-type assessment.

These foundations of confidence assessment offer some insight into the practical issues involved with confidence assessment. Next, we give a toolkit for performing these assessments, including a complete set of procedures to apply and on formal and limited confidence assessment methodologies.

Chapter 3

Assessment Activities

> **CONCEPTS - Details of the five assessment processes and supporting activities. Recommended especially for quality assurance experts and confidence assessment team members; managers may want to review material.**

Confidence assessment is an effective way to characterize the model's capabilities and a risk assessment for potential users. The CA methodology is intended to be implemented via five processes: concept validation, software verification, operational validation, data validation, and internal security verification.

These processes, or activities, provide five different perspectives on a model and help evaluate the concepts and data underlying the model to compare the declared capability versus the demonstrable capability of the model. This is accomplished through the scrutiny of the various aspects of the model including:

- the logical implementation of the conceptual model into code,
- the soundness of the actual coding practices and the quality of the software development process itself,
- the configuration management and the code security practices, and
- the model's operation, reliability, and accuracy – via rigorous and methodical testing.

The CA approach addresses and resolves the companion issues of the intended use, the specific version being assessed, the specific elements or functions being examined, and the relation of the assessment to previous efforts.

Of course these perspectives of model development and functionality are not disjoint; they are interactive processes of the assessment effort. The tools and methods of these five activities usually must be employed dynamically to fully assess the characterization and performance of the model under consideration.

It should be mentioned here that a new generation of simulation languages present a breakthrough in the field. These languages support graphical model development using iconic displays. These include Schruben's Sigma,[27] Pritsker's Slam II/Tess and Slamsystem,[28] Pegden's Siman,[29] and CACI's Simfactory, Comnet, and Lannett.[30-32] These packages allow creation of the logic flow in a graphical format, which is then automatically translated into software code. This can greatly streamline the assessment process. For example, assuming that the underlying generation of code has been already verified, then the tasks of tracing program logic and software debugging are greatly simplified. Some languages support animation of element interactions and simulation output, which also provides an efficient means to assess simulation models. Thus, graphics-based languages provide a superb link between development, functionality, and model assessment.

Care should be taken in applying these features in the assessment of a simulation. Law and Kelton point out several shortcomings of animation that also apply to graphical model development, including

- animated output presents only a snapshot of results and not a valid statistical analysis,
- one cannot assume that a system is well-defined by watching the animation,
- only part of the simulation model's logic is displayed, and
- there is no guarantee of a valid or debugged model.[8]

The five processes

Concept validation attempts to establish the reliability of the model design and the integrity of its development, facilitated by completeness of documentation and augmented by expertise and training of the CA analysts. Consideration is given to development history, level of detail, level of fidelity, inputs, outputs/measures of effectiveness (MOEs), ranges/specifications, and premises of design.

The aspects of *software verification* (to include implementation analysis) include completeness and compatibility of functions and concepts within the model, development integrity and thoroughness of documentation, as well as maintainability, level of fidelity, ease of use, overall runtime, implementation of design elements and system components. Moreover this method uses computer-aided software evaluation techniques (computer-aided software engineering tools) and applies metrics like Gandalf,[33] Analyze,[34] Logiscope,[35] and

McCabe.[36] Within this analysis, modules of code are identified as candidates for detailed analysis based on criticality or in response to any concern raised during a phase of the assessment.

Operational validation is based on a rigorously-defined operational test plan, and provides documentation for all procedures and results; the plan incorporates excursions as deemed necessary, and in general is designed to 1) baseline the model, 2) stress the model, and 3) establish parametric comparisons with previous testing efforts as well as with known or accepted results.

Data validation includes an analysis of data derivation, trustworthiness of data origin, consistency throughout the model and code, and output, as well as analysis of the representation of constants and variable definition, units of measure and ranges.

Internal security verification is a process of investigating the code security plans that were drafted, those that were actually implemented, accurate and current identification of model versions, and other aspects of configuration management.

Table 3-1 briefly outlines the tools/methods relevant to these activities, which are discussed in detail in the following sections of this chapter. It should be kept in mind that these methods are most effective when used interactively throughout the assessment effort.

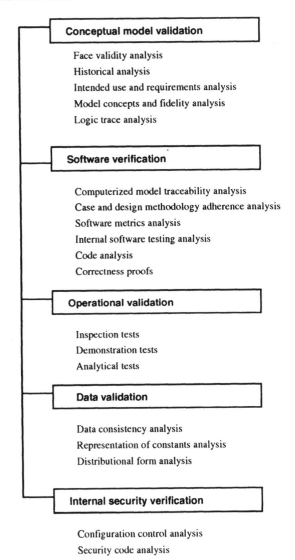

Conceptual model validation

Face validity analysis
Historical analysis
Intended use and requirements analysis
Model concepts and fidelity analysis
Logic trace analysis

Software verification

Computerized model traceability analysis
Case and design methodology adherence analysis
Software metrics analysis
Internal software testing analysis
Code analysis
Correctness proofs

Operational validation

Inspection tests
Demonstration tests
Analytical tests

Data validation

Data consistency analysis
Representation of constants analysis
Distributional form analysis

Internal security verification

Configuration control analysis
Security code analysis

Table 3-1. Outline of the five assessment activities.

Conceptual model validation

Prior to analyzing the actual computerized model, the underlying conceptual model needs to be analyzed to validate its assumptions, theories, fidelity, derivation, logic, and interfaces. The developer's justifications of the concepts, assumptions, and algorithms that comprise the conceptual model are key elements in this examination. In this section we detail the methods for performing these analyses.

If the documentation for a model is incomplete, then some of these analyses can be conducted by using the code. This is a higher risk approach but it can provide at least some understanding and validation of the conceptual model. If this approach becomes necessary, there will be considerable overlap between these methods and those used for software verification. To support this possibility, we listed model source code as a *useful data item* on many of the methods in this section.

```
Face validity analysis

Historical analysis
•  Development history analysis
     Requirements
     Interface standards
     Development plans
     Verification and validation plans
     QA/CM plans
     Design standards and specifications
     Coding standards
     Test plans, procedures, and results
     Data collection plan and procedures
     Data generation plan and procedures
     Data validation plan and procedures
     Internal security verification plans
     Problem reports/discrepancy report history
     Studies and analysis
•  IV & V support analysis
•  Model derivative analysis
•  Previous model use analysis

Intended use and requirements analysis
•  Criticality analysis
     Definition of criticality classes
     Classification of requirements
     Definition of assessment levels
     Correlation of assessment levels with criticality classes
     Assignment of assessment levels to requirements
•  System analysis
     Derivation of submodel requirements
     Comparison of submodel requirements to similar modes
     Traceability analysis

Model concepts and fidelity analysis
•  Modeling concepts analysis
•  Input/output analysis
•  Algorithm analysis

Logic trace analysis
```

Table 3-2. Conceptual model validation analysis tools.

Face validity analysis. Face validity analysis is a subjective review of all of the information available on a model to determine areas where additional analysis is required to raise the confidence level in the model to an acceptable level. It evaluates the overall behavior of the model at an observer level. It gives a subjective analysis of whether or not the model behaves as expected by system experts based on the model's outputs and/or assumptions. During the *planning phase* this analysis provides information on the areas in the conceptual model that have inherent credibility and areas that require further analysis. This helps to identify procedures that need to be applied during the *application phase*. One of the real benefits of this method is the relatively low cost and short time frame required for its application. This method, however, provides little benefit during the application phase since it is a subjective, high-level analysis versus an objective, detailed analysis.

The manual process of face validity analysis may be augmented by graphics routines to present the data in a user-friendly format. The information about the conceptual model is presented to a group of knowledgeable people to detect areas where the conceptual model may be weak and need more analysis. This is similar to Delphi Testing, which we discuss later in this chapter, in the section on operational validation.

Face validity analysis is constrained by the quantity and quality of the information available on the conceptual model. Also, due to the subjective nature of this method, the validity and application of this method are highly dependent on the knowledge base of the analysts involved.

To use this procedure, two groups of data are essential:

- a conceptual model description and
- a known and accepted scenario description.

In this analysis, the inputs, outputs, and logic flow are presented (often in graphic form) to the knowledgeable people mentioned earlier for known or accepted scenarios, as well as any assumptions or algorithms used in the model. After presentation of the model, the group is polled for their opinions as to areas of weakness within the model. The weaknesses identified are then used in development of potential risk areas requiring further assessment.

This method produces the following outputs:

- descriptions of areas of potential weakness in the conceptual model,
- descriptions of areas of perceived strengths in the conceptual model, and
- early, subjective evaluation of the credibility of the model.

Historical analysis. Historical analysis involves review of historical information on a model to determine additional analyses required to raise the confidence in the model to an acceptable level and to provide an early indication of the model's appropriateness for the intended use. The procedures involved are development history analysis, independent verification and validation (IV&V) support analysis, model derivative analysis, and previous model use analysis.

Historical analysis evaluates the model development data and any other data available on past uses of the model (or a similar model on which the one under study is based). It provides a preliminary assessment of the model's appropriateness for use (based on historical documentation) and identifies areas where further analysis is required. During the planning phase, this method provides information on areas in the model that need to be analyzed further due to the lack of previous analysis or to documented problems. This helps identify procedures that need to be applied during the application phase. This method also familiarizes the analysts with the model and the history of its development and use, providing a strong basis for further analyses. Historical analysis also provides an early recommendation on the appropriateness of the model for the intended use since documented uses may show evidence for or against the current intended use. During the application phase, this method can be carried into the code to determine if the standards specified for the development phase were correctly employed.

Historical analysis is a manual process involving review of all of the information available on a model and any information on the model it is derived from (if applicable). This analysis can feed the rest of the analyses by providing concise, up-front information on what testing or analysis has been performed in the past. It will also allow the confidence assessment effort to focus on weak and unknown areas.

Historical analysis is constrained by the quantity and quality of the documentation retained from the model's development, IV&V, previous uses, and the related versions of the model. A lack of documentation in any area drives the choice of some application phase procedures to provide the needed analysis to increase confidence in the model. A lack of documentation on the model itself will severely impact other analyses to be conducted during the planning and application phases.

The following items are needed to use these procedures:

Data Items	Development history analysis	IV&V support analysis	
Development cycle documentation	X		
Host's interface standards	O		X = essential data
Model source code (Application phase only)	O		O = useful data
Documentation		X	

Data items	Model derivative analysis	Previous model use analysis	
Previous use documentation		X	
Previous model documentation	X	O	
Differences between current model and previous model	O	O	X = essential data
Intended use description		X	O = useful data

The way a model is developed affects the credibility and internal security of the resultant simulation. If a strict program of quality assurance steps, good standards, a design methodology (possibly including the use of computer aided software engineering tools), and thorough testing are employed during the development cycle, the model may have greater initial credibility and require less confidence assessment analysis before it is used. However, if no rigorous standards were followed during the development, more analysis may be necessary during the confidence assessment process.

Development history analysis. Development history analysis is a manual review of the developer's documentation of the development effort. The goal of this analysis is to determine how rigorous the model's development was and to note any areas of deficiency. The analyst reviews this documentation, looking for evidence of sound development practices including scheduled reviews, enforced use of good programming and design standards, controlled interfaces between programs, and thorough testing at all levels from module level through system. A lack of evidence for any of these is factored into the analysis strategy that is developed for the application phase. The analyst also reviews any plans and any information available on how closely the plans were followed to determine areas where the plans or non-adherence to the plans do not support the creation of a credible model. During the application phase, any coding standards or interface standards employed are compared with the code to determine how closely they were followed during the development. The following information provides some guidance on what to look for in various types of model documentation.

- *Requirements specifications*. These documents should contain a complete and unambiguous specification of the model requirements.

- *Interface standards and documents.* The following items need to be reviewed: mechanisms for controlling changes to the interfaces, mechanisms for defining generic interfaces, mechanisms for controlling access to internal devices (such as databases), mechanisms for designing compatible unique interfaces, and completeness and accuracy of defined interfaces.

The interface standards used for a model's development can affect how easily the model can be integrated into the user's environment. One goal of this review is to detect interfaces used in the model that cannot be easily integrated into the host's environment based on comparison with the applicable interface standards.

The model's inputs and outputs (at both the conceptual model and the computerized model levels) are examined versus the required interface standards to detect areas where the model does not support easy integration into the host's environment. The following items need to be verified in relation to the standards: the structure of the interfaces, the content of the interfaces, and the techniques by which the interfaces are passed and controlled. Areas where the coded interfaces do not follow the standards are listed and made available for incorporation into the user's integration effort.

While this is primarily a manual process, the static analysis tools described later in this chapter, in the section on software verification, may be useful for checking the implementation of the standards.

- *Development plans.* You must verify logical and structured techniques employed, mechanisms for controlling data exchange, mechanisms for handling changes to the model, and mechanisms for controlling development progress.

- *Verification and validation plans.* Verify the use of reasonable verification and validation methods and sufficient verification and validation of each portion of the conceptual and computerized models.

- *Quality assurance and configuration management plans.* The following items need to be verified: use and effectiveness of scheduled walk-throughs, control of changes to established baselines, technical content of quality assurance/configuration management (QA/CM) reviews, and correct employment of any tools used to verify the internal security of the original code or any changes to it.

- *Design standards and specifications.* The following items need to be verified: logical and structured techniques employed, mechanisms for centralizing information flow, mechanisms for controlling changes to the design baseline and for reflecting those changes in the documentation, and completeness and accuracy of design details.

- *Coding standards.* The following items need to be verified: definition of module sizes, definition of acceptable coding constructs, definition of acceptable programming languages, mechanisms for defining and controlling generic interfaces, and mechanisms for defining and controlling generic data. While this is primarily a manual review process, static analysis tools may be useful in checking the implementation of the standards. (See the next section, on software verification, for further information on the applicable static analysis tools.)

- *Test plans, procedures, and results.* The following items need to be verified during this analysis: control and documentation of the test data, control and documentation of the test drivers and test tools, the use of reasonable testing methods and strategies, correct generation of expected results, completeness of the testing effort, and results of the testing effort. In addition, test inputs that have not been covered may be identified and factored into the independent testing portion of the application phase.

- *Data collection plan and procedures.* The following items need to be verified: a controlled collection mechanism, complete and accurate specification of data needed, and correct identification of sources for that data. During the application phase, the analyst reviews the data collection procedures to detect areas where the data requested was inaccurately specified or incorrectly interpreted by the external data source. This may include not specifying units, coordinate systems, or exact data needs. Potential problems may be detected by incomplete data specifications or by data that appears to be out of range for the model.

- *Data generation plans and procedures.* The data used in a model may be derived from previous studies or generated solely for the model's development. These studies can range from analytic (paper) studies to other models and actual testing. The following items need to be verified: controlled generation mechanisms, complete and accurate specification of the data needed, and identification of correct generation methods to use. During the application phase, the analyst reviews the studies and tests that were run to generate the model's data to detect inaccurate, inappropriate, or incomplete derivations.

- *Data validation plan and procedures.* The following items need to be verified: control of the data, verification mechanisms (perhaps by walk-throughs) for the generated data, and verification mechanisms (perhaps by outlier analysis) of the collected data. In addition, for collected data, the history of the data is investigated. The credibility of the data may be increased by wide community acceptance of the data. This is especially true for models involving specific physical, structural, or statistical data.

- *Internal security verification plan.* The following items need to be verified: configuration management mechanisms for controlling, verifying, and documenting changes to the model.
- *Problem and discrepancy report history.* The following items need to be verified: complete specification of the problem, correct actions taken, and complete retesting done where necessary.
- *Studies and analyses.* Trade-off studies and various analyses may have been conducted in support of model development. If they are available, the following items need to be verified: complete specification of item investigated, description of procedures, and accuracy of conclusions.

IV&V support analysis. An IV&V activity undertaken during or after the development effort can increase the credibility of the model by enriching the quality and availability of documentation and other information concerning the model. The goal of IV&V support analysis is to determine the level of IV&V support provided and assess the results.

Support analysis involves a manual review of the IV&V contractor's documentation to assess the level of review provided by the IV&V contractor during each phase of the development. This includes review of the analytical studies, test results, and problem report discrepancy report histories maintained by the IV&V contractor. Also assessed, if possible, is the level of impact that the IV&V agency had on the development effort. Any code analysis or testing is evaluated for its contribution to the credibility of the model. This information is factored into the analysis strategy that is developed for the application phase.

Model derivative analysis. If a model is primarily a modification of a previously assessed model it may have greater credibility than if it is derived from first principles. The goal of model derivative analysis is to review any confidence assessment that was done on the model from which the current one is derived, determine the differences between the two models, and factor that into the analysis strategy being developed.

Model derivative analysis is a manual process whereby the analyst reviews the information from any assessments of a previous model upon which the current model is based. This assessment includes the use for which the model was assessed, the depth of that assessment, and the results of the analysis. In addition, the changes between the two models need to be compared to determine what areas need to be reassessed. This allows the current assessment effort to focus on new software, old open risk areas, and old risk areas that should be mitigated by fixes. The information derived from this analysis is factored into the development of the analysis strategy for the application phase. (This is essentially the first step in performing a maintenance assessment.)

Previous model use analysis. If a model has been used for previous studies (whether the model was assessed or not) it may have greater initial credibility than a new model. The goal of previous model use analysis is to review previous uses of the model and any information on how completely the user accepted those results.

Previous model use analysis is a manual process in which the analyst reviews the information available on previous uses of the model including any data available on the subjective response of the user to the model and its results. This assessment includes how the model was used, how closely that use corresponds to the current intended use, and how completely the results were accepted by the previous users and reviewing agencies. Areas where results were not accepted need to be investigated to determine the reason for non-acceptance. Any deficient areas discovered during this review need to be factored into the analysis strategy developed for the application phase. In addition, if any data are available relating previous results achieved with the model to operational data collected since, that also is assessed. Any areas uncovered where the model and the operational data conflict are factored into the analysis strategy developed for the application phase.

This method produces the following outputs:

- early recommendation on the appropriateness of the model for the intended use;
- initial characterization of the model;
- descriptions of deficiencies in the development cycle, previous testing, previous use results, and IV&V analysis that need to be covered in the confidence assessment analysis;
- descriptions of areas where the current model has changed sufficiently from a previously assessed model to require reassessment;

- a list of documented interfaces that do not conform to the host's interface standards and that may impact the integration of the model into the user environment;
- a list of coded interfaces that do not conform to the host's interface standards and that will impact the integration of the model into the user environment;
- a list of collected data items that are incorrect and an assessment of their impact on the intended use of the model; and
- a list of generated data items that are incorrect (due to inaccurate or incomplete derivation studies) and an assessment of impact on the intended use of the model.

Intended use and requirements analysis. Intended use and requirements analysis involves review of the intended use to determine critical requirements in an effort to effectively use resources. In addition, the model's program requirements are evaluated against the intended use of the model to determine whether any intended use requirements are not supported. The procedures involved are criticality analysis and system analysis.

Intended use and requirements analysis provides a basis for all subsequent analysis and testing activities. During the planning phase, this method familiarizes the analyst with the capabilities of the model, verifies that the requirements of the intended use are supported by the model, and provides a mechanism to focus the efforts during the application phase on the critical portions of the model. This allows for a more efficient and effective use of resources during the application phase. This method may effectively use automated requirement-tracing tools and database tools designed to support tracking and reporting the requirements. These tools can create a requirements cross-reference matrix when this method is combined with traceability analysis. (See section on software verification.)

The limitations of intended use and requirements analysis include
- the subjective nature of classifying the criticality classes in criticality analysis,
- the limitations of any tools used to support the analysis,
- the possibility that the requirements might be vague or so broadly stated that the analysis loses significance, and
- the cost in time and effort to perform the analysis.

The following items are needed to use these procedures:

Data items	Criticality analysis	System analysis
Intended use description	X	X
Model requirements specification		X
Conceptual model description		X

X = essential data

Criticality analysis. An essential aspect of intended use and requirements analysis is determining the criticality of each intended use requirement. The cost of an assessment in both money and time often prohibits its application to the entire model, and in these cases only the requirements deemed critical are subjected to detailed analysis. In all cases it is useful to identify the requirements most critical to the intended use to establish an effective analysis approach.

The first step in criticality analysis is to *define criticality classes* meaningful to the assessment. These classes define different levels of criticality appropriate to the intended use of the model. These classes may be based on failure impact, technical risk, or other criteria. Criticality analysis based on failure impact classifies each requirement according to the consequences of failing to satisfy it. The four criticality classes for this approach are:

- class 1: invalidation of the entire experiment,
- class 2: serious credibility risk to the experiment or to the validity of experiment results,
- class 3: slight credibility risk to the experiment or to the validity of experiment results, and
- class 4: minor inconvenience in performing experiments but no impact on credibility.

Criticality analysis based on technical risk classifies each requirement according to the degree of innovation needed or difficulty involved in implementing it. This may be especially applicable if modifications are required to the model. Criticality classes for this type of analysis are:

- class 1: new technical area that appears difficult,
- class 2: new technical area that appears simple,
- class 3: current technical area, but difficult, and
- class 4: current technical area and simple.

Once criticality classes have been selected, they form the basis for *requirement classification*. This process requires an understanding of the experiment's needs, the host's environment in which the program will operate, and similar models and experiments to judge the relative importance or risk associated with each requirement. The criticality classification may be applied to individual requirements or to groups of related requirements.

The third step of criticality analysis is *defining a series of assessment levels* appropriate to the current model assessment effort. The levels are defined in terms of the intensity of effort involved, the types of assessment activities and tools to be employed, and other factors.

Each criticality class permits the analyst to consider other factors such as complexity or results of previous phases, in addition to the primary criticality criterion, when selecting the assessment level for each requirement.

The final step is *assigning an assessment level to each requirement or group of requirements*. The analyst considers the criticality class plus any other relevant factors and selects an appropriate assessment level. The result is an assessment approach tailored to the specific assessment and making optimal use of available resources.

System analysis. One step beneath a system-level model is a submodel. As discussed in Chapter 2, these subsystem-level models describe how parts of a component operate. While these can be stand-alone models during development, these models are usually contained in a component-level model.

The system-level model incorporates numerous discrete and interrelated components and subsystems, as was illustrated by the model of the product distribution problem presented in Figure 2-2. A *subsystem model*, in that example, might be the personnel component of the transport simulation, which would describe payroll, labor structure, job functions, management-employee relations, chain-of-command, working environments and conditions, training, job safety, and so on. The development of the submodels, as well as their integration into the system-level model, must be analyzed during an assessment.

System analysis is the process of evaluating the requirements for a submodel against the requirements for the intended use. The objectives of this analysis are to ensure that the submodel requirements are complete and to establish traceability between the submodel and the intended use.

One method that may be used in system analysis is independent *derivation of the submodel requirements*. This method studies the model and intended use requirements and independently identifies the requirements that should be established for the submodel. The independently derived requirements are then compared with the actual requirements of the submodel. This method identifies omissions, extraneous requirements, and incorrectly defined requirements.

A second method is *comparison of the submodel requirements to standard references or to similar models*. If the submodel implements a standard function or resembles an existing model of known integrity, its requirements may be compared with those of the standard or existing model to identify omissions, errors, and extraneous requirements.

A third method is *traceability analysis*, which may be performed either manually or with the aid of automated tools. Each submodel requirement is cross-referenced to the model-level requirement from which it was derived and to any intended use requirements that it supports. This information may be represented in tabular form or entered into the database of a software tool designed to store and report such information. Analysis of the model traceability relationships helps to identify incomplete, missing, and incorrectly allocated requirements.

Several types of tools may be used to aid in submodel analysis. These include (but are not limited to)

- *requirements tracers*, which provide a trace of requirements through the requirements specification into any design documentation and into the code, and
- *database managers*, which control and manipulate database records, thereby providing insight into the input/output function of the submodel.

This method produces the following outputs:

- characterization of the intended use,
- initial characterization of the model,
- criticality matrix for use in planning the application phase procedures, and
- a list of intended use requirements not fully supported by the model.

Model concept and fidelity analysis. Model concept and fidelity analysis is a method involving review of the algorithms and submodels underlying a model to identify premises that do not apply or are too restrictive for the intended use of the model, and to determine if the fidelity of the components is sufficient to support the intended use of the model. The procedures involved are modeling concepts analysis, input/output analysis, and algorithm analysis.

Model concept and fidelity analysis evaluates the algorithms and submodels underlying a model and the fidelity of each such component. It is used to ensure that the conceptual model is scientifically reasonable, internally consistent in its representations of the physical world, and compatible (both in functionality and fidelity) with the intended use of the model. During the planning phase this method provides an early indication of whether or not the model has sufficient fidelity to support the intended use. It also provides indications of areas where the fidelity of different submodels does not appear to be supported. These areas are factored into the analysis plan developed for the application phase.

During the application phase, this method is used to verify that the algorithms, range of inputs, and fidelity of the model support the intended use of the model. This procedure provides the analysts with a detailed understanding of the underlying assumptions used in the model and verifies their correctness. During this phase, the analyst may be aided by the use of static software analysis tools (see the next section on software verification). The analyst reviews all of the information available on the algorithms and submodels of the model to detect inappropriate, inconsistent and restrictive assumptions. Results of this analysis can be used in preparation for equation reconstruction during code analysis, where the coded implementation of the algorithm is checked to ensure that further restrictions have not been introduced.

Model concept and fidelity analysis is constrained by the quality and appropriateness of the data available on the conceptual model, the computerized model, the algorithms used, and the interfaces of the model. It is also constrained by how well the systems and physical phenomena that were modeled are understood. If the model is very detailed or contains many different algorithms, then this method will be relatively time-consuming and will also be constrained by the capabilities of the analyst and the tools used in the analysis.

To use these procedures, you need the following:

- a conceptual model description (essential data),
- a model source code for the application phase only (useful data), and
- an intended-use description (essential data).

Data items	Modeling concepts analysis	Input/output analysis	Algorithm analysis
Data flow diagrams	O	O	
Model interface documents		X	X
Trade-off studies (if applicable)			O
Algorithm references (if applicable)			O
Physical experiment data (if applicable)			O

X = essential data   O = useful data

Modeling concepts analysis. Modeling concepts analysis identifies the concepts employed in development of a model and the ways they affect the fidelity and level of detail for the model. Most simulations have a target level of detail in development of the conceptual model. For example, when modeling a production line, the underlying concept of constant demand will force constant resource requirements; adding cyclical demand inputs increases the level of detail for resource requirements. Modification of the model to support other uses can alter the level of detail and thereby introduce modeling concepts inconsistent with other components of the model.

Common modeling concepts range from simplistic approaches and simple random draws to modeling each element using mathematical representations. Examples of the extremes are probabilistic look-up tables and *n*-degree-of-freedom dynamic models. The level of detail available from each of the different model types can only support a fairly narrow range of intended uses. A second issue is that the level of detail expressed by the model must be accurate enough to meet the requirements. As particular subsystems are developed, more inferences can be made concerning the detailed workings of the actual system. The model must be compared to the level of knowledge concerning the actual system's functions to determine if the level of detail modeled is reasonable.

The conceptual model descriptions and, where necessary, the computerized model, are examined to determine the modeling concepts used. Selection of modeling concepts should be similar across the model components. In this analysis, the concepts are examined to assure consistency. Not every model component needs to use the same concept, it is only important that the component level of detail used by the model is similar. Another key to this is the compatibility of data transferred between the modules. Compatibility of data transfer is covered next in a discussion of input/output analysis.

The level of detail modeled must also be commensurate with the intended use. Characterizations of the model and the modeling concepts used are compared to a characterization of the intended use. Any mismatches are examined to determine the impact to the user in meeting the stated goals. If the real-world system being modeled is under development, then some contact with the actual component developers may be required to assure that the detail modeled is representative of that system. For low-detail models, this requirement is mitigated somewhat because of the gross level of aggregation used in the modeling concept. More detailed models require more verification from the system developer to assure that the concepts modeled are correct.

Input/output analysis. Input/output analysis has a multifold purpose. First, it determines if the level of fidelity of the model matches the level of fidelity stated in the documentation for the model. Second, it determines if the fidelity level of the model can meet the requirements of the intended use. Third, it determines if the input domain of the model can support the intended use.

Since a large simulation may be composed of several models controlled by a more general simulation framework, it is important that the components of the simulation pass compatible levels of information in the interfaces of the submodels. The actual fidelity of the submodels need not be the same, but the interfaces must support the full range of element fidelity. During conceptual model validation, this will involve review of any available interface documentation, the data flow diagrams (DFDs) (if they are available), and any other design description documentation. The DFDs show the major decomposition of the functions of the models and can be used as one method of checking the level of information both within a submodel and passed between submodels. Code review will contribute additional information during software verification by providing data on the fidelity of the model input/output as they were actually coded.

The input conditions under which a given model produces valid outputs are also constrained by the assumptions inherent in the conceptual model and its implementation. An experiment may be designed to test a given hypothesis in a particular range of possible input data and this range of input data may not be compatible with the assumptions inherent in the conceptual model. Input/output analysis is designed to detect those points at which the desired experiment is outside the valid range of the conceptual model by reviewing the inputs and processing to detect limitations (both documented and undocumented) in the input domain. This procedure is related to the code analysis techniques of program interface analysis and program constraint analysis. Application of this procedure involves checking the correctness of the DFDs (or other design description documentation), their organization, and their logic. In addition, it involves checking the DFDs against each other and analyzing the interface documents for completeness and compatibility of the data passed between submodels. For example, if one section of the model uses a range of values for the given entity of 0 to 100 while an interfacing section only accepts the range 0 to 10, then the experiment may not be supportable. Values of the input domain are mapped through the conceptual model to detect possible internal conflicts from that set of inputs. The result of this analysis is a map of the boundary of the valid input domain or verification that none of the proposed experiment's inputs are outside the range of the model.

Also involved in this analysis is the explicit verification of the stated limitations of the conceptual model while detecting, documenting, and verifying unstated limitations. Any area where the fidelity of a submodel is insufficient for the experiment, unsupported by the other submodels, or where the intended use inputs are not supported by the model, needs to be analyzed for its impact on the intended use of the model and a risk level needs to be assigned. During the software verification phase this process may be aided by the use of static analysis tools. (See the next section on software verification for further details in this area.)

Algorithm analysis. Analysis of the algorithms in a conceptual model detects incompatible, inappropriate, or restrictive premises imbedded in the algorithms used in the model and submodels. These submodels may include parameters used to describe the operational characteristics of a particular element including architectures, strategies, and system components. They may also be used to handle generation of various pieces of non-hardware related data. These include entity characteristics, various scenarios, and the physical environment or dynamic phenomena. Each of these contain a number of parameters that may include a variety of assumptions.

Each of these details needs to be examined to assess its accuracy and limitations, and the correctness of its implementation. This analysis may include comparison of a particular algorithm or constant against an accepted standard to verify that the correct modeling is being done. If any trade-off studies are available on a particular algorithm, they can be used to help guide a portion of the analysis. The interfaces between two sections of the model are compared to verify that both sections are working under equivalent premises. Areas where the premises are limiting need to be analyzed to determine the impact on the intended use of the model to assign a risk associated with it.

This method produces the following outputs.

- Additions to the model's characterization
- Identification of those model elements not consistent with the advertised level of fidelity
- Descriptions of areas where the level of information passed from one component to another does not support the fidelity of the receiving component and an assessment of the risk associated with that non-support
- Descriptions of areas where the fidelity of a component is insufficient to support the proposed experiment
- Identification of data "lost" from a high fidelity submodel that is not processed by the other submodels
- A list of areas where the input domain of validity of the model is insufficient for the proposed experiment
- Descriptions of areas where the internal premises are inconsistent and may cause errors during the model's use (including runtime errors or erroneous data output) and an assessment of the risk level associated with the problem
- Descriptions of premises in the algorithms that may be problematic in the conduct of an experiment and an assessment of the risk level associated with the problem (including incorrectly modeled pieces of hardware and mismodeled physical phenomena)
- Measure of the fidelity of the model and the individual submodels

Logic trace analysis. Logic trace analysis involves review of the behavior of specific entities in the model as they are traced through the model's logic to determine whether the behavior is what is expected for that entity.

Logic trace analysis evaluates the behavior of the model for specific entities as they are traced through the model's logic. It is used to ensure that the conceptual model correctly handles specific entities and to determine if the logic maintains the accuracy necessary for the intended use.

This method is related to the code analysis technique of program logic analysis, which is conducted on the code. (See the next section on software verification for further information on that related analysis.) Due to the detailed nature of this analysis, it is only useful during the application phase. During that phase it provides the analyst with an increased understanding of the structure and logic in the conceptual model that will be useful when analyzing the computerized model. In addition, it provides verification on the correct handling of the important entities in the conceptual model. For this method, the analyst may be aided by tools designed to trace requirements-level information. These tools are related to the CASE tools covered under software verification. Graphical support tools may also be used to depict some of the relationships between various modeled entities.

Logic trace analysis is constrained by the quality and appropriateness of the information available on the conceptual model, and by the depth of understanding that exists for the entity being studied and any physical phenomena related to it. This method can be relatively time-consuming if several different entities are traced.

To use this procedure, you need the following three types of essential data:

- a conceptual model description,
- information on entities of interest,
- and expected behavior of entities.

The procedure used in logic trace analysis is the tracing of entities through the description of the conceptual model. Entities are chosen that may include reaction times, transit times, or other measures of performance. These may be determined by the assessment team using criticality analysis (earlier in this section), or they may be provided by outside sources. These are then followed through the conceptual model information to see if the model's logic is correct in its handling of the entity and if the model maintains the accuracy of the entity at or above the required level. Any such areas discovered are evaluated for their impact on the intended use of the model and a level of risk associated with each one.

To aid in this analysis, you can use requirement tracers or graphical display packages, which display the relationships between various entities being traced. This method produces the following outputs:

- additions to the model's characterization,
- identification of areas where the behavior of a specific entity within the model is not reasonable and an assessment of the impact of that on the intended use, and
- identification of areas where the model's logic degrades the accuracy of an entity below an acceptable threshold and an assessment of the impact of that on the intended use.

Software verification

Using the information derived from conceptual model validation, the actual computerized model can be verified. The goal of this phase is to verify that the validated conceptual model has been correctly implemented and tested. In general, the same attributes that were examined during conceptual model validation will be examined in the code to verify their implementation. This involves methods commonly employed for standard software verification, including traceability to model documentation, internal testing of the software, correctness proofs of the code and code analysis, as outlined in Table 3-3.

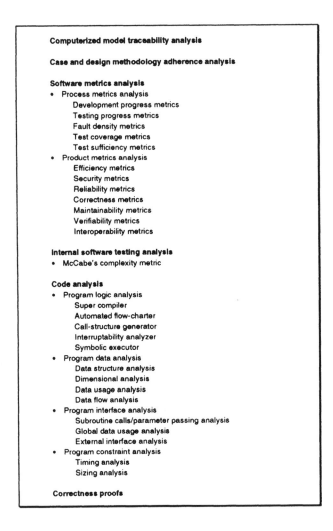

Table 3-3. Software verification analysis tools.

Computerized analysis tools. Several powerful automated tools are commercially available that can be applied in code verification. These automated tools include metrics products that monitor software reliability and development quality from early stages of code design through system integration and testing.

Moreover, in addition to software V&V during model development, several of these tools are flexible enough to support other activities, including: code maintenance (via analysis of modification impact), project managements (through progress measurement), and testing. The following specific tools are mentioned in the bibliography, to provide an appreciation of the capabilities available:

- *Logiscope.* This software quality analysis tool provides code diagnostics for the range of uses from code development to project management. Like many of the other commercial products, it has powerful graphic display capability to depict program architecture and module performance. The module performance is displayed by means of distinctive Kiviat diagrams (as illustrated in Figure 3-1) that represent how well the program conforms to given standards.[35]

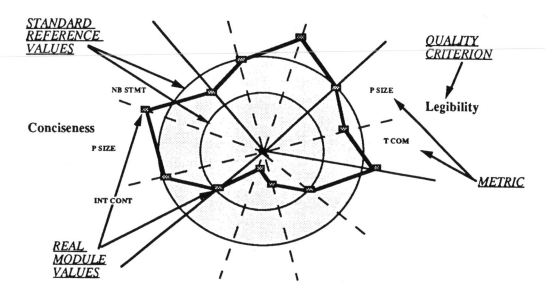

Reprinted from *LOGISCOPE*, Verilog USA, Alexandria, VA.

Figure 3-1. Kiviat diagram (Logiscope).

- *AdaMAT* is a static code analyzer (for code written in Ada) that collects data on numerous data items. It measures the adherence of code to given software standards, and reports on the quality of the code at any time during its life cycle.[37]
- *Analyze and McCabe* static code analyzer tools calculate several metrics (such as cyclomatic complexity and control flow) to verify the software as it is developed and provide insight into the quality of the code development process itself.[34,36] A discussion of complexity metrics can be found in the documentation for these tools and in the National Bureau of Standard's *Structure Testing*.[38]
- *SQMS* is an automated code analyzer that provides, in addition to code quality metrics, projected data on time and expense to meet requirements for code/program management.[39]

Computerized model traceability analysis. Traceability analysis involves tracing the elements, inputs, outputs, and algorithms in the computerized model back to the conceptual model. It also involves the intended use of the model to determine if the validated conceptual model has been faithfully translated into the computerized model and if the computerized model supports the intended use of the model. The procedures involved are *traceability of computerized model to conceptual model analysis* and *traceability of computerized model to intended use analysis.*

Traceability analysis evaluates how well the computerized model traces to the conceptual model and to the intended use of the model. This method ensures that the computerized model's elements, inputs, outputs, level of detail and fidelity, and algorithms support the needs of the intended use and the requirements of the conceptual model. During the planning phase, this tracing is conducted using documentation on the code (versus the code itself) to provide preliminary verification that the model supports the intended use and tracks to the conceptual model. Areas where there is a lack of data, contradictory data, or where the data does not support this verification drive the choice of procedures to use during the application phase. In addition, the analyst gains increased understanding of the model that is useful during further analysis.

During the application phase, this tracing is conducted using the actual code. This provides confirmation of the findings from the planning phase as well as verification that the code contains the elements necessary to support the intended use. When this method is combined with requirements analysis (covered in the preceding section), a requirements cross-reference matrix can be created to aid further analysis.

Traceability analysis is constrained by the quality and appropriateness of the information available on the conceptual model, the computerized model, and the intended use of the model. In addition, it is constrained by how completely the conceptual model has been validated and how valid that model was determined to be.

To support the two procedures involved with traceability analysis, the following items are needed.

For both procedures:
- model source code (essential data)
- CASE tools-generated information (useful data)

For traceability of computerized model to conceptual model analysis:
- conceptual model description (essential data)
- conceptual model validated procedures/results (useful data)

For traceability of computerized model to intended use analysis:
- intended use description (essential data)

Traceability of the computerized model's capabilities back to the (validated) conceptual model is necessary to verify the computerized model. If the conceptual model has not been correctly translated (or the invalid sections of the conceptual model have been translated correctly) the computerized model will not be credible.

Traceability of computerized model to conceptual model analysis involves review and comparison of the data available on the conceptual model and the model source code to detect areas where the computerized model does not support the conceptual model. Among the areas that need to be compared between the two sets of information are the input/output/MOE definitions and their associated ranges of values, the entities involved and their fidelity, the algorithms employed, and the limitations, restrictions, and assumptions made during the development. In addition, the model is checked for the attributes listed in appendix D. This part of the tracing helps to fill in the simulation characterization attribute and matrix illustrated in the sample Tables 4-1 and 4-2. (See also Chapter 8.) If the conceptual model was developed to a requirements specification (or the equivalent of that was developed during conceptual model validation) then an automated requirements tracing tool may be used to conduct this analysis. Any potential deficiencies discovered by this procedure during the planning phase are factored into the application phase analysis strategy as risk areas. Deficiencies discovered during the application phase are analyzed for their impact on the intended use so that appropriate risk levels can be assigned. Requirement tracers can be used to aid this analysis.

The traceability of the characteristics in the computerized model back to the intended use specification is necessary to verify that the model can support that intended use. Traceability of computerized model to intended use analysis involves review and comparison of the data available on the computerized model and the intended use to locate areas where the computerized model cannot support the intended use of the model. Among the areas that need to be compared are the input/output/MOE definitions and their associated ranges of values, and the entities involved and their fidelity. In addition, any special user requirements need to be verified in the computerized model. Any potential deficiencies discovered by this procedure during the planning phase are factored into the application phase analysis strategy as risk areas. Deficiencies discovered during the application phase are analyzed for their impact on the intended use so that appropriate risk levels can be assigned.

This method produces the following outputs.
- A list of areas where the computerized model does not trace to the valid sections of the conceptual model and an assessment of the impact of the lack of traceability on the intended use of the model
- A list of areas where the computerized model traces to the invalid sections of the conceptual model and an assessment of the impact of that tracing on the intended use of the model
- A list of areas where the computerized model does not trace to the intended use of the model and an assessment of the impact of that on the proposed experiment
- A requirements cross-reference matrix
- Additions to the characterization of the model

CASE and design methodology adherence analysis. CASE and design methodology adherence analysis is a method involving review of the design methodology and any CASE tools used during the development process to determine whether they were correctly employed.

CASE and design methodology adherence analysis evaluates how well the developer employed any design methodologies and/or CASE tools utilized during simulation development. Specifically, this analysis verifies that the engineering tools, capabilities, and guidelines provided by CASE tools and design methodologies were not ignored or misused. This verification is important in two respects. First, CASE tools and design methodologies can provide a great deal of information about the simulation. This analysis helps verify that this information is correct. Second, if some or all of this information is incorrect, this analysis determines the impact on the intended use requirements.

During the planning phase this method provides data on the employed CASE tools and design methodologies, and the information they provide. During the application phase, CASE and design methodology adherence analysis provides information on the weaknesses in the application and capabilities of the tools and methodologies, and the impact of those weaknesses on the intended use requirements.

The usefulness of this method is limited by the availability of the CASE tools used during development, and the assessment team's knowledge of the design methodology and CASE tool capabilities.

These procedure requires

- CASE tools (essential data),
- design methodology (essential data),
- model requirements specification (essential data), and
- CASE tool-generated information (essential data).

The term CASE encompasses all software tools that aid or automate system development throughout the life cycle. Several categories of CASE tools exist ranging from design methodology support to program management. Design methodology support tools provide a platform for the use of modeling languages that specify system requirements and design. These modeling languages are based upon the various design methods such as top-down structured design, data-structure design, and object-oriented design.

Errors can occur using design methodologies and CASE tools when the developer

- does not fully understand the syntax and semantics of the modeling language,
- ignores the warnings of noncompliance produced by the tools,
- fails to use tool capabilities, or
- manages configuration in a faulty way.

There are two approaches in CASE and design methodology adherence analysis for verifying the correct use of the CASE tools and the correct employment of the design methodology. The choice of approach is dictated by the types of CASE tools used during the development.

The first approach is to look for logical mappings between the documentation, conceptual model, and computerized model. This is useful for identifying areas where the developer's understanding of the modeling language is faulty, and for verifying the correct use of documentation generation and code generation tools. There are several ways to perform this task. The first is to conduct reviews of the models involving people well-versed in the design methodology and modeling language. Second, reverse engineering tools (if available) can be used to translate the code into low-level design models. These design models are compared with the original models for consistency. Last, since the correct use of the tools and a clear understanding of the modeling language leads to direct traceability between the conceptual and computerized models, adherence to the design methodology and correct use of the CASE tools is straightforward to check. Areas where the models do not trace are analyzed for their impact on the intended use of the model. This approach is closely related to traceability analysis (covered earlier in this section).

The second approach to CASE and design methodology adherence analysis is designed to verify the correct use of traceability and model analysis tools. These tools produce a repeatable, automated output. In this approach, the generation of this output is repeated by the assessment team to verify that all warning and errors generated by the tools were properly dealt with by the developer. Errors or warnings generated by these tools during the assessment indicate incorrect use of the tools and each such message is analyzed to determine the effect of the noncompliance on the intended use of the model.

This method produces
- a list of areas where the design methodology was not adhered to and the impact of that non-adherence on the intended use of the model, and
- a list of areas where the CASE tools used during the development were not correctly employed and the impact of that misuse on the intended use of the model.

Software metrics analysis. Software metrics analysis involves reviewing data and derived metrics that characterize attributes of the model development or product to identify potential risk areas associated with using the model. The procedures involved are process metrics analysis and product metrics analysis.

Software metrics analysis evaluates measurable characteristics of the model collected during or after its development. Primitive data on which the metrics are based are directly measurable, countable, or constant attributes relating to the development or use of the model. During the planning phase, the analyst selects and examines software metrics for which data are available to identify potential risk areas and to assist in formulating evaluation objectives for the application phase. During the application phase, the analyst selects software metrics that relate to accomplishing the evaluation objectives, collects or derives the required data using other assessment procedures, and analyzes the metrics to assist with understanding and documenting assessment results.

There are four main limitations inherent to software metrics analysis. First, many metrics are linked to the structure of the development software and may not be applicable to all models. Second, process metrics are based on data measured periodically throughout the development process; if this data was not collected, it may not be possible to reconstruct it, and the associated process metrics cannot be evaluated. Third, although many software metrics provide a relative measure of software quality, values of metrics need to be calibrated against an accepted standard to discern absolute measures of quality. In many cases, such a standard may not exist. Fourth, most product measures require detailed data about the model's design and structure that must be collected manually or by automated tools. If the required tools are not available or do not exist, data collection becomes a very time- and staff-intensive effort.

The following items are needed to use these procedures.

Process metrics analysis
- design documentation (essential data)
- module test documentation (essential data)
- previous use documentation (essential data)
- development cycle documentation (essential data)
- unit test documentation (essential data)
- development test reports (essential data)
- documentation supporting adherence/non-adherence to plans and standards (essential data)

Product metrics analysis
- design documentation (essential data)
- algorithm references (essential data)
- model source code (essential data)
- previous use documentation (useful data)
- model interface documents (essential data)
- computer resource utilization statistics (essential data)
- compilers/assemblers - for certain static analysis tools (useful data)

Process metrics. Process metrics used during the software development can provide an early indication of areas that do not support a credible model. Specifically, these metrics offer insight into such areas as the sufficiency of testing and the degree of adherence to the development plan. This procedure involves review of these metrics and would best be used in conjunction with the other procedures listed in this section. (These metrics and their definitions were gleaned from various references on software quality indicators.[33,40-43] The following paragraphs describe process metrics useful in the assessment effort as well as associated assessment procedures.

Development progress metrics monitor the developer's adherence to schedule throughout the software development. Development progress metrics are normally measured in both absolute terms (such as the number of software units completed) and relative terms (for example, the percentage of units completed). Comparison of actual progress to planned progress sheds considerable light on the orderliness of the development. The rate of development progress typically starts slow as development personnel climb the learning curve for the software, accelerates as development progresses, then slows again as development nears completion, possibly in response to delays encountered in difficult software units or to normal staff reductions. Deviations from such a development progress profile (such as a premature leveling off of development progress) may signal that unanticipated software difficulties were encountered during the development that could have led to degraded software quality. This metric can be used with the development history analysis' development plans, discussed earlier in this chapter.

Testing progress metrics monitor the developer's adherence to schedule throughout the software testing and integration. The number of units integrated measures the rate at which software interfaces were checked out, and the number of tests completed measures the rate at which software requirements were validated. Comparisons of actual and planned unit integration and requirement tests reveal the extent to which testing progressed and may provide an indirect reflection of the degree to which software problems were uncovered. In particular, an increasing rate for new or unresolved problem reports may have been an indication of software quality problems. Testing progress metrics are also related to the development history analysis' verification and validation plans; test plans, procedures, and results; and problem reports/discrepancy reports history.

Fault density metrics indicate how well the requirements were implemented in testable software products. This indicator can be used with test coverage metrics (covered later) to assess software reliability and maturity qualitatively. Specifically, these metrics consist of the cumulative faults discovered divided by the total number of software units and the cumulative faults corrected divided by the total number of software units. Fault density metrics should level off during testing and gradually flatten as testing nears completion. Failure to match such a profile may be an indication of immature software or inadequate testing. Fault density metrics are related to development history analysis' QA/CM plans and internal software testing analysis (covered earlier in this section).

Test coverage metrics measure the completeness of the test process. They look at both the percentage of requirements tested and the percentage of software structure tested against the planned test coverage objectives. This indicator provides insight into how well the software was stressed during testing. The metric used is the percentage of implemented requirements tested multiplied by the percentage of software structure tested. Several measures of test coverage of software structure have been formulated within the software testing community. Some of the more commonly used test coverage metrics are described in this section. Test coverage metrics are related to development history analysis' QA/CM plans and internal software testing analysis.

Test sufficiency metrics address how successful the developer's test processes were in detecting software errors before the software became operational. When used with fault density metrics, the number of errors remaining in developed software can be estimated. The metrics used by this indicator are an estimate of remaining faults (based on the numbers of faults predicted and detected) and maximum and minimum tolerances (which are subjective estimates of the number of remaining faults that would be operationally acceptable). If the indicator falls outside the tolerance band, the software being assessed may require additional testing. Test sufficiency metrics are related to development history analysis' QA/CM plans and internal software testing analysis.

Product metrics. Product metrics can be used to characterize the attributes of previously developed software. Collecting or deriving product metrics assists in identifying risk areas and documenting assessment results. Details on product metrics can be found in references suggested in the bibliography. The following paragraphs briefly describe metrics useful in the assessment effort as well as associated assessment procedures. (This is by no means intended to be an exhaustive list, nor a robust treatment of each metric. It should however expose those users concerned with such tools to the variety and capabilities available).

Efficiency metrics quantify the relative extent to which a software product utilizes system resources effectively. Relevant measurements include processing effectiveness, storage effectiveness, and communication effectiveness. Simple efficiency metrics are measured in units of actual resource utilization divided by total resource availability. Additional efficiency metrics can be constructed based on various primitive design criteria considered important to the efficiency of the software product. Efficiency metrics are related to code analysis.

Security metrics assess the degree to which a software product controls unauthorized access to or modifications of system software and data. Simple security metrics are measured in units of the number of security-related software failures occurring during a given time period divided by the total number of executable lines of source code. Security metrics are related to code locking method analysis and security code analysis, both covered later in this chapter, in the section on internal security verification.

Reliability metrics assess the degree to which a software product consistently performs its intended function without failures. Draft IEEE Standard P982, "Software Reliability Measurement," provides a set of metrics indicative of software reliability that can be applied to the software product as well as to the development and support processes. Reliability metrics in this context are primarily concerned with accuracy, although software design and implementation considerations of complexity also pertain to reliability. Simple reliability metrics are measured in units of the number of software failures occurring during a given time period divided by the total number of executable lines of source code. Reliability metrics can be used with analytical tests, extreme-condition testing, limited standards testing, and input-output relationship testing, all covered in the next section.

Correctness metrics assess the degree to which a software product satisfies its specified requirements. This type of metric is concerned primarily with completeness, consistency, and traceability. Simple correctness metrics are measured in units of total errors occurring during a given period of time divided by the total number of executable lines of source code. Other correctness metrics can be constructed based on various primitive design criteria considered important to the correctness of developed software. Correctness metrics are related to code analysis and traceability of computerized model to conceptual model analysis.

Maintainability metrics assess the effort required to locate and correct any error in a software product. Maintainability metrics are concerned primarily with self-descriptiveness and complexity, although software design and implementation considerations of consistency, visibility, and modularity also pertain. Simple maintainability metrics are measured in units of average labor days to fix a detected software fault. Other maintainability metrics can be constructed based on various primitive design criteria considered important to the maintainability of developed software. For example, the McCabe Complexity Metric (discussed in earlier in the section on computerized analysis tools) may be used for assessing maintainability. Maintainability metrics are related to code analysis and development history analysis' coding standards.

Verifiability metrics assess the effort required to ensure a software product performs its intended functions. Verifiability metrics are concerned primarily with visibility, modularity, self-descriptiveness, and complexity. Simple verifiability metrics are measured in units of effort to verify software operation and performance divided by the original development effort. These metrics are related to code analysis, input-output relationship testing (covered in the next section), and internal software testing analysis.

Interoperability metrics assess the degree to which the software can interface with other systems. Interoperability metrics are concerned primarily with commonality, functional overlap, and system compatibility, although software design and implementation considerations of independence and modularity also pertain to software interoperability. Simple interoperability metrics are measured in units of effort to couple divided by effort to develop. Other interoperability metrics can be constructed based on various primitive design criteria considered important to the interoperability of developed software. These metrics are related to development history analysis' interface standards/documents (covered earlier in this chapter).

This method produces the following outputs:

- a list of potential risk areas based on the metric values, and
- quantitative measures that characterize attributes of the software development or product.

Internal software testing analysis. Internal software testing analysis involves the conduct of some additional low-level testing to support the confidence assessment effort. Internal software testing analysis augments the developer's efforts in the area of module, unit, and integration testing where necessary. During the application phase, the conduct of extra, low-level tests can be used to add more credibility to the model. Internal software testing analysis requires runs of the computerized model (possibly using test tools) during the application phase.

This analysis is limited by how many of the test tools were kept by the developer or can be recreated by the assessment team.

The following items are needed to use this procedure:

- model source code (essential data),
- model executable code (essential data), and
- test tools (essential data).

The extent to which the pieces of a model have been tested individually can affect the credibility of the model. Areas where the model has not received sufficient attention at a low-level are tested during the assessment. This process is designed both to augment the development testing and to repeat some of the developer's tests as a sanity check. These tests are closely related to development history analysis' verification and validation plans, and test plans, procedures, and results. This process relies on running portions of the model standing alone or as small units to verify that details (such as algorithms or error handling) contained in those portions are correct. If the developer has maintained controlled copies of all test drivers and test tools that were used during the development, then this analysis can be conducted using those tools. Otherwise, test drivers may have to be developed to support module and unit level testing. Any portions of the model that do not provide correct responses are analyzed to determine their impact on the intended use of the model so that correct risk levels can be assigned.

A common element with all testing approaches is the need to choose test case inputs. There are several strategies for determining sets of inputs to run for a given testing program. These include path, domain, structured, and fault tree analysis strategies.

For the path strategy, test data are chosen to cause selected paths in the model to be executed. These data may be generated manually or with the aid of test data generation tools. These tools can either select the path and let the analyst generate the test data, or take an analyst-selected path and generate the test data. In some cases, the tool may be capable of both generating the path and the equivalent test data.

For the domain strategy, test data are chosen to reveal domain errors. A domain error occurs when a specific input follows an incorrect path in the program due to an error in the control flow of the program. This strategy is based on the premise that the control flow statements of a model partition its input space into mutually exclusive domains, each of which corresponds to a particular program path. By selecting inputs from each of the domains, complete coverage of the program paths can be achieved.

McCabe's complexity metric. The structured strategy is based on McCabe's complexity metric, which can identify suitable paths and test data for effective testing.[36] McCabe's metric represents a computer program by its associated control graph G and uses the mathematical concept of the cyclomatic number $V(G)$ of the graph as a measure of complexity of the program. Every outcome of each decision must be executed at least once. At least V distinct paths must be executed, where V is the cyclomatic number of the control graph for the program.

McCabe has derived several alternative ways to compute the cyclomatic number and has also developed a methodology for selecting test cases that satisfy the structured testing criteria. This methodology is based on systematic variation of a baseline functional path.

The software fault tree analysis strategy is adapted from the corresponding methods used for hardware. Fault tree methods seek to determine potentially hazardous events that could result from software errors and to identify the conditions under which such events could occur. Software fault trees can be derived from an analysis of a program's structure or directly from knowledge of the program's operational environment and requirements.

The extent to which these strategies cover the modes of the model's behavior can be constructed by using test coverage measures. Several criteria have been proposed for characterizing the thoroughness of test coverage for a particular set of tests. These criteria include

- executing every instruction at least once,
- exercising every program segment (every decisional outcome) at least once (commonly known as the C1 measure),
- exercising every program segment at least once, and evaluating every predicate term in each decisional outcome to each possible truth value,
- executing together at least once every dependent pair of program segments, and
- exercising every iteration up to and including k repetitions of a loop.

None of the criteria, however, ensures complete testing. This method produces descriptions of areas in the simulation that provide incorrect responses at a low-level and the impact of each on the intended use of the model.

Code analysis. Code analysis involves a detailed review of the coded representation of the model to detect problem areas, incorrect logic, and mishandled extreme conditions in the code that affect the model's acceptability for the intended use.

Code analysis evaluates the coded representation of the model. It ensures that the coded model correctly implements the validated conceptual model and familiarizes the analyst with the coded simulation. The analyst examines the code with a skeptical, questioning attitude, trying to detect possible problem areas and to identify unexpected or extreme conditions that could cause the program to perform incorrectly. The selected implementation is evaluated in terms of correctness, efficiency, accuracy, understandability, and compliance with known constraints. Programming practices are evaluated, and adherence to programming standards is evaluated.

(See the section on conceptual model validation earlier in this chapter.) Also evaluated is the effect of each subroutine's implementation on interfacing subroutines and on the system as a whole. Software tools can help in this process by identifying error-prone constructions and providing other information that would be tedious or impractical to obtain manually. The key ingredient, however, remains the analyst's ability to become thoroughly acquainted with the program and to identify problems and improvements. While code analysis is primarily used during software verification, it is also useful during operational validation, data validation, and internal security verification, all detailed later in this chapter.

During the application phase, code analysis greatly increases the analyst's understanding of the model and ensures that the code is a correct implementation of the validated conceptual model. Without a validated conceptual model, only intrinsic correctness can be verified, not correctness for the original purpose. This method is also designed to provide the information on if the coded model can truly support the entities and ranges of values specified for the intended use.

There are four main limitations inherent in code analysis. First, it requires a stable, controlled version of the code to be completely effective. Second, it requires a validated conceptual model. If the conceptual model is not validated or is not available, then the code analysis effort will be constrained to providing verification that the code faithfully implements what the developer thought he was to implement (valid or not), and correctness for the intended use only. The third limitation is that run-time related errors cannot necessarily be detected during this static analysis. The last limitation is the amount of time and manpower that can be consumed by this activity. Detailed code analysis is a very time- and staff-intensive effort.

The following items are needed to use this procedure:

- model source code (essential data),
- conceptual model validation procedures and results (useful data),
- target computer and language references (useful data),
- user's manual, if available (useful data),
- algorithm references, if applicable (useful data),
- design documentation (useful data), and
- compilers and assemblers for certain static analysis tools (useful data).

Any deficiencies that are discovered by application of the procedure are examined to determine their impact on the intended use of the model so that an appropriate risk level can be assigned to each. Code analysis typically covers four main areas: program logic analysis, program data analysis, program interface analysis, and program constraint analysis. These are not normally performed as separate procedures but are, instead, a single procedure with four separate sections.

Program logic analysis. A typical program is made up of thousands of instructions. The branching and looping operations included in these instructions can create a profusion of program paths, and the complexity of the resulting logic is the source of most programming errors.

Logic reconstruction consists of preparing flowcharts from the code and comparing them to the descriptions and flowcharts in the design materials. The program call structure may be diagrammed and analyzed in the same way. Automated flowcharters and call structure generators may be used in this process. A similar technique, equation reconstruction, consists of reconstructing equations from the code and comparing them with those in the design materials. These reconstruction techniques help the analyst assess the correctness of the coding. Factors considered in the comparison include efficiency of operation in terms of both time and memory use, accuracy of results, and impact of the selected implementation on interfacing subroutines and subsystems.

In assumptions analysis, the analyst follows a program path and identifies the assumptions made by the programmer in writing the code. Included may be assumptions that a given variable is already initialized, that two variables are compatible in type and units, or that inputs are in a particular format. Analysis of these assumptions helps to identify subtle errors in program logic and to suggest improved program implementations.

Interruptability analysis, performed on real-time programs, looks at the effect of interrupts on program operation. The source, purpose, type, and effect of each interrupt must be understood to analyze this aspect of the program. Of particular concern is the potential for resource conflicts caused by interrupts. An interruptability analyzer may be used to identify possible conflicts for further analysis.

In *path analysis*, the analyst identifies every logical condition that must be met for a particular path to be executed, determines the output of the path for selected inputs, and determines whether this set of conditions and outputs represents the true intent for the path. A symbolic executor aids in this process by analyzing program logic, identifying the conditions for selected paths, and generating symbolic expressions that represent path outputs.

Various static analysis tools can aid this analysis. These include (but are not limited to) the following.

- *Super compiler.* Provides global cross-references, set/use and initialization information for all variables, cross-checks of data typing and interface parameters, and other general information to aid manual analysis
- *Automated flowcharter.* Automatically generates flowcharts to aid in manual analysis
- *Call structure generator.* Automatically generates call structures (some automatically output information in a structure chart format)
- *Interruptability analyzer.* Identifies possible conflicts in the use of computer resources as a result of interrupts during program execution
- *Symbolic executor.* Provides algebraic expressions representing the transformations performed and conditions imposed on program variables as a result of executing a particular path.

Program data analysis. Analysis of the data items used by the program is usually performed in conjunction with logic analysis. Program logic defines the actions that the program will take; program data are the items acted on. Ensuring that these data items are defined and used properly and optimally is the objective of program data analysis. This process is closely related to data validation, which is covered later in this chapter, in the section on data validation.

Data structure analysis focuses on the way in which data items are defined and organized. This analysis includes verifying the value of all constants defined by the program and checking the consistency of program data definitions with the descriptions given in design materials. If the programming language includes data types, such as integer, floating point, complex, and logical, the analysis may include ensuring that each data item has been defined in the appropriate category. Particular attention may be given to data organized into arrays to ensure that each array has been defined correctly, that an appropriate method is used for accessing information in the array, and that any pointers related to the array are used correctly.

Dimensional analysis is another technique concerned with data definition. This technique consists of verifying that data items have been assigned appropriate units and scaling factors. The analysis is frequently performed in conjunction with equation reconstruction to ensure that the mathematical quantities used in an expression are compatible in units and scaling and will result in the calculation of a quantity that has the required precision.

Data usage analysis ensures that each data item is used compatibly with its definition and with its description in the design materials. A logical flag used as a mathematical entity, for example, would indicate a data usage error. This technique also focuses on such problems as addressing errors, use of mixed-mode expressions, and faulty indexing into arrays. A set-use matrix may be prepared from the code and compared with the set-use information in the design materials. Useful tools include a global cross-reference generator and a program editor providing annotated listings.

Data flow analysis scrutinizes both the logical structure of the program and the data usage properties of each program statement. It uses this information to identify data usage errors such as failing to initialize variables before they are used, failing to use variables once they are set, and resetting variables before previous values are used. A data flow analyzer can aid in identifying these errors and can also respond to user requests to identify all variable settings that may affect, or be affected by, a given setting. This information helps to identify errors and inefficiencies in the handling of program data.

The tools listed under program logic analysis are also useful for this form of analysis. You can also use a data flow analyzer, which identifies errors (such as variables used before they are set or variables set but never used) and can list all variable settings that affect, or are affected by, a specified variable setting.

Program interface analysis. Most programs comprise a number of subroutines working together to perform the necessary processing. These subroutines frequently pass data to one another and have access to common data areas. In addition, they often interface with system components external to the program, such as hardware devices relaying inputs to the program, other software operating within the system, or a system database. Each of these interfaces is a source of potential problems. Program interface analysis verifies that the interfaces have been implemented properly and optimally.

One aspect of program interface analysis is verifying that subroutine calls and parameter passing are handled correctly and efficiently. Subroutine calls are checked for proper format, and for correct number and order of parameters. The analyst also verifies that each parameter is defined and used correctly in all subroutines that refer to it, and that one subroutine's handling of a parameter does not degrade another's. Special attention may be given to such error-prone constructions as variably dimensioned arrays and equivalenced parameters.

Another aspect of this is ensuring proper use of global data, such as Commons in Fortran. This analysis identifies all the subroutines that reference each global data item and ensures that each is using the item correctly and in a way that does not degrade the data item's use by other subroutines. The analysis is also designed to detect possible conflicts in the use of global data due to interrupts or other situations in which a subroutine inadvertently destroys data needed by another subroutine. A global cross-reference generator is useful in this analysis.

External interface analysis focuses on the program's interfaces with hardware, software, and database components external to the program. This analysis involves determining the interface characteristics of each external component, and ensuring that the program complies with these characteristics. Interfacing hardware may affect data formats, impose time limits on processing, and impact data-handling methods. Interfacing software may have similar effects. An external database will affect data formats and may have special procedures that must be followed to gain access to data. Each of these aspects must be considered to ensure that the external interfaces do not degrade the performance of the program, the interfacing element, or the system as a whole. The tools listed under program logic analysis are also useful for this form of the analysis.

Program constraint analysis. Every program has limitations within which it must operate. These may be imposed by the system or program requirements, by the design solutions selected for the program, or by the hardware characteristics of the computer system on which the program executes. This technique identifies these limitations and ensures that the program operates as efficiently as possible within them.

Timing analysis may be applied if the program must perform some or all of its functions within a given amount of time. This technique is most effectively applied with the use of a timing analyzer. The results can identify paths that are unacceptably time consuming or that are candidates for optimization. Timing analysis can also be used to compare the execution times required for alternate implementations of a given algorithm.

Sizing analysis ensures that the program does not exceed limits placed on the amount of computer memory or secondary storage it may use. Computer memory usage is easily determined from statistics output by such support software as assemblers, compilers, and loaders. Usage of secondary storage may require an analysis of program logic and data structures to determine the frequency with which data are stored into secondary memory and the amount of data stored each time. A memory decode program able to locate all such storing instructions is useful in this analysis. Alternate implementations may be evaluated to identify more size-efficient approaches, including memory overlay methods.

A frequent source of program errors is improper handling of the limitations imposed by the target computer system. Potential problem areas include the program's sensing and handling of overflow and underflow conditions, its use of extension registers to address desired memory locations, the measures it takes to handle rounding and truncation of data values, and the checks it performs to ensure that data and registers are within allowable ranges before using them. Program limitations may also be imposed by peripheral equipment and the operating system. Program errors and inefficiencies resulting from such limitations are frequently subtle and difficult to detect. Analysis aimed at locating them requires a detailed understanding of the computer system and its characteristics. The characteristics of the compiler or assembler used for translating source code to object code must also be understood. Software tools such as memory decode programs may be used in the analysis.

The tools listed under program logic analysis are also useful for this form of analysis. The following tools may also be useful.

- A timing analyzer calculates execution times for selected program paths using a table of timing formulas. Other timing analyzers monitor a program during runtime and provide statistics on the actual runtime of each section of the code.
- A memory decoder translates object code back to symbolic notation and identifies all instances of selected bit patterns, such as critical instructions that may be disguised as data in the source code.

This method produces the following outputs:

- a description of areas where the code does not correctly implement the conceptual model and an assessment of the impact of that on the intended use of the model,

- descriptions of coding and interface errors and an assessment of the impact of them on the intended use of the model,
- descriptions of inefficient code and its effect upon the intended use of the model, and
- additions to the characterization of the model.

Correctness proofs. Correctness proofs involve construction through assertion-checking of an actual proof of a program's correctness. They prove the correctness of a portion of a model. During the application phase it provides a high-level of certainty that a given section of the model is correct.

The proofs are constrained by the fact that the model must be specified in an axiomatically rigorous language. In addition, they are very difficult and time-consuming to construct. Because of these limitations, this method will probably have very limited utility in many application environments.

The procedure requires

- model source code (essential data) and
- model requirements specification (essential data).

The basic procedure used to prove program correctness is assertion checking. Under this procedure, the correct behaviors (or, requirements) of a program are specified in the form of input/output assertions. An input assertion characterizes conditions expected to be true upon entry to the program, and an output assertion characterizes conditions expected to be true upon exit. Symbolic execution techniques, possibly employing symbolic executors (refer to the sections on code analysis and program logic analysis) are then employed to show the truth of an input assertion upon entry guarantees the truth of the corresponding output assertion upon exit. When all such assertions (specification requirements) have been checked, the program is considered successfully proved. This method produces a proof of correctness for a portion of the model.

Operational validation

The goal of operational validation is to assure that the model compares well to perceived reality. This process uses methods for software testing that are commonly employed during software validation. These include all levels of tests, from inspection to demonstration, to analytical tests. A common element with all testing approaches is the need to choose test case inputs. We covered several strategies for doing this in the section on software verification analysis. In this section we detail the operational validation testing methods.

```
Inspection tests
 •  Delphi tests
 •  Turing tests
 •  Input/output relationship tests
        Static analysis
        Dynamic approach
 •  Event-sequencing tests
        Static analysis
        Dynamic approach

Demonstration tests
        Animation tests
        Fixed-value tests
        Simplified tests
        Predictive validation tests
        Internal validity tests
        Extreme-condition tests
        N-version tests
        Limited standards tests

Analytical tests
        Predictive validation
        Comparison to test data
        Sensitivity analysis
        Feedback loop analysis
```

Table 3-4. Operational validation analysis tools.

Inspection tests. Inspection tests involve a heuristic comparison of a model's outputs to how the real system is expected to operate to determine if the model is functioning in a similar fashion. The procedures involved are Delphi tests, Turing tests, input-output relationship testing, and event sequencing testing.

Inspection tests evaluate the model and its outputs using visual examination procedures ranging from ones that use a panel of people knowledgeable on the system reviewing relatively unstructured data to procedures that use only a few analysts with very structured data. They are used to provide a check on the level of realism available from the model. In some cases, software tools may aid in the generation and/or analysis of the test data. During the planning phase, these tests can be used to provide preliminary evidence that the model is providing reasonable outputs. In addition, they increase the analyst's understanding about the model and the system being modeled. Areas that do not appear to be providing the correct output contribute to the selection of analysis procedures for the application phase. During the application phase, these tests provide preliminary verification of the internal relationships in the model.

Inspection tests are constrained by the level of knowledge available on the system being modeled, the availability of other models with which to compare, and the ability to gather intermediate data from the model runs. In addition, they do not provide rigorous, objective data about the model, only subjective data with bits and pieces of objective data. All these procedures require model executable code.

Data items	Delphi tests	Turing tests	
Model documentation	X		
Model run inputs/outputs		X	
System behavior information	X	O	X = essential data
Inputs/outputs of accepted models/real system		X	O = useful data
Model source code	O	O	

Data items	Input-output Relationship testing	Event-sequencing testing	
Model run inputs/outputs	X		
System behavior information	X	X	X = essential data
Model source code	X	X	

Delphi tests are used to evaluate the model in its entirety but in a non-rigorous fashion. This procedure involves the assembling of a panel of people who are knowledgeable about the system being modeled. Using all of the information available, including their own expertise on the real system, the panel makes a decision as to what areas of the model seem to behave like the real system and which do not. This procedure is very similar to face validity, covered earlier in this chapter. Any model areas that are flagged by the group as not behaving correctly are listed as risk areas and procedures to understand them are added to the application phase analysis plan.

Turing tests are used to evaluate the outputs of the model in a similar fashion to the way the whole model is evaluated during Delphi Tests. The general procedure is for the analyst to run the model and collect inputs and corresponding outputs. Equivalent runs of either the real system (if it is available) or of an accepted other model are also made. People knowledgeable on the system being modeled then compare the two sets of data and attempt to determine which set of data is the *real* data and which set is from the model. If there are any items that the panel can determine the real system data from the model data, how they detected the difference can be used to improve the model. These areas are flagged as risk areas and procedures to understand those risks are added to the application phase analysis strategy.

Input-output relationship testing evaluates the causal relationships between the inputs to a model, and the outputs and MOEs from the model. This procedure may either be performed in a static analysis fashion or in a dynamic environment. Both approaches are designed to detect relationships in the model that are not reasonable.

For the *static analysis approach* to input-output relationship testing, tools may be used to generate flowcharts or global cross-reference tables. (More information on these tools may be found in the section on software validation.) The inputs to the model are manually or automatically traced through the source code to their resultant outputs. These relationships may then be placed on a diagram or in a table to aid further analysis. These relationships are then inspected to see if they are reasonable for the system that is being modeled. Symbolic executors may be used to aid this analysis.

The *dynamic environment approach* to input-output relationship testing involves running the model to collect the data on the inputs and their resultant outputs (instead of generating them by code analysis). The main difference between these two approaches is that no internal path information is provided by the dynamic approach whereas that data is provided by the static approach. As in the static approach, the results of these runs are then tabulated and reviewed by the analysts familiar with the system to detect areas where the model does not correctly describe the input-output relationships of the real system. In both cases, any paths that do not produce reasonable relationships are labeled as risk areas and procedures to understand those risks are added to the application phase analysis strategy.

Event-sequencing testing is used to evaluate the occurrence and internal ordering of events in the model by tracing the events through their generation, evolution and demise. This analysis may be performed using either a static or a dynamic approach. Both approaches are designed to detect areas in the model that do not order the events in the same fashion as expected in the real system.

For the static analysis approach to event-sequencing testing, the analyst reviews the source code looking for the flow of events throughout the model. The tools that are useful for general code analysis (discussed under software verification) are also useful for this analysis. These events are then ordered and related (either graphically or in a table) to show the causal relationships between the various events. These relationships are then reviewed to determine if they represent reasonable relationships for the system being modeled. This procedure is related to program logic analysis (see software verification) and would normally be performed with that analysis.

The dynamic environment approach to event-sequencing testing, involves using runs of the model to trace the flow of events. Intermediate data may need to be collected from the model to provide the level of detail necessary for the analysis. This information is then handled just as the manually collected information was handled in the static analysis approach above. Any areas where the event ordering is not as expected are labeled as risk areas and procedures to understand the risks are added to the application phase analysis plan.

This method produces the following outputs.

- additions to the characterization of the model
- a list of areas that do not seem to provide the correct representation of the system being modeled and a list of procedures to understand those risks
- a list of areas where the causal relationships between the inputs and outputs of the model are not reasonable and a list of procedures to understand those risks
- a list of areas in the model that do not correctly order the events in the system and a list of procedures to understand those risks

Demonstration tests. Demonstration tests evaluate a model by generation of positive examples of its operation. The procedures involved are animation tests, fixed-value tests, simplified testing, predictive-validation testing, internal validity testing, extreme-condition testing, *n*-version testing, and limited standards testing.

Demonstration tests ensure that the model is providing reasonable output by using the model to perform some of the specific operations for which it was designed. The analyst then reviews the outputs and MOEs against other models, hand-calculated results, or the expected behavior of the system. During the planning phase, these tests can provide an early indication of the capabilities of the model and can provide some confidence that it is at least up to a certain minimal standard of operation. During the application phase, these tests can be used to gain an increased understanding of the complex interrelationships in the model and to validate certain portions of the model for limited test conditions. They can also supply information necessary for internal validation of the statistical nature of the model.

All of these procedures are impacted by the degree of randomness associated with the model. In addition, there are different constraints for each of the procedures. Animation tests are constrained by the capabilities of the graphics tools that are available. They require real-time graphics support plus off-line data reduction graphics. Fixed-value tests (and in some cases simplified assumption testing) are limited by how much of the model can be predicted mathematically. Simplified testing is dependent upon having a multilevel model that has validated lower fidelity versions of it available with which to compare the results. Predictive validation testing and limited standards testing are constrained by the availability of similar, accepted models with which to compare the output data. Internal validity testing is limited by the time necessary to get a statistically significant number of runs completed. And *n*-version testing is constrained by the amount of time it takes to construct the independent versions of the model that are required.

Model executable code is required to use these procedures.

Data items	Animation tests	Fixed-value tests	Simplified testing
Model source code			X
Model documentation		O	O
Inputs/outputs of other accepted models/real system			X
Graphical tools	X		
Conceptual model description	O		

X = essential data

O = useful data

Data items	Predictive validation testing	Internal validity testing	*N*-version testing	Limited standards testing
Model source code			X	
Inputs/outputs of other accepted models or real systems	X			X
Statistical item information		X		
Other model versions			X	

X = essential data

O = useful dat

Animation tests are a graphical procedure for understanding the complex, time-dependent interrelationships present in a model. For this procedure, data are collected as the model runs and displayed graphically to the analyst. Ideally, these graphics should be available both real time and for post-processing. This procedure is related to event sequencing testing (covered earlier in this section) however, this normally traces only high-level events. Automated tools may be used to portray the relationships in a variety of ways including histograms and device maps. Using this data, the analyst reviews the relationships in the model looking for inconsistent or inaccurate connections. Any problems detected are analyzed to determine their impact on the intended use of the model so that appropriate risk levels can be assigned.

One procedure for determining the reasonableness of the output of a model is to strictly control the inputs so that very simple cases are run. Running the model under these controlled (degenerated) conditions allows the analyst to compare the outputs with accurate, hand-calculated expected results. Fixed-value tests detect areas where the behavior of the model is incorrect for very specific, simple cases. Any areas where the model does not provide the same output as the expected results are analyzed to determine their impact on the intended use of the model so that appropriate risk levels can be assigned.

Simplified testing involves either removing portions of a model or setting the input values such that sections of the model are not exercised. In this way, the expected behavior can be determined in advance by hand calculation or from accepted lower fidelity models. Then, any areas where the model does not provide the same output as the calculated expected results are analyzed to determine their impact on the intended use of the model so that appropriate risk levels can be assigned. This procedure is related to internal software testing analysis.

Another procedure for demonstrating that a model is providing reasonable data is to compare the results from the model with results from real system field tests or physical models that are distinct from the model under test. This procedure, *predictive validation testing*, is designed to detect sections of the model (such as algorithms) that do not provide correct results. Any tests for which the model does not provide the expected results are analyzed to determine their impact on the intended use of the model so that appropriate risk levels can be assigned. This procedure is related to Turing tests (covered earlier in this section) but is designed to provide more objective results than that procedure.

One factor influencing the confidence level that can be achieved for a model is the level of random variability in the model. A high amount of variability (which corresponds to a lack of consistency) may cause the model's results to be questioned unless the real system is inherently variable. Also, a low degree of variability in the model of an inherently variable system may also raise a risk.

Internal validity testing involves making several replicated runs (using different random number seeds) of a probabilistic model to determine the amount of internal random variability present. Runs that produce a different degree of variability (either higher or lower) than expected are analyzed to determine their impact on the intended use of the model so that appropriate risk levels can be assigned. The way a model handles extreme and unlikely input data can affect the acceptance of outputs generated from nominal inputs.

Extreme-condition testing demonstrates that a model correctly handles non-nominal input conditions. Extreme-condition testing is a process involving running the model with inputs out of the normal range, on the extremes of the normal range, or combinations of inputs that would not normally occur. The handling of those inputs is compared to either an accepted standard or to hand-derived expected results. Any areas of the model that do not correctly handle extreme conditions are analyzed to determine their impact on the intended use of the model so that appropriate risk levels can be assigned.

N-version programming is the software version of hardware fault tolerance testing. Independent software development is conducted on the model or submodels under test by either the assessment team or another independent group. These alternate models provide an independent estimate of the system behavior for comparison with the output of the model under test. If the test results from the two independently developed software modules are identical, there is an increased likelihood that the software is valid. If the test results differ, further analysis of the differences is necessary to determine the problems and their impact on the intended use of the model so that appropriate risk levels can be assigned.

If the average behavior of a group of accepted models is available, the general behavior of the model being assessed can be compared to that standard. This comparison can provide an estimate of whether or not the model is operating in the correct region or if it is out of range.

Limited standard testing runs a set of standard tests through the model in question looking for areas where it provides different answers than the average behavior of a group of accepted models. This set of tests is pre-run through the accepted models to provide the comparison set of data. This data can be set up to provide a limited form of sensitivity analysis by varying key parameters that are common to all of the models. Any areas where the model does not follow the behavior expected contribute to the choice of procedures for the application phase analysis strategy.

This method produces the following outputs:

- Additions to the characterization of the model
- A list of areas in the model where the time-dependent interrelationships are incorrect and an assessment of the risk level associated with each one (animation tests)
- A list of areas that do not correctly process degenerate/simplified cases and an assessment of the risk level associated with each one (fixed-value tests and simplified assumption testing)
- A list of areas that do not provide output equivalent to other models used and an assessment of the risk level associated with each one (predictive validation testing and *n*-version testing)
- A list of areas in the model that have a higher or lower level of random variability than what the real system is expected to have (internal validity testing)
- A list of areas that do not correctly handle extreme inputs and the impact of each one on the intended use of the model (extreme-condition testing)
- A list of areas where the output of the model is wildly different than what is expected and an assessment of the risk level associated with each one (limited standards testing).

Analytical tests. Analytical tests examine a model's outputs to determine if they are comparable to some standard – another model, expected outputs, or actual test data. The procedures involved are predictive validation, comparison to test data, sensitivity analysis, and feedback loop analysis.

Analytical tests ensure that the model is providing statistically consistent outputs. They are accomplished by using the model to repeatedly perform the specific operations for which it was designed. The analyst then compares the outputs to some form of standard (with the real system, an accepted other model, or other runs of the same model). During the application phase, these procedures validate portions of the model (either outputs or feedback mechanisms) statistically and provide the analyst with an increased understanding of the model.

Analytical tests are constrained by the availability of a comparison standard and the amount of time necessary to get a large enough number of sample runs for the statistical analysis. Feedback loop analysis is constrained by the amount of information available on the feedback systems employed in the model and in the real system. The following items are needed to use these procedures.

Data items	Predictive validation	Comparison to test data	Sensitivity analysis	Feedback loop analysis
Model executable code	X	X	X	X
Model source code		X		
Inputs/outputs of other accepted models or real systems	X	X		
Feedback loop information				X

X = essential data

Many of the procedures employ statistical tests to analyze the results. Among the usable methods are
- regression analysis,
- analysis of variance (ANOVA),
- analysis of covariance,
- discriminant analysis,
- response-surface methods, and
- T-tests.

Other procedures to be employed include robust and non-parametric analogs to the methods as well as their multivariate extensions. These procedures are common statistical procedures and can be found in most standard statistics packages.

One procedure for validating the outputs of a model is to use the model to predict the results from runs of an accepted standard. The standard may be derived from the real system or physical probabilities and earlier runs of the model. This case of predictive validation differs from that discussed in this section under demonstration tests by the degree of analysis performed on the data. In that treatment, the runs are used to demonstrate that the model is performing as expected, whereas the procedure here is to statistically analyze the outputs. Allowances must be made for the statistical uncertainties in both the model and either the real system or the accepted standard. Any statistically significant differences between the model and the accepted standard are analyzed to determine their impact on the intended use of the model so that appropriate risk levels can be assigned.

When experimental data are available for a subsystem or component, the results of the model under study can be compared to that data to help validate the outputs of the model. *Comparison to test data* is a process whereby the analyst sets up runs of the model to approximate as closely as possible the conditions under which the experimental data was collected. In some cases, the scope of the model may exceed the scope of the experimental data. For these cases, the extraneous sections of the model will need to be controlled. This may involve setting certain internal variables or external inputs to nominal fixed values (see fixed value tests, under demonstration tests, for a similar method) or removing sections of the model. Care must be exercised when doing this to avoid biasing the results or invalidating empirically derived sections of the model. The analyst then compares the results to the experimental data either directly or by statistical methods. Any significant differences between the two sets of data are analyzed to determine their impact on the intended use of the model so that appropriate risk levels can be assigned.

The sensitivity of a model to changes in its input or internal variables needs to be analyzed. Any variable to which the model is particularly sensitive needs to be carefully reviewed to ensure that it has been modeled to an acceptable fidelity. Sensitivity analysis is performed by systematically varying key inputs or internal values while keeping the rest of the model constant. In this way, the statistical behavior of the model can be analyzed in relation to key variables. Any variable for which the model responds incorrectly is analyzed to determine its impact on the intended use of the model so that appropriate risk levels can be assigned.

One characteristic of many dynamic systems is the presence of *feedback loops* in which effects of one system element are fed through other system elements with a resulting effect on the original element. Feedback loops can be positive (amplifying) or negative (attenuating), and net effects of feedback loops are moderated through counteracting positive and negative loops, as well as by delays. The structure of the real system may translate to a similar structure in the model under review.

Through analysis of this modeled feedback loop structure, the analyst predicts the steady-state behavior of the model. This is then used to validate model assumptions, and to uncover potential differences between the modeled feedback structure and the expected behavior of the real system. Any differences discovered are analyzed to determine their impact on the model's intended use so that appropriate risk levels can be assigned to each item.

This method produces the following outputs:
- additions to the characterization of the model,
- list of statistically significant problems in the model and their impact on the intended use of the model, and
- list of input processing variables to which the model is overly sensitive and the impact of each on the intended use of the model (sensitivity analysis).

Data validation

In addition to validating the conceptual and computerized models, the data used with the model needs to be validated. This includes internal variables as well as inputs and data used to generate the model. The use of invalid or inconsistent data can invalidate the use of an otherwise credible model. All of these methods are related to program data analysis (discussed earlier). The methods for validating data are outlined in the following table.

```
┌─────────────────────────────────────────────────────────┐
│  Data consistency analysis                               │
│  •  Embedded data analysis                               │
│  •  Input  data analysis                                 │
│  •  Consistency analysis                                 │
│                                                          │
│  Representation of constants analysis                    │
│  •  Dimensional and numerical verification analysis      │
│  •  Location and retrieval verification analysis         │
│                                                          │
│  Distributional form analysis                            │
│  •  Graphical analysis                                   │
│  •  Statistical analysis                                 │
└─────────────────────────────────────────────────────────┘
```

Table 3-5. Data validation analysis tools.

Data consistency analysis. Data consistency analysis reviews the data used in the model and the data used as input to the model to verify that the sets of data are consistent with themselves and each other. The procedures involved are embedded data analysis, input data analysis, and consistency analysis.

Data consistency analysis evaluates the consistency of the data used in the model. During the application phase, it provides a mechanism for ensuring that the data used as inputs and the data internal to the model are self-consistent and consistent between the two sets of data. Data consistency analysis is constrained by the quality and appropriateness of the information available on the data used in the model and the interrelationships among that data.

The following items are needed to use these procedures:

Data items	Embedded data analysis	Input data analysis	Consistency analysis
Model source code	X		X
Model input data		X	X
Data support documentation	X	X	X

X = essential data

The data embedded within the model need to be analyzed to show that they are self-consistent. One area of a model should not use one set of data while another area uses a non-equivalent copy of that data. This can lead to serious representation problems within the model and can invalidate the results available from the model.

Embedded data analysis is a procedure designed to detect areas where the internal data used in the model is inconsistent. This procedure involves review of the data contained in the model to find areas where equivalent items are being used but are not represented or set in an equivalent manner. Any sets of such data that are discovered are analyzed to determine their impact on the intended use of the model so that appropriate risk levels can be assigned.

The data used as input to the model need to be analyzed to show that they are self-consistent. One area of the input should not require data inconsistent with data requested in another section of the input. This can lead to inconsistencies in the processing performed and can invalidate the results of the model.

Input consistency analysis detects sections of the input data that are inconsistent. It reviews the input data specifications in general and specifically (if the input data is available). The analyst reviews all of the input specification areas in the model and verifies the correspondence of the input items to each other. Any inconsistent data discovered are analyzed to determine their impact on the intended use of the model so that appropriate risk levels can be assigned.

The consistency of the data between the input data and the model data needs to be verified. If the type or use of the data is not consistent, then the results provided by the model may be invalid.

In *consistency analysis* the analyst compares the input data and the embedded data to find areas where the two sets of data are inconsistent. This may include areas where the model needs one set of data but requests it incorrectly so that the input data does not provide the needed information. Or it may be where the information used to generate the two sets of data are incompatible (such as when the model wants some data in a particular reference frame while the input data provides it in a nearly equivalent frame that is incompatible). Any inconsistent data discovered during this procedure are analyzed to determine their impact on the intended use of the model so that appropriate risk levels can be assigned to each.

This method produces the following outputs:

- a list of embedded data items that are not consistent with each other and an assessment of the impact of each set on the intended use of the model,
- a list of input data items that are not consistent with each other and an assessment of the impact of each set on the intended use of the model, and
- a list of data items (both input and embedded) that are not consistent with each other and an assessment of the impact of each set on the intended use of the model.

Representation of constants analysis. Representation of constants analysis is a method involving review of the locations, units, retrieval, and actual values of the constants used in the model to verify the correctness of the representations. The procedures involved are dimensional and numerical verification analysis and location and retrieval verification analysis.

The analyst evaluates the constants used in the model to ensure that the data used in the model are correctly portrayed in the code. During the application phase, it provides a mechanism for verifying that the units, value, location, and retrieval of the data in the model are all correct. This is primarily a manual process although some sections of the analysis may be aided by software tools. (See the section on software verification for further information on these tools.) This method is closely related to program data analysis.

Representation of constants analysis is constrained by the quality and appropriateness of the information available on the constants used in the model. In addition, due to the difficulties that exist in tracking some of the constants in the code to verify their location and the retrieval methods used with them, this method can be relatively time-consuming.

The following items are needed to use these procedures:

Data items	Dimensional and numerical verification analysis	Location and retrieval verification analysis
Model source code	X	X
Constants documentation	O	O
Constants memory map		O

X = essential data   O = useful data

The constants used in the model need to have both numerically correct values and the correct units employed to integrate with the rest of the model. In *dimensional and numerical validation analysis* the analyst reviews available documentation to determine what the correct constants should be and then reviews the code to determine if those values and units have been correctly translated into the code. This procedure can be effectively combined with the equation reconstruction technique discussed earlier to determine the validity of the representation of complete algorithms. Any constants incorrectly represented in the code are analyzed to determine their impact on the intended use of the model so that appropriate risk levels can be assigned for each one.

Another aspect of constants that needs to be validated is that the constants are being loaded into the correct locations and that they are being accessed correctly. *Location and retrieval verification analysis* is designed to detect constants that may not be located in the correct place in the model or may be being misretrieved before being used. This is primarily a manual process but it may be aided by employing static analysis tools covered under software verification for locating the locations and accesses for a given constant. The analyst verifies the memory locations used for a constant, the retrieval points used to access that constant, and the variable size (integer, double precision, logical, and so on) used to retrieve the constant. This procedure analyzes memory maps for static memory, and databases and the access to them (if applicable). This procedure can be effectively combined with program data analysis. Any incorrect constants or retrievals of constants are analyzed for their impact on the intended use of the model so that appropriate risk levels can be assigned.

This method produces the following outputs.

- A list of constants incorrectly represented in the model and an assessment of the impact of them on the intended use of the model
- A list of constants not loaded into the correct location in the model and an assessment of the impact of them on the intended use of the model
- A list of constants incorrectly retrieved from their storage location and an assessment of the impact of them on the intended use of the model

Distributional form analysis. Distributional form analysis reviews the distributional forms used in, and as input to, the model to verify the reasonableness of each choice. The procedures involved are graphical analysis and statistical analysis.

Distributional form analysis ensures that the random components used in or input to the model are correctly derived, implemented, and used by the model. During the application phase, it provides a mechanism for verifying that the correct distributional forms are being used in the model. In addition, it provides verification of the implementation.

Two main limitations are inherent in distributional form analysis. First, it is constrained by the quantity and quality of the information available on the random components in question. Second, it is constrained by the level of understanding the analysts have for the statistical issues and their impacts.

The following items are needed to use these procedures:

- model source code (essential data),
- statistical items information (useful data), and
- physical experiment data (useful data).

There are two general issues to be addressed in determining whether a distribution in a model is correct.

- Is the distribution representative of the theoretical system behavior?
- Was the distribution correctly implemented in the model?

The first question is a subject that must be addressed in examination of the model's construct and is covered under modeling concept analysis earlier in this chapter. There, the distributional form modeled is compared to actual system knowledge and physical theory governing the system. The second question is investigated in this section.

Verifying the correctness of distributional form can be accomplished using two general procedures: graphical and statistical goodness of fit. Techniques in each class are covered in the following sections.

Graphical methods are the most common and easiest means of verifying a distributional form, for example, plots of the observed distribution against percentiles of the candidate distribution. These are quantile-percentile (QP) plots. The distributional form is correct when the plot forms a roughly straight line. QP plots can be very sensitive. As more data are available from the observed distribution, very small deviations from a straight line can be an indication of lack of fit. An experienced analyst can examine the deviations and determine another class of distributions or parameter variations (in the case of exponential-classes) that may better fit the observed data.

The question of how close is close enough must be raised. Depending on the intended use, the model may perform adequately using a slightly wrong distribution that is easy to model. Appropriate selection of distributional forms can make the model more efficient and easier to implement. A key area to check a distributional form is in the tail where extreme values of the data may occur. Typically, engineering test data have *spikes* at extreme values. This is often difficult to model and modeling shortcuts are common. Unfortunately, the extreme behavior of the data often forces extreme behavior of the system and can be the points of most interest. Care should be taken in examination of the regions of the graph that reflect the extreme values of the distribution.

There are many *statistical methods* that quantitatively measure how well an observed set of data fit a distributional form. Techniques commonly used include the chi-square test, Scheffe test, Blackman-Tukey test, and many others. Each will compare observed data to any distributional form. These methods are commonly documented and their statistical properties well understood. The chi-square test is the oldest and perhaps the most widely used. The other methods were derived in attempts to improve the statistical power over the chi-square test, that is, to make the tests more sensitive to deviations from the distributional form.

These methods are available on most standard statistical software. They can be easily applied but they have some significant shortcomings. If the test result indicates the distributional form is not representative of the data, the analyst must use other means to determine how close the fit was and where in the range the deviation was significant. Most often, the other means used is the graphical procedure listed above. For large data sets, statistical methods can be too sensitive and force additional analysis to assure the analyst of the validity of the procedure conclusions. Statistical goodness-of-fit procedures should be applied carefully in attempts to quantify results from graphical means.

This method produces the following outputs:

- a list of data modeled by incorrect distributional forms and
- a list of data modeled by correct distributional forms, but with incorrectly modeled forms.

Internal security verification

For critical-application models, the internal security of the model needs to be verified. Compromises of the model (and thereby its outputs) need to be prevented. The existence or nonexistence of potential ways to breach the code needs to be investigated. The following paragraphs detail methods that can be used to detect internal security problems in a model.

```
Configuration control analysis
•  CM procedure analysis
•  CM tool analysis
•  Code-locking technique analysis

Security code analysis
•  Undocumented inputs analysis
•  Virus analysis
```

Table 3-6. Internal security verification analysis tools.

Configuration control analysis. Configuration control analysis reviews the configuration management (CM) procedures and tools that were used during development and use of the model to ensure that these controls enhance (not degrade) the internal security of the model. The procedures involved are CM procedure analysis, CM tool analysis, and code locking technique analysis.

Configuration control analysis evaluates the configuration management procedures and tools used to control changes to the code to ensure that they support the maintenance of internal security in the model. During the planning phase, this method provides a mechanism for verifying that the documented procedures and tools used for configuration control during the development and use cycles of the model contribute to the internal security of the model. Areas that do not contribute to this are used to choose procedures that need to be employed during the application phase to understand the risks associated with the internal security of the model. While configuration control analysis is primarily a manual process, some of the CM procedures and tools involved may best be analyzed by actually operating them in the computer environment.

Configuration control analysis is constrained by the quality and appropriateness of the information available on the CM procedures and tools used during the development and use cycles of the model. In addition, full analysis of the tools and procedures requires the availability of a system and the requisite tools to test them.

The following items are needed to use these procedures:

Data items	CM procedure analysis	CM tool analysis	Code-locking technique analysis
CM procedures	X		O
CM tools documentation		X	
CM tools		X	
Code locking data			X

X = essential data   O = useful data

The CM procedures that control changes to a model or its databases can contribute to or detract from the internal security of the model. *CM procedure analysis* detects areas in the CM procedures that do not support maintenance of internal security in the model. In CM procedure analysis the analyst reviews the stated procedures for implementing changes into the model or its databases looking for areas where the procedures allow for the input of uncontrolled changes into the baseline. This analysis may be supplemented by actually performing the steps necessary to determine ways to circumvent the controls provided. Any areas where the procedures do not support internal security contribute to the choice of procedures to be applied during the application phase.

The tools that control changes to a model or its databases can also contribute to or detract from the internal security of the model. *CM tool analysis* detects the weaknesses in the tools used to control these changes. In CM tool analysis the analyst reviews the documentation for the tools being used for CM control of the changes to the baseline. This manual analysis may be supplemented by actually exercising the tools to determine ways to bypass the control provided and make uncontrolled changes to the code. Any areas where the tools do not support internal security contribute to the choice of procedures to be applied during the application phase.

A method employed to enhance the internal security of a model may include locking the baselined code with crypto locks. *Code locking technique analysis* is a procedure designed to verify the effectiveness of the particular locking scheme employed for the model. In code locking method analysis the analyst reviews the information on how the code is locked looking for areas of weakness in the method employed. This involves a review of the crypto-key generation procedures, the completeness of the lock-out, and any bypass methods available. Any areas of weakness in the method contribute to the choice of procedures for the application phase analysis.

This method produces

- a list of areas in the configuration management procedures that may allow compromise of the internal security of the model,
- a list of the configuration management tools used that may allow compromise of the internal security of the model, and
- a list of areas of weakness in any code locking schemes used.

Security code analysis. Security code analysis reviews the source code for a model to ensure that it does not contain any way to defeat its own internal security. The procedures involved are undocumented inputs analysis and virus analysis. (This serves as a good introduction to the area of the security of code, but is by no means complete. Several references on this subject have been suggested in the bibliography for further examination of viruses and trusted code.)

Security code analysis evaluates the source code for the model to ensure that the coded model does not provide a means to defeat its own internal security. During the application phase, it provides a mechanism to detect areas in the code that affect the internal security of the model and thereby provides a measure of the internal security of the model. In addition, it familiarizes the analyst with some of the critical sections of the code. This knowledge can be used during the other analyses that are conducted on the model. While security code analysis is primarily a manual process, some of the tools available to aid general code analysis can also be used here. (See the section on software verification for further details on those tools and general code analysis.)

Security code analysis is constrained by the quality and appropriateness of the information available on the inputs to the code, the outputs of the code, and any unique constructs used in the model. In addition, it is limited by the capabilities of the virus-detecting tools available.

The following items are needed to use these procedures:

Data items	Undocumented inputs analysis	Virus analysis
Model source code	X	X
Input/ output specification	X	
Unique constructs information		O

X = essential data   O = useful data

One method that exists to defeat the internal security of a model is to build into the code undocumented, "illegal" inputs that allow a person to bypass the usual controls on the model.

Undocumented inputs analysis detects undocumented inputs and determines if they just require documentation or if they can compromise the internal security of the model. Undocumented inputs analysis is primarily a manual procedure although static analysis tools that provide global cross-references may be used to aid the analysis. (See the section on data validation for further information on these tools.) The analyst reviews the code looking for all of the inputs into the model. These are then compared to the documented inputs to verify that they are actually required inputs to the model. The analyst traces any undocumented inputs to see how they affect the model. If they do not contribute to a needed output or they actively provide a security breach, they are analyzed to determine their impact on the intended use of the model so that appropriate risk levels can be assigned. Any that are simply undocumented inputs are documented to aid further analyses. This procedure is related to program interface analysis, found in the section on software verification.

Another method for bypassing the internal security of the model is to build in sections of undocumented code that perform the bypass. This may include trap-door constructs (which might operate with the inputs discovered during the analysis in this section) or self-modifying code. Virus analysis is designed to detect these undocumented, unique sections of code.

Virus analysis is a code review process that is aided (whenever possible) by virus-detecting tools. Other static analysis tools and logic flow analyzers may also aid this process. The analyst reviews the code and the outputs of the tools looking for all sections of code that do not appear to be normal in the context of the model under review. Any abnormal sections are reviewed to see if they contribute to the required outputs of the model or if they bypass the internal security of the model. Any sections of code that bypass the internal security of the model by allowing illegal accesses, by providing illegal outputs or by modifying the code, are analyzed to determine their impact on the intended use of the model so that appropriate risk levels can be assigned. Any unique constructs relevant to the model are annotated to aid further analyses. This procedure is also related to program interface analysis.

In addition to the tools listed under software verification, virus detectors may prove useful in this analysis. These tools identify constructs in the code that perform illegal actions such as providing illegal outputs and overwriting critical sections of memory.

This method produces
- a list of areas in the code that contain unused or illegal inputs that degrade internal security and
- a list of areas in the code where the constructs used can compromise the internal security of the model.

Review of the five processes of the formal assessment

The following chart condenses the preceding information of this chapter, as a handy synopsis of the tools suggested for each of the processes of a formal assessment.

Conceptual model validation

Face validity analysis

Historical analysis
- Development history analysis
    - Requirements
    - Interface standards
    - Development plans
    - Verification and validation plans
    - QA/CM plans
    - Design standards and specifications
    - Coding standards
    - Test plans, procedures, and results
    - Data collection plan and procedures
    - Data generation plan and procedures
    - Data validation plan and procedures
    - Internal security verification plans
    - Problem reports/discrepancy report history
    - Studies and analysis
- IV & V support analysis
- Model derivative analysis
- Previous model use analysis

Intended use and requirements analysis
- Criticality analysis
    - Definition of criticality classes
    - Classification of requirements
    - Definition of assessment levels
    - Correlation of assessment levels with criticality classes
    - Assignment of assessment levels to requirements
- System analysis
    - Derivation of submodel requirements
    - Comparison of submodel requirements to similar modes
    - Traceability analysis

Model concepts and fidelity analysis
- Modeling concepts analysis
- Input/output analysis
- Algorithm analysis

Logic trace analysis

Operational validation

Inspection tests
- Delphi tests
- Turing tests
- Input/output relationship tests
    - Static analysis
    - Dynamic approach
- Event-sequencing tests
    - Static analysis
    - Dynamic approach

Demonstration tests
- Animation tests
- Fixed-value tests
- Simplified tests
- Predictive validation tests
- Internal validity tests
- Extreme-condition tests
- N-version tests
- Limited standards tests

Analytical tests
- Predictive validation
- Comparison to test data
- Sensitivity analysis
- Feedback loop analysis

Software verification

Computerized model traceability analysis

Case and design methodology adherence analysis

Software metrics analysis
- Process metrics analysis
    - Development progress metrics
    - Testing progress metrics
    - Fault density metrics
    - Test coverage metrics
    - Test sufficiency metrics
- Product metrics analysis
    - Efficiency metrics
    - Security metrics
    - Reliability metrics
    - Correctness metrics
    - Maintainability metrics
    - Verifiability metrics
    - Interoperability metrics

Internal software testing analysis
- McCabe's complexity metric

Code analysis
- Program logic analysis
    - Super compiler
    - Automated flow-charter
    - Call-structure generator
    - Interruptability analyzer
    - Symbolic executor
- Program data analysis
    - Data structure analysis
    - Dimensional analysis
    - Data usage analysis
    - Data flow analysis
- Program interface analysis
    - Subroutine calls/parameter passing analysis
    - Global data usage analysis
    - External interface analysis
- Program constraint analysis
    - Timing analysis
    - Sizing analysis

Correctness proofs

Data validation

Data consistency analysis
- Embedded data analysis
- Input data analysis
- Consistency analysis

Representation of constants analysis
- Dimensional and numerical verification analysis
- Location and retrieval verification analysis

Distributional form analysis
- Graphical analysis
- Statistical analysis

Internal security verification

Configuration control analysis
- CM procedure analysis
- CM tool analysis
- Code-locking technique analysis

Security code analysis
- Undocumented inputs analysis
- Virus analysis

Chapter 4

A Guide to Formal Assessment

METHODOLOGIES - Description of a complete assessment effort. Recommended for technical experts, software engineers, quality assurance personnel, and confidence assessment team members.

In Chapter 2, we detailed the activities of confidence assessment. As indicated in that chapter, these activities can be undertaken at different levels depending on the purpose and constraints governing the effort. The methodology followed in greatest depth and scope was defined as formal assessment and was introduced schematically in Figure 2-3. In this chapter, we detail the procedures for formal assessment of simulation models. We provide an overview of the assessment methodology to introduce assessment concepts and the structure and composition of the formal assessment process. The remaining sections explore the methodology's four phases.

Formal assessment

Different activities are performed in each of the four phases of formal assessment.
- *Preparation.* Gather the required information about the simulation and its intended use and confirm that the assessment can be reasonably accomplished with the information available.
- *Planning.* Review the simulation, its development, testing, and documentation, and the simulation's intended use to form an initial determination of whether the simulation can meet the intended use. Perform limited independent testing of the simulation to investigate apparent problem areas in its performance. Plan the rest of the assessment based on open problem areas identified during this process.
- *Application.* Complete the simulation assessment by applying assessment procedures based on requirements identified in the planning phase.
- *Evaluation.* Evaluate information compiled from the previous phases to form a recommendation concerning use of the candidate simulation.

Note that each phase involves management review of the assessment status and requirements. The incremental reviews also provide an opportunity to present assessment findings and allow management direction of the assessment effort. This review process is chaired by management and should include the CA team of analysts and representatives of: the user, the developer, independent consultants, and experts from associated firms, organizations or agencies. It is also useful to include potential users. If the assessment is being conducted by the developer organization, the members of a review team and CA assessment team must be as objective and impartial as possible.

Figure 4-1 shows the functions that must be accomplished in each phase. Management reviews are listed for each phase.

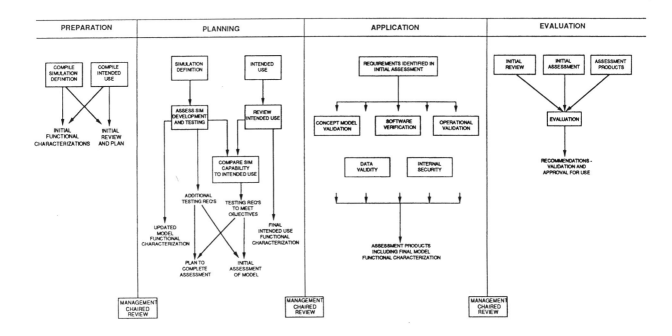

Figure 4-1. Confidence assessment overview.

Preparation phase. During the preparation phase, the information required for the assessment is identified and assembled. In gathering the information, a cursory review will help determine the scope of the data and develop an initial schedule for the assessment. Information required for the assessment includes a description of the simulation and a statement of its intended use.

The objectives for the preparation phase are to
- organize the assessment team,
- gather the information required, and
- develop an initial plan to accomplish the assessment including specific objectives, schedule, and resources, as well as requirements for format and degree of formality in reporting final results.

These activities are described in detail in the next section.

The information required to perform the assessment is difficult to completely specify. Usually, no standards for documentation of a simulation were applied and the information will, most likely, have to be gathered from multiple sources. The objective is to gather the available information describing a simulation and use it to develop the initial assessment plan.

The simulation description includes a wide variety of information concerning the specification, development, testing, and capabilities of the simulation. Consult developers and past users when possible to obtain information describing the model. This is especially desirable if there is inadequate documentation available in any of the stages of the model development or testing, or whenever questions arise concerning the scope of functionality or the model's intended use.

Information needed for an assessment can be found in the following types of documentation:
- specification documents,
- design documents,
- user's manuals,
- operations manuals,
- analyst's manuals,
- technical reference manuals,
- programmer's manuals,
- verification and validation test plans, procedures, and reports,
- source code, and
- histories of the simulation's use.

If the information is not available, it must be derived if possible (see data description, Appendix B). However, information derivation is a higher risk approach to simulation assessment.

Additional information is required regarding the availability of the model, the classification, and versions to be used. The model should be hosted at the assessment site, or as a second choice, via modem or other remote access. Any slip in the hosting schedule may cause responsive slips in the assessment schedule. (A suggested format for the assessment schedule is presented in Chapter 8).

The model version being assessed orients the assessment with respect to specific capabilities and intended use. As mentioned in Chapter 2, model development is often evolutionary, reflecting significant differences between model versions. Therefore, an assessment of one model version may have limited bearing on another. New versions of models are commonly developed to meet additional capability required for an upcoming intended use. This makes assessment of more than one model version advantageous in allowing the assessment process to parallel development efforts for the subsequent versions.

The intended use of the simulation may be specified by a general statement of a set of potential uses or specified in a detailed test plan including an experiment design and scenario. A list of the required functional model capabilities are developed with the users and model developer. As with the simulation definition, the more specific the description of the intended use, the more precise the assessment of the model.

The management review at the conclusion of the preparation phase concentrates on determining whether the simulation can be assessed for the intended use within the resources and time available. The review board evaluates the assessment team's recommendations concerning the adequacy of information to address the assessment issues defined and directs the priority and emphasis for the remainder of the assessment.

Planning phase. The planning phase consists of a detailed review of all available information on the simulation and its intended use, and a comparison of the simulation capabilities with the intended use. Reviewing the available information determines the strengths and weaknesses in the model's development and testing. This review pivots on the technical areas discussed in Chapter 2, under simulation model characteristics. Planning phase assessment procedures structure the review and indicate important areas to be reviewed including the development, past testing or assessment efforts, and the history of the simulation's use. This process includes review of test results and fixes applied to the model. A long, well-documented history of accepted use for a model can contribute to the credibility of the simulation.

The objectives of the planning phase are to

- review the simulation's development, testing, history, and intended use;
- perform some limited testing of the simulation to investigate some apparent problem areas,
- further develop the functional characterization of the intended use;
- further develop the functional characterization of the model;
- identify open problem areas from the developer's effort; and
- develop a plan to investigate open problem areas.

Meeting these objectives requires review and analysis of the information gathered in the preparation phase. Activity in this phase is accomplished according to the initial plan. The plan developed in this phase represents a revision to the initial plan that includes application of specific additional assessment procedures to investigate open problem areas. The activities performed in this phase are described in detail later in this chapter.

Review of the simulation description and intended use is guided by a set of detailed questions. Answers to the questions define areas of the model's strength and areas where there appear to be concerns about the model's credibility. Potential weaknesses in the development or testing of the model indicate where additional assessment must be accomplished. The questions posed during this phase must investigate areas of the model used such as

- model functionality, functional elements, and the interaction between elements supported by the model;
- the level of fidelity and detail;
- model input data types, threat, environment, and so on;
- parameter variations;
- the domain of applicability for the simulation;
- model outputs, MOEs, and intermediate results;
- historical use in comparison with the intended use; and
- required accuracy of model performance.

By examining these technical areas an assessment can be made as to how well the simulation's documented capabilities meet the technical needs of the intended use. Areas where the required model functionality is not supported by demonstrated capability receive particular attention during the assessment.

A summary of the additional analysis and test requirements from these reviews is developed and the assessment team formulates a plan for the remainder of the assessment. This plan is a modification of the plan developed during the preparation phase with more details on resource requirements and scheduling. Results of the initial assessment, including the established capabilities of the simulation and additional assessment requirements are presented to the management review board. The board determines whether to proceed with the assessment and selects or modifies the assessment plan to address the simulation at the level required for the intended use.

Application phase. The application phase entails the execution of the specific assessment plan laid out during the planning phase. Attention is paid throughout to ensure that efforts and interim results are well documented.

The objectives of the application phase are to
- apply assessment procedures to understand problem areas identified in the planning phase,
- document assessment findings, and
- prepare information for the evaluation phase.

The plan developed during the planning phase provides the information required to accomplish this phase of the assessment. This section describes the process of managing and documenting procedure applications and findings. The activities of this phase are described in detail later in this chapter.

As introduced in Chapter 2, the assessment procedures employed during this phase are broken down into the five major categories which are the primary areas where additional effort can enhance the credibility of a model:
- conceptual model validation,
- software verification,
- operational validation,
- data validation, and
- internal security verification.

Based on the specific requirements identified in the planning phase, selected assessment procedures within the new categories are applied to complete the assessment during this phase. Detailed information for each assessment procedure was presented in Chapter 3.

Almost all of the simulations assessed will require application of some procedures if for no other reason than to verify the integrity of the developer's processes. Each of the assessment procedures selected are applied to the simulation as described in the initial assessment plan. The results of the application of specific procedures are compiled for later evaluation. Areas may be revisited several times during the analysis, either by design or in response to needs identified during earlier stages of the assessment.

Evaluation phase. During the evaluation phase, assessment results through the first three phases are compiled and evaluated. The steps required in arriving at the final assessment include developing the relative weightings of problem areas addressed, identification of major problems (potential show stoppers), and development of the appropriate representation of the results and collateral findings. The summary of findings includes a list of the potential risk areas in using the model and their consequences.

The objectives of the evaluation phase are to compile and analyze the results of the previous phases and to develop a recommendation for use or validation. The details of the process used in the assessment, catalogues of the open risk areas for potential users of the model, characterizations of the model and of its intended use are documented to support the final recommendations. This phase involves three distinct steps. First the assessment team compiles the results from all of the previous phases of the assessment. Preliminary findings are discussed in a findings meeting and then assigned to individual team members for development, consolidation, and grouping. These results are then evaluated and conclusions are formulated to support the recommendations. Lastly, based on the assessment report, the final recommendation is drafted for further determinations by management.

These steps are summarized as follows.
- Review open risk areas and determine which are major and minor.
- Assess the impact of the open areas and their criticality to the intended use of the model.
- Form the draft recommendations concerning validation and model use.

- The evaluation phase of the methodology calls for a management-chaired evaluation team. The team is responsible for final evaluation of the assessment results and for developing recommendations for model validation. The activities performed in this phase are described in detail later in this chapter.

Reporting results. The final results and a description of the assessment can be compiled and summarized in a final report. This report contains the detailed assessment procedures followed, the results, and final recommendations. All assessment information is available to experiment planners and future assessment teams, as well as the developer. This will facilitate their efforts to find credible simulations for experiments; in assessing simulations for a particular experiment; and in establishing reference for upgrades.

As was recommended in Chapter 2, it is important to identify the needs, conditions and criteria governing the final report. This effort should be made early in the assessment to avoid any ambiguities or unmet expectations. These issues include the following.

- Who will receive the final results? Who will have access to those results?
- Who is the final approving authority? Who determines the dissemination of results?
- What are the politics? What risks or stakes attend possible findings? Whose neck is on the line?
- What is the desired level of detail?
- How will the results and supporting data be archived? How will the information be secured?
- What degree of formality is required for presentation of findings?
- What format is preferred for presentation of the final results? Options include formal report with full documented substantiation, executive briefing, an executive summary for the read-file, or memorandum for record.

Follow-on assessment efforts. A formal assessment can be reaccomplished on a smaller scale, the concept defined earlier as a maintenance assessment. The purpose of a maintenance assessment is to reexamine a model that has undergone changes since the model's last assessment or is being considered for a different intended use. These changes include the following.

- *Changes to a previously approved or validated model.* If changes have been made to a model that was previously validated, a maintenance assessment may be conducted on the updated model to accomplish revalidation.
- *Changes to a model that failed previous approval for use.* If changes have been made, in an attempt to correct a model that failed to perform as intended, a maintenance assessment may be conducted on the updated model to establish credibility.
- *Changes to the intended uses of the model.* If the intended uses of a model have changed, regardless of whether changes have been made or the model was validated and approved for use or not, a maintenance assessment may be conducted.

A maintenance assessment conducted subsequent to a formal assessment should use all data from previous assessments. The direction of the assessment will be geared more towards investigating the changes to the model rather than reexamining sections of the model that were previously examined. The results from the previous assessment will be reexamined and combined with any new results.

Preparation phase activities

Establish assessment team and identify expertise. A simulation assessment team is established during the preparation phase. The specialized knowledge of the simulation and of its intended use must be contained within the team for the assessment effort. Team members include confidence assessment analysts and representatives of the developer and users, as appropriate. The team leader is normally selected from the assessment staff because of the staff's familiarity with the assessment process. This convention may be varied when specific technical knowledge is required to lead the assessment effort for a particular simulation.

The designated team leader then identifies assessment team members. Team members are selected from the following technical groups:

- confidence assessment group,
- management,
- affiliated personnel,

- developers,
- potential users,
- technical experts for the simulation, or hardware/software consultants, and
- technical experts in certain specific model areas.

Assessment requirements and the technical level of the model dictate the composition of the team and not all of these technical areas provide members for every assessment. However, maintaining access to the appropriate technical areas is essential to assure credibility of the assessment. These technical areas are represented at appropriate reviews and consulted as necessary during the assessment process.

The assessment team makes recommendations for periodic management-chaired reviews of the assessment process. These reviews are intended to provide visibility into the assessment process, intermediate results, and progress and plans. Members reviewing the effort are selected to review the entire assessment process from initiation to final report and to provide insight into the model, its origin, past uses, and its intended uses. The team may include analysts from

- management,
- simulation developer,
- potential simulation users, and
- technical experts for simulation specific areas.

The composition of the group is determined by the interest in the model and the technical requirements of the model itself.

As soon as possible, a kickoff meeting is scheduled and chaired by the team leader. Other parties requiring an overview of the direction to be taken during the analysis or having the ability to provide unique inputs at the outset of the assessment are invited.

The agenda of the meeting includes

- a comprehensive background overview brief containing both top-level directional guidance and scope definition, as well as a general description of the model to be assessed,
- setting initial milestones and target dates for the assessment, including phase completion dates, interim report deadlines, and other required progress brief dates (Figure 8-1 provides a sample schedule),
- identification of the government review requirements and scheduling of the first meeting,
- assignment of general responsibilities to team members to be carried out during all phases of the methodology implementation and of specific tasks to be accomplished during the preparation phase, and
- additionally, it is advisable to determine the desired venue of reporting results.

Other issues of concern include: who will receive results, who is the final approving authority, who disseminates assessment findings, what is the desired level of detail and formality of the presentation of those findings (formal report vs. executive brief), who will brief the results, who will draft the formal copy, how will results be archived and preserved?

Example. Because of the importance of this activity, we provide the following example as motivation of the methods defining the preparation phase.

A discrete-event simulation, PLANT, was developed to model an assembly plant for the production of widgets by the manufacturing company Clangen, Banger & Associates. The CEO, R.U. Clangen, asked his industrial engineering division to study their operations under certain product demand scenarios. Because the PLANT simulation is ten years old, Clangen also hired the consulting firm of Goodbytes Corporation to validate the simulation. Goodbytes held a meeting with Clangen and his industrial engineers. From this initial conference the scope and level of detail that could be committed to the effort was identified. A second significant result of this meeting was that they all determined the use for which the simulation was intended. They concurred that the intended use of PLANT in their application was to evaluate the cost-effectiveness trade-offs of various production schedules given specific product demand conditions. They also determined an acceptable range of model accuracy especially in light of the importance of decisions based on simulation results. Goodbytes then listed PLANT's attributes (see Table 4-1) and formulated the shell of a model characterization matrix (Table 4-2), and modified the characterization of the model's intended use (compiled in Table 4-3). This information was given to the industrial engineers for their review and comment.

As this example illustrates, to assess a simulation it is essential to determine a model's intended use. Equipped with this understanding at the outset, subsequent model characterization can be effectively undertaken.

Compile a simulation description. Three sets of information describing a simulation are used during the assessment process: specification and descriptive documents, procedural documents, and historical documents. Each of these sets provides a different kind of data used in the assessment process. The list of documents in each area includes but is not limited to the following.

Specification and descriptive documents
- requirements, design, and software specifications
- conceptual and computerized model descriptions
- design documents
- functional description
- algorithm references and justification
- maintenance manual
- data descriptions and justification
- trade-off studies
- source code

Procedural documents
- design methodology
- design standards
- coding standards
- programmer's manual
- quality assurance plans
- development plans
- verification plans
- operational validation plans
- test plans, procedures, and results
- data collection, generation, and validation plans
- internal security verification plan
- conceptual model validation plan
- user's manual

Historical documents
- documented relationship to previously assessed model
- documented uses of the model
- configuration management history
- history of problems reported and fixed
- independent verification and validation reports
- model functional characterization previously developed

While not all of this data is absolutely essential to perform an assessment, the greater the body of data available at the outset of the analysis, the more complete the analysis will be. The actual data required for any application phase assessment procedure is found on the application phase procedures information requirements matrix in Chapter 8. The procedure descriptions contain the data requirements for all procedures. In addition, the data item description table in Appendix B contains more complete information as to what data are expected in the documents listed above.

As a realistic minimum, the documentation that the assessment team needs to obtain from the model developer, simulation custodian, configuration manager, or user during this phase includes
- a baselined version of the source code,
- user's manual,
- verification and validation test plans, procedures, and results,
- model specifications, and

- conceptual model documentation.

This set provides the core data required to determine what the model is, what it's supposed to do, how to make it do it, and how it has been tested. This gives the assessment team some data from which to start deriving model capabilities and risk areas associated with using the model. Information contained in these documents can be derived from the code or other available data. However, derivation can be a very intensive, risky effort. Whenever possible more data should be collected to include

- a programmer's manual,
- history of problems reported and how they were resolved,
- documentation on previous uses of the model (including inputs and results where possible), and
- algorithm references.

Characterize the model's intended use. The intended use for the model is summarized by creating a short statement in coordination and agreement with the assessment team, the users, and the developers. This effort is of paramount importance early in the assessment. Agreeing on the intended use helps in establishing the focus of the assessment, in setting realistic goals, and in communicating the expectations of the various players. After this is accomplished, the model can be summarized by listing its attributes and creating a characterization matrix (refer to Tables 4-1 and 4-2). These summaries provide textual, tabular descriptions of the required model capability.

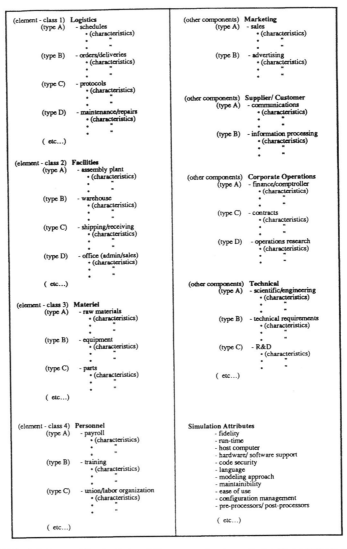

Table 4-1. Assembly plant simulation: sample characterization attributes.

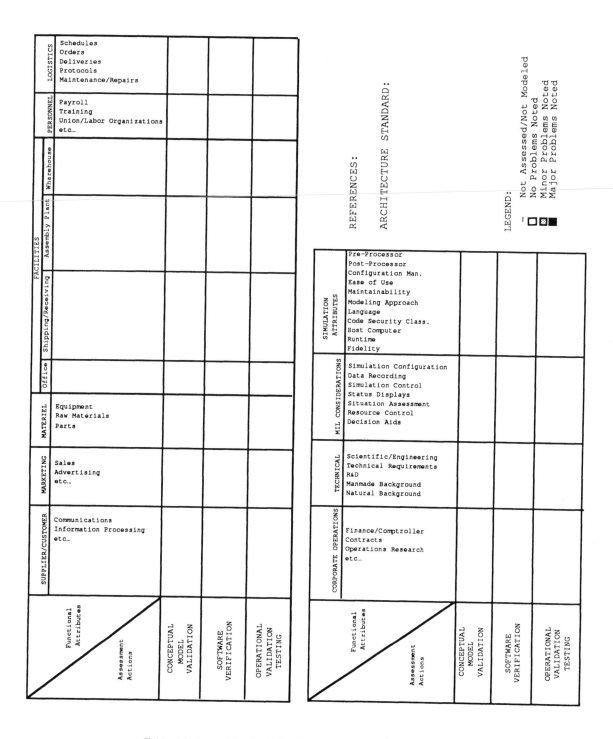

Table 4-2. Assembly plant simulation: sample characterization matrix.

As needed, the characterization of model attributes will be altered appropriately at this point in the assessment. Examples of the general intended uses foreseen for various models include those shown in Table 4-3. A new set of characterization attributes, or a significant modification to the attributes as suggested in Tables 4-1 and 4-2, will be required to address some of these general intended uses. Changes may also be required as the fundamental concepts and system configuration evolve.

ASSEMBLY PLANT SIMULATION

Performance and system design evaluation
Costing analysis
Productivity analysis

ELEMENT SIMULATION
Engineering development model
Personnel/ management
Facilities design
Scheduling/queueing

TEST SUPPORT

TECHNOLOGY SIMULATION
Retool/product development
Operations analysis

SIMULATION SUPPORT TOOL
Shipping/receiving model
Marketing/advertising model
Machine design/ scheduling model
Logistics
Maintenance
Parts and equipment Requisition
Product demand model
Warehousing model

TRAINING AND EDUCATION

Table 4-3. Sample table of model's intended uses.

The model capabilities are also characterized using the attributes illustrated in Table 4-1 and in the characterization matrix in Table 4-2. This summary provides a textual description of the developer's claims for model capability. This information is drawn from such documents as the functional description, user's manual, and programmer's manual. Discussion with the developer can provide additional information to complete the characterization, particularly when the model is under development. This information is updated during the course of the assessment as capabilities are assessed and entries are made to the characterization matrix. These attributes are oriented towards a specific end-to-end simulation model, to be used only for illustration. As described for the attributes used to characterize intended uses, the list of attributes may have to change and evolve to meet model capabilities and system concepts. Justifications and back-up data for the assessment values are provided as supporting data to the final assessment report (discussed later in this chapter).

Define assessment objectives. The assessment attempts to evaluate particular areas of the model or its capability. These can be critical areas of the model design or important aspects of the intended use. Development of the assessment objectives is aided by characterizing the intended use and the model in the same terms.

Defining the assessment objectives focuses a model assessment. Whereas the questions and assessment procedures define the general areas to be examined in a formal assessment, the assessment objectives define those specific issues that must be tested and closely examined for the given model. Some additional depth may be added to the assessment process to address the objective, but no additional scope is expected to address them.

Characterization of the model and its intended use as described above identifies key areas of the model that must be emphasized during the assessment. These areas are where model performance is essential to meeting the study or experiment objectives. Specifically, does the model provide the degree of accuracy required so that the operational results will adequately represent the real-world system? Key areas identified are considered in planning the assessment and in selection of assessment procedures to be applied. Understanding the assessment objectives and their origin is essential for the assessment team to make proper judgments in selecting assessment procedures. The more specific this information is, the more concrete the assessment process can become.

The assessment objectives are derived from comparison of the model and intended use characterizations. These are listed as model capabilities that must be proven to meet the intended use. As assessment procedures are applied during the planning and application phases, additional knowledge becomes available that may update the characterizations and the list of objectives. Any updates represent changes in the focus for the assessment and can influence selection of assessment procedures or direct additional effort into new areas.

Generate an initial assessment plan. Once the information on the simulation has been gathered, the intended use of the simulation has been defined, and the assessment objectives have been compiled, the initial assessment plan is created. The objectives are used to provide an initial estimate of the resources that will be required for the planning and application phases of the assessment, including the following.

- *A model description.* This is a high-level description of the model capabilities. The text will be expanded in later phases to state the model capabilities in detail for the briefing and report.
- *An assessment approach.* The assessment approach contained in the plan highlights the areas of the model that are key to the assessment and procedures to be employed.
- *An initial schedule.* The relationship between assessment tasks is different for each assessment. Factors such as model size, complexity, classification, amount of supporting information, ease of use, intended model uses, and model runtime influence the schedule.
- *Identification of confidence assessment group functions and personnel.* This covers the assessment team composition and assignments. Of particular importance is the availability and tasking of system experts outside of the confidence assessment team including those people from other areas of the hosting organization, the developer, and user agencies.
- *Compilation of simulation documentation and data,* and additional data requirements, which is a gathering of available information for the assessment.
- *Statement of intended use of the simulation,* preferably in the context of the particular experiment or study to be conducted. The intended use for the simulation, along with the model description, serves as the basis for the assessment. This statement of the intended use of the model may be expanded during the assessment in cooperation with the model user.
- *Identification of hardware resources required.* Hardware resources are limited and their utilization must be planned and coordinated with other users.

Management should review the progress of the assessment at the completion of the preparation phase. The assessment team provides the following information:

- composition of the assessment team,
- initial assessment plan, and
- assessment issues concerning the model or information availability that could impact the decision to go ahead with the assessment.

Planning phase activities

Determining the assessment requirements is a three-step procedure.

First step. Apply planning phase procedures that provide
- a functional characterization of the model,
- an evaluation of the development and testing efforts,
- limited additional testing of the model,
- a review of the simulation's intended use, and
- a comparison of the simulation's capabilities with the intended use.

Second step. Compile procedure results and formulation of open problem areas that require additional assessment

Third step. Identify assessment procedures that can be applied during the application phase to understand the problem areas. In some cases, this step will include identification of additional information required to apply the procedures.

At the conclusion of the planning phase, management should review the results and the plan developed. The review requires prioritization of the open assessment areas and identification of resources that can be applied.

Following these three steps, an *initial assessment* of the model is formulated by compiling the problem areas found in review of the development and testing efforts and the capabilities of the simulation to meet its intended use. The initial assessment is part of the material reviewed at the end of this phase.

The assessment is guided by a set of detailed questions that force examination of key attributes of the model development and testing processes, the intended use, and the capabilities demonstrated by the model. Table 4-4 contains a partial list of the questions; the complete list is provided in Chapter 8. Each question is addressed by application of one or more planning phase procedures. A method to select appropriate procedures to address each question is covered later in this section. Most planning phase procedures are performance of specific reviews or other observer-oriented actions. The same planning phase procedure might address more than one question. Table 4-5 is a list of the planning phase procedures that can be applied to address the questions. The entries on the table are grouped by related procedures. Products of the procedures provide answers to the questions. The answers define the model areas for which additional assessment action is required. These areas form the basis for the application phase assessment plan.

Review of intended use

Is the intended use to be supported documented?
Are the elements needing to be modeled documented?
Is the level of detail and fidelity needed for each entity documented?
Are the outputs and measures of effectiveness (MOEs) needed documented?
Are the required key inputs documented?
Are the ranges of values necessary for the key inputs documented?
Were special requirements to be levied on the model documented?

Review of simulation developer's effort problem entity

Was the original intended use to be supported documented?
Were the elements needing to be modeled documented?
Was the level of detail and fidelity needed for each entity documented?
Were the outputs and MOEs needed documented?
Were the required key inputs documented?
Were the ranges of values necessary for the key inputs documented?

Conceptual model derivation

Was there a plan developed for deriving the conceptual model?
Does the conceptual model provide the level of detail and fidelity for each element that was required for the problem entity?
Does the conceptual model provide the outputs and MOEs needed for the problem entity?
Does the conceptual model provide the key inputs that the problem entity required?
Does the conceptual model provide the ranges of values for key inputs that the problem entity required?
Were the assumptions made and theories used during the derivation of the conceptual model documented?
Were the assumptions made and theories used during the derivation of the conceptual model supported?

Table 4-4. Partial question list for formal assessments. (A complete question list is contained in Chapter 8.)

Conceptual model validation
Face validity analysis
Historical analysis
      Development history analysis
      IV&V support analysis
      Model derivative analysis
      Previous model use analysis
Requirements analysis
      Criticality analysis
      System analysis
Model assumptions and fidelity analysis
      Modeling concepts analysis
      Input/output analysis

Software verification
Traceability analysis
      Traceability of computerized model to conceptual model analysis
      Traceability of computerized model to intended use analysis
Case and design methodology adherence analysis
Software metrics analysis
      Process metrics analysis
      Product metrics analysis

Operational validation
Inspection tests
      Delphi tests
      Turing tests
      Input-output relationship testing
      Event sequencing testing
Demonstration tests
      Limited standards testing

Internal security verification
Configuration control analysis
      CM procedure analysis
      CM tool analysis
      Code-locking technique analysis

Table 4-5. Planning phase procedures

Results of the assessment procedures applied to the questions can be summarized into three categories. (We recommend a coding scheme in summary forms, such as the shading method depicted in Table 4-6.)

- *No problems noted.* The documented information satisfactorily answers the question. No further assessment actions are required for the question topic and no problem areas were identified. These can be coded white on summary forms (no shading).
- *Minor problems noted.* The documented information indicates some weakness, absence, or other problem concerning the question topic and raised some minor concern. Further assessment actions are required to allow better understanding of the user risk. These can be coded gray on summary forms (partial shading).
- *Major problems noted.* The documented information indicates some weakness, absence, or other problem concerning the question topic and raised serious concern. Further assessment actions are required to allow better understanding of the user risk. These can be coded black on summary forms (completely filled-in).

As responses for each question are developed from the planning phase procedures, they can be summarized using the form shown in Table 4-6. Application of each procedure is also documented to describe the information reviewed, questions addressed, findings, and description of any problem areas identified. Both the summary table and individual write-ups should be included in a final assessment report.

Question	Planning phase procedure	Related procedure report	Question response (by procedure)	Question summary code
	Table 4-5	Figure 4-2		

    ○   No problems noted
    ◉   Minor problems noted
    ●   Major problems noted

Table 4-6. Question-response summary table.

The method for selecting appropriate planning phase procedures, summarizing their results, and identifying procedures to apply during the application phase is guided by tables identifying potential procedures and summarizing the planning phase results. Figure 4-2 summarizes the steps required to use the tables.

- The first step involves the *Questions to planning phase procedures* table that relates the question list to the appropriate planning phase procedures that can be used to answer each question. This table is provided to the analysts to guide their selection of planning phase procedures to apply.
- The second step involves application of the planning phase procedures to answer the questions. Additional activities during this step include the updating of the model functional characterization (Tables 4-1 and 4-2), and initial creation of assessment finding charts.
- The last step in the process is the development of the *Application phase planning* table by the analysts. The responses recorded in this table help identify risk areas. This table is used to fill out the rest of the *Application phase planning* table. (Chapter 8 contains examples of the tables used in this process.)

The following flow diagram illustrates the step-wise process.

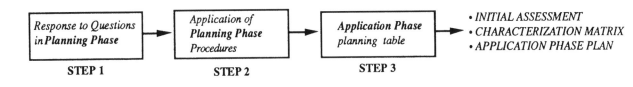

Figure 4-2. Planning phase process.

Develop application phase plan. The application phase assessment plan developed during the planning phase consists of a summary of the open problem areas identified, and prioritized assessment actions that can be used to understand them. Key elements in the formalization are identification of resource requirements and development of a schedule.

This plan provides the starting point from which a resource-constrained plan is developed and also provides information to the government on what a full assessment would entail. Priorities (which reflect knowledge of the model and assessment objectives) assigned to the application phase procedures are used to refine the scope of the assessment to what can be accomplished within the constraints. This process must be done carefully because any procedure not applied may force one or more of the problem areas to remain open after the assessment is completed. These can represent important risk areas and can affect certification actions. If critical questions must remain unanswered because of the constraints, this becomes an issue requiring resolution during the management review. If deemed necessary, an impact statement concerning partial implementation of the assessment procedures is prepared to support requests for additional funding or time to complete the assessment.

At this point, the plan includes

> *a list of assessment procedures* to be applied;
> *resources required to apply the procedures*, including
> - personnel required and approximate time frames for any unique expertise needed,
> - data needed (beyond that presently available) that must be derived by the assessment team,
> - computer resources needed, and
> - additional tools required; and
> *a schedule for the application phase*, including
> - showing when each of the procedures is to be applied and
> - completing the assessment within time and resource constraints.

A management board reviews the results of the planning phase. A summary of the planning phase procedures applied and the application phase plan developed is briefed to the government to provide a forum to address questions and concerns. The assessment team provides the following information.

- Answers to each of the questions addressed
- Procedures used in the investigation and any problem areas identified
- Detailed model characterization, including discrepancies between the model capabilities and intended uses, and areas of capability not thoroughly tested
- Prioritization of the open problem areas including rationale
- Application phase procedures selected and why each was chosen
- Application phase plan including a summary of the procedures to be applied, resources required, and schedule. The plan must also address the impact of resource non-availability, list key planning assumptions, and schedule contingencies.
- Assessment issues concerning the model that could impact any decision to go ahead with the assessment

The second and third items document the initial assessment of the model and can be used by potential users to guide their experiment planning and analysis until the formal assessment is complete. This information has roughly the same scope as a limited assessment and can be used in a similar manner.

Application phase activities

The assessment plan developed during the planning phase describes each of the open problem areas, assessment procedures to be applied to address each problem area, a schedule to follow, and the resource allocations. The problem areas contained in the plan and the schedule specified reflect the priority assigned to the problem areas by the assessment team and management review.

A management review should be held at the end of this phase to communicate results of the assessment procedures. Informal reviews are held during the phase to cover intermediate results and to surface important issues that affect the assessment.

The assessment procedures will be applied according to the schedule developed in the planning phase. Instructions for application of each of the procedures are contained in Chapter 3. That chapter is organized by the major areas of assessment: conceptual model validation, software verification, operational validation, data validation, and internal security. Procedures contained in Chapter 3 for this phase are shown in Table 4-7. Notice the different emphasis reflected here compared with that shown in Table 4-5.

As assessment procedures are applied and more is learned about the model, additional problem areas may be uncovered. These new problem areas must be incorporated into the plan. Schedule and resource restrictions reflected in the plan must be relaxed or the priorities of the problem areas reexamined to consider the new areas. The assessment team performs the initial step to determine if the plan must be modified. A decision may be to let the new areas remain as open risk areas in the final assessment and no changes are required. If, however, some realignment of the assessment priorities is required, the management review board should be asked to review the proposed changes and take part in forming the plan change.

Conceptual model validation
Historical analysis
Model assumptions and fidelity analysis
    Modeling concepts analysis
    Input/output analysis
    Algorithm analysis
Logic trace analysis

Software verification
Traceability analysis
    Traceability of computerized model to conceptual model analysis
    Traceability of computerized model to intended use analysis
Case and design methodology adherence analysis
Software metrics analysis
Internal software testing analysis
Code analysis
Correctness proofs

Operational validation
Inspection tests
    Input-output relationship testing
    Event-sequencing testing
    Demonstration tests
    Animation tests
    Fixed-value tests
    Simplified-assumption testing
    Predictive-validation testing
    Internal-validity testing
    Extreme-condition testing
    N-version testing
    Limited-standards testing
Analytical tests
    Predictive validation
    Comparison to test data
    Sensitivity analysis
    Feedback loop analysis

Data validation
Data consistency analysis
    Embedded data analysis
    Input data analysis
    Consistency analysis
Portrayal of constants analysis
    Dimensional and numerical verification analysis
    Location and retrieval verification analysis
Distributional form analysis
    Graphical analysis
    Statistical analysis

Internal security verification
Security code analysis
    Undocumented inputs analysis
    Virus analysis

Table 4-7. Application phase procedures

Documentation of assessment findings is crucial and it is important to examine problem areas as they are discovered. Table 4-8 illustrates an assessment finding sheet that would assist in documenting and addressing findings. Its purpose is to list specific procedures that could be employed and identify those areas where additional assessment could be fruitful. This sheet will also help in deciding whether new problem areas should be incorporated into the assessment or left as open problem areas in the final assessment.

Model assessment finding

Finding # :

Conceptual model validation:

Software verification:

Operational validation:

Internal security verification:

Data validation:

Risk:

Table 4-8. Assessment findings.

Documenting assessment results. The final product of each assessment procedure is a short report describing application of each assessment procedure used. These reports document the assessment accomplished and form a document trail describing the assessment. This level of information is very valuable to future assessments of the same model and to support assessment conclusions. These reports also contain the level of detail required to specify changes or enhancements to the model to better support the model's credibility. The reports are developed during the assessment process. The analysts involved in application of a procedure prepare the associated report as the procedure is applied. Related procedures may be documented in a single report.

Figure 4-3 shows a general report format. Key elements of the report are a summary of the problem area (either from application of planning phase procedures or from statement of the assessment questions being answered), the purpose of the procedure application, a summary of expected results, a description of how the procedure was applied, findings and observations, and a risk assessment. The purpose of applying the procedure describes what the procedure is intended to investigate in general terms and why the particular procedure has been selected. This is primarily a restatement of the problem area and procedure selection described in the plan. The analyst will have some familiarity with the simulation and will develop a summary of the expected findings. These findings describe particular areas of investigation and concentration the analyst will use to guide the assessment. Each of the steps used in applying the procedure will be documented to describe what was done in assessing the model. Description of the steps taken is important to document decisions made and intermediate results found during the assessment. A summary of the assessment procedure results will include any observations made by the analyst during the assessment. The results are compiled by the analyst to form conclusions that address the problem area being investigated. This level of evaluation may require discussion with other members of the assessment team and management.

```
                                    Analyst:
                Title               Date:

1. Purpose
        1.1 Description of Problem Area
        1.2 Procedures to be Employed

2. Expected results

3. Procedures
        3.X Procedure Implemented
                3.X.1 Description of Effort
                3.X.2 Results

4. Summary of results
        4.1 Findings and Limitations
        4.2 Open Risk Areas
        4.3 Further Assessment Action
```

Figure 4-3. Assessment procedure report outline.

Assessment procedure results are also summarized according to the functional characterization developed in the planning phase. Procedure results are assessments of the correctness of the derivation and implementation of the model attributes described in the textual characterization of the model (Table 4-1). Table 4-2 documents these results. Assessment results are placed in the appropriate row of the matrix based on the assessment area being covered (conceptual model validation, software verification, and so on). The possible categories of assessment results are: *not assessed*, *no problems noted*, *minor problems noted*, and *major problems noted*.

References to the findings that correspond to each of the *minor* and *major problems noted* entries and the related procedure reports are added to the appropriate element of the textual characterization in Table 4-1. Table 4-9 is a portion of Table 4-1 that has been expanded to illustrate this technique.

```
Model characteristic/feature
        Sub-feature - Finding #n

                (text describing model
                capabilities & limitations)

        References: procedure report x
        Operational test log
```

Table 4-9. Expanded textual characterization.

Management review. At the completion of the application phase, management should review the progress of the assessment. The basic issue is to determine if the assessment is complete and final conclusions can be reached based on the information available. The agenda of the meeting includes an overview of the assessment process, including

- problems encountered that hindered the analysis,
- a summary of the application phase analyses, categorized as findings in given areas,
- a list of deviations from the planning phase plan including the rationale for modifications and findings,
- a statement of problem areas or simulation topics not assessed, including impact projections, and
- a list of risk areas arising from the assessment. Refinement and evaluation of this list is accomplished during the evaluation phase, which we address in the next in section.

The agenda should also include reviewing the schedule for the evaluation phase and ensuring that all information required for the evaluation is available from the assessment.

Evaluation phase activities

During this phase of the assessment, a management-chaired evaluation team is formed. It is essentially the CA assessment team augmented with other players as deemed appropriate or necessary for the evaluation effort.

Compile assessment results. The structure imposed during the assessment facilitates compilation of assessment results. Reporting mechanisms that are required during the application of the assessment procedures and the tables used to track and manage the assessment process provide much of the information required. Results of applying the assessment procedures are in terms of the risks involved in using the model. Each assessment procedure was applied to understand a problem area and the results of the effort are expressed in terms of remaining risk areas.

Compiling these results forms a draft of the final assessment report, described in the next section. Most of the assessment results and associated documentation form the technical appendices of the document. A draft of the entire document is developed by the assessment team during this phase of the assessment. This draft is provided to the management-chaired evaluation team as input to the final evaluation process. Other forms of the results are also developed to facilitate group discussion.

Assess problem and risk areas. The assessment team reviews each open problem area to determine its criticality to the model's operation and the extent of its effect on simulation results. Classification of a particular issue is not always a clear-cut decision. Each issue is reviewed by all concerned to ensure that support for a classification is objectively based and not motivated by any predisposition toward enhancing a case for either model approval or rejection.

Problem areas are classified as follows.
- *Major problem area.* Problems in this area individually impact the model's credibility. These are problems that point to incorrect or dishonest model development and test practices or model implementations. Code them black on summary forms. Existence of one or more of these is sufficient reason for denying certification or limiting the potential uses of the model.
- *Minor problem area.* Problems in this area point to weaknesses in model development, testing, or implementation and indicate possible modifications to the model that would improve its credibility. Identification of a reasonably small number of minor problem areas in the absence of more serious concerns is normally acceptable. However, the presence of an unusually large number of minor problems may itself become major. These will be coded gray on the summary forms. The presence of more than one minor problem area may be grounds for forwarding a recommendation to not certify.
- *No problem area.* This area does not seem to affect the simulation's results. These areas indicate correct model implementation providing realistic results. These will be coded white on the summary forms.

Reviews of these problem areas are used to update the form shown in Table 4-2.

The wide variety of simulation models makes it difficult to impose a fixed set of evaluation standards for model certification, as is documented in the literature. The decision to recommend certification may be clear cut. That is, the presence of one or more major concerns may preclude certification. Or, the absence of any major or minor problem areas may make the decision to recommend certification straightforward. More often, however, meticulous implementation of a structured, objective methodology as outlined herein uncovers a number of major and minor issues which must be considered individually and in aggregate to form a final evaluation of a model.

The impact of open problem areas must be examined in light of the model's intended use. Table 4-2 contains the functional characterization of the model reflecting the assessment findings. These products are developed in the planning and application phases of the assessment. Presence of problem areas concerning an attribute are summarized by their criticality (major and minor) to indicate the importance of the problem area.

The following example illustrates how this coding scheme is used as the major and minor problem areas are examined to determine their contributions to the final recommendation.

- Existence of major problem areas is sufficient for the model to fail validation or recommendation for use, unless those problems are tempered by a very general intended use of the model.
- The number, nature, and synergy of the major and minor problem areas contribute to the validation or use recommendation. A number of highly related areas can be more important than a similar number of independent ones. The collective impact on the simulation's results is a determining factor on whether the model should be approved.
- Most of the minor problem areas define areas where the model's credibility could be better supported. A large number of these issues can impact the validation/use decision, mainly in combination with other, more major concerns.

The evaluation is supported by this list of open problem areas, their descriptions, impact, and individual codes. Compiling the codes for the individual problem areas into an overall code for the model is accomplished by selecting the model's most severe rating. The decision to support validation is based on this evaluation.

This evaluation process yields a list of areas that should be improved, enhanced, or corrected in the model. The model developer and users also make recommendations for modifications.

Develop recommendations concerning use. The evaluation team develops the final recommendation for model use. The group evaluates the assessment results and ensures that the assessment was complete and unbiased and that the assessment results are justified. The following is a partial list of issues that they examine concerning conduct of the assessment.

- *Completeness of the assessment.* Verify that all critical areas of the model were assessed.
- *Consistency of results in overlapping areas of coverage.* Ensure that procedures examining related areas show consistent results.
- *Aggregation of results.* Ensure that the grouping of results across procedures and subsets of the model is appropriate.
- *Synergistic evaluations.* Ensure that the joint consideration of related areas was correctly accomplished and that the synergism between them is appropriately represented.
- *Quantitative versus qualitative issues.* Ensure proper application of procedures in each case.

This evaluation is based on the draft evaluation and supporting assessment results provided by the assessment team. Because of the wider purview of this group, there may be additional insight available concerning potential model uses or other information that can contribute to the final assessment. Thus, the group should not be bound by the draft evaluation results.

This group updates and revises the draft evaluation summaries and report. The assessment team incorporates these revisions and prepares the final draft of the report for signature by the evaluation team's chair. The evaluation team then issues a report for dissemination to management.

Reporting activities

At the completion of the evaluation phase, a confidence assessment report and annotated brief are developed to document the assessment effort. (As mentioned in Chapter 2, the expectations for the content, format, and dissemination of the assessment results should be clearly stipulated early in the preparation phase.) Assessment results are also stored in a database or archived on tape for future use and further evaluation.

At its final meeting, the evaluation team coordinates the report and briefing content. Figure 4-4 is a guide for writing the report. Documentation at each step in the evaluation process, as has been emphasized throughout the guide, facilitates compilation of the report. Key elements of the report are: introductory information for the assessment, a summary of the approach followed in each area of the assessment (such as the conceptual model validation or software verification), a list of assessment findings (Table 4-8), a summary of problem areas involved in using the model, and characterization of the model. The model characterization includes the model characterization matrix and the model description (For an example, see Tables 4-1 and 4-2. For general form, refer to Chapter 8.) The intent of the model description is to highlight model functional characteristics, to identify sections of the model where problems were not found, and to address problem areas found during the assessment.

---

1. Preliminary
    1.1 Document purpose
    1.2 Organization of document

2. Assessment introduction
    2.1 Assessment background
    2.2 Model description
    2.3 Assessment scope
    2.4 Assessment team

3. Assessment approach
    3.1 Overview of assessment process
    3.2 Conceptual model validation approach
    3.3 Software verification approach
    3.4 Operational validation test approach
            1) Operational validation test concept
            2) Synopsis of operational validation test plan
    3.5 Data validation approach
    3.6 Internal security verification approach

4. Model characterization

5. Assessment findings

6. Summary of major problem areas

Appendices and enclosures:
    A. Operational validation test log
    B. Assessment procedure reports
    C. Assessment management reports
    D. Model characterization back-up data
    E. Developer comments

Figure 4-4. Confidence assessment report outline.

To develop sections two through six of the report, we can expand the text from the executive summary briefing, which is sometimes terse and not always self-evident. The appendices contain detailed test information, procedure reports, management reports, and the complete characterization data. In addition, an appendix is provided for the developer of the model to supply comments on the assessment and the assessment findings. These comments are added to the confidence assessment report in the form received from the developer.

In a typical assessment report, Appendix A is the assessment test log. It includes the test plan and test results. Each test case is described in terms of purpose, scenario, and expected and observed results, including any anomalies in implementation. Cases are grouped functionally and results may additionally be depicted in summary form. The final report's Appendix B contains all assessment procedure reports. Each analyst participating in the assessment completes one or more procedure reports, structured in accordance with the guidance in the preceding sections.

Appendix C includes assessment characterization back-up data. Each line item on the model characterization attributes (Table 4-1) is expanded with the material presented in the order depicted on the characterization matrix. Brief notations on what specific references support each functional characterization area are included. Appendix D contains model characterization back-up data. Appendix E contains developer comments, at the developer's discretion. Most model developers have chosen to address each assessment finding individually, in the order of presentation during the brief with notations as to the status from developer perspective.

Presentation of findings. The confidence assessment and recommendations package should be submitted to management. The package may then be distributed to developers and users other than the host, for review and comment. Comments from users and developers can be consolidated in a memorandum. The memorandum should contain a statement of approval or disapproval (with supporting rationale) of the model's use.

Chapter 5

A Guide to Limited and Maintenance Assessments

> **METHODOLOGIES - Description of a limited approach to
> the confidence assessment methodology.
> Recommended for technical experts, software engineers, quality
> assurance personnel, and confidence assessment team members.**

As mentioned in Chapters 2 and 3 – and as its name suggests – the limited assessment process is a limited application of formal assessment. A variation, maintenance assessment, permits further flexibility in assessing a model that has been previously assessed or is being continually assessed during its development. In general, this type of assessment can be treated as a special application of the limited assessment methodology. While it would therefore be sufficient to merely highlight the differences between the formal and limited levels of the confidence assessment methodology, this chapter is intended rather to present a complete description of the limited assessment process and the maintenance assessment variation. This description is provided independent of the foregoing treatment of the formal assessment process, with reference to significant differences in the two.

The following section covers the derivation and objectives of this assessment type, and the remaining sections will present the four phases of the process: preparation, planning, application, and evaluation. In addition, we discuss reporting and presenting the findings.

Limited assessment

The basic structure of the limited and maintenance assessment processes is similar to that of formal assessment described in Chapter 4, but with reduced depth (or, detail) and breadth (scope). Another distinction is that, for the sake of expediency, the review process (which had figured so prominently in the formal implementation) is not as prevalent in a limited or maintenance assessment. Although intermediate reviews are eliminated from the assessment process, management participation in the effort is desirable, but the emphasis on quick response minimizes the luxury of frequent reviews. Furthermore, limited and maintenance assessment consist chiefly of only three of the five formal assessment activities: conceptual model validation, software verification, and operational validation. Internal security verification and data validation are optional activities to be included as time and resources permit, or as model use or design specifications require.

Objectives of limited assessment. A limited assessment provides a level of confidence in a model for potential users, and identifies potential areas of risk associated with using the model, especially within time or cost constraints.

The limited assessment process is predominantly a risk analysis and model characterization whose objectives are consistent with those of the formal assessment, though limited in scope and detail. These objectives are
- to determine the degree of credibility that can be attributed to a simulation primarily by assessing the development efforts,
- to characterize the model to identify capabilities for potential users of the model,
- to identify and quantify risk areas in applying the simulation to its intended use, and
- to provide an analytical basis for further assessment, possibly in conjunction with a different experiment. The limited assessment, when properly conducted, provides the groundwork for, and initial stages of, a formal assessment. A limited assessment can also be followed by one or more maintenance assessments to track evolution and development of a model.

A limited assessment is appropriate in those instances when a formal assessment would prove too time consuming or costly and when a less formal implementation of the process, of reduced scope or detail, may provide enough credibility analysis. A formal assessment can be accomplished at a later date as needed, or as time and resources permit.

A limited assessment of a model is designed to be performed during the model development or use. The assessment team can perform their functions in close cooperation with the model developer and/or the experiment team. Discrepancies that are noted and enhancements to the model that are proposed need not await the completion of the limited assessment to be presented to the model builders or users.

Objectives of maintenance assessment. A maintenance assessment reexamines a model that has been previously assessed. There are two reasons for considering a maintenance assessment.
- *Changes to a previously assessed model.* If changes have been made to a model that was previously assessed, a maintenance assessment will be conducted on the updated model.
- *Changes to the intended uses of the model.* If the intended uses of a model have changed, regardless of whether changes have been made to the model or not, a maintenance assessment may be conducted.

A maintenance assessment after a limited assessment can follow the limited assessment methodology. All data from previous assessments would be used. The direction of the assessment will be geared more towards investigating the changes to the model rather than revisiting sections of the model that were previously examined. However, the results from the previous assessment will be reexamined and combined with any new results.

For the sake of brevity in the remainder of this chapter, we will refer to only limited assessments, with the understanding that all discussions pertain as well to the maintenance assessment process.

Assessment phase. As with formal assessment, a limited assessment's four phases have distinct objectives.
- *Preparation.* Gather the required information about the simulation and its intended use and confirm that the assessment can be reasonably accomplished with the time and information available.
- *Planning.* Review the simulation, its development, testing, and documentation, and the simulation's intended use to form an initial determination of whether the simulation can meet the intended use. Plan the remainder of the assessment based on open problem areas identified during this process.
- *Application.* Complete the simulation assessment by applying assessment procedures based on requirements identified in the planning phase.
- *Evaluation.* Evaluate information compiled from the previous phases to form a list of risk areas and a model characterization.

These phases overlap during limited assessments due to the nature of the process and its time constraints.

Figure 5-1 illustrates the functions that must be accomplished in each of these phases. The risk analysis concentrates on the model's capability to meet its intended use. The risk assessment identifies the problem areas and summarizes the procedures used to assess them. Functional characterization defines the areas critical to the model meeting specific requirements, which are those areas that must receive attention during the assessment.

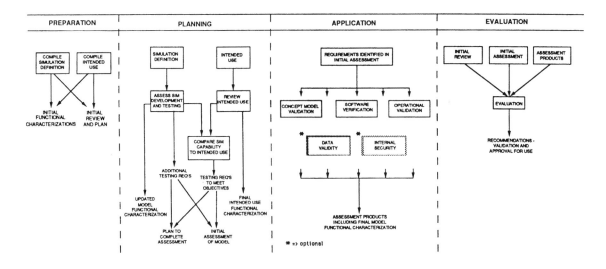

Figure 5-1. Limited assessment process overview.

Preparation phase. During the preparation phase, the information required for the assessment is identified and assembled. While assembling the information, a cursory review is conducted to determine the scope of the data and to develop an initial schedule for the assessment. Information required for the assessment includes a description of the simulation and a statement of the simulation's intended use.

The preparation phase of a limited assessment is significantly reduced in scope compared to formal assessment. At this level of effort, the assessment team is smaller. The objectives for the preparation phase are to

- organize the assessment team,
- gather the information required, and
- develop a plan to accomplish the assessment, including specific objectives, schedule, and resources, as well as requirements for the format, detail, and formality of reporting results.

We describe this phase in detail later in this chapter.

The simulation description includes a wide variety of information concerning the specification, development, testing, and capabilities of the simulation. Both developers and past users should be consulted when possible to obtain information describing the model. This is especially desirable if there is inadequate documentation available in any of the stages of the model development or testing, or whenever questions arise concerning the scope of functionality or the intended use of the model.

The information will most likely be available in the following types of documentation:

- specification documents,
- design documents,
- user's manuals,
- operations manuals,
- analyst's manuals,
- technical reference manuals,
- programmer's manuals,
- verification and validation test plans, procedures, and reports,
- source code, and
- history of the simulation's use.

These items generally contain the information desired when performing an assessment. If the information is not available, it must be derived if possible (see data description, Appendix B). However, information-derivation is a higher-risk approach to simulation assessment.

Additional information is required regarding the availability of the model, the classification, and versions to be used. The model should be hosted at the assessment site, or as a second choice, via modem or other remote access. Any slip in the hosting schedule may cause responsive slips in the assessment schedule. (A suggested format for the assessment schedule is presented in Chapter 8.)

The model version being assessed orients the assessment with respect to specific capabilities and intended use. As mentioned in Chapter 2, model development is often evolutionary, reflecting significant differences between model versions. Therefore, an assessment of one model version may have limited bearing on another. New versions of models are commonly developed to meet additional capability required for an upcoming intended use. This makes assessment of more than one model version advantageous in allowing the assessment process to parallel development efforts for the subsequent versions.

The intended use of the simulation may be specified by a general statement of a set of potential uses, or specified in a detailed test plan including an experiment design, and scenario. A list of the functional model capabilities required are developed with the users and model developer. As with the simulation definition, the more specific the description of the intended use, the more precise the assessment of the model.

If a management-chaired board conducts a review at the conclusion of the preparation phase, it should concentrate on determining whether the simulation can be assessed for the intended use within the resources and time available. This review board should evaluate the assessment team's recommendations concerning the adequacy of information to address the assessment issues defined. The board also directs the priority and emphasis for the remainder of the assessment.

Planning phase. The planning phase consists of a detailed review of all available information on the simulation and its intended use, and a comparison of the simulation capabilities with the intended use. Reviewing the available information determines the strengths and weaknesses in the model's development and testing. This review pivots on the technical areas discussed in Chapter 2, under simulation model characteristics. Planning phase assessment procedures structure the review and indicate important areas to be reviewed including the development, past testing or assessment efforts, and the history of the simulation's use. This process includes a review of test results and the fixes applied to the model. A long, well-documented history of accepted use for a model can contribute to the credibility of the simulation.

The objectives of the planning phase for a limited assessment are a limited version of those for a formal assessment:

- review the simulation's development, testing, history, and intended use;
- further develop the functional characterization of the model;
- identify problem areas from the developer's effort and develop a plan to understand them through additional analysis; and
- develop a plan to investigate all open problem areas.

From the outcome of these objectives a revision to the initial plan may be required, including application of specific additional assessment procedures to investigate open problem areas. (Note that this effort is more concentrated and selective than the formal process, as described in Chapter 4.) The activities performed in this phase are described in detail later in this chapter.

Review of the simulation description and intended use is guided by a set of detailed questions. Answers to the questions define areas of the model's strength and areas where there appear to be concerns about the model's credibility. Potential weaknesses in the development or testing of the model indicate where additional assessment must be accomplished. The questions posed during this phase must investigate areas of model used such as:

- model functionality, the functional elements, and the interaction between elements that are supported by the model,
- level of fidelity and detail,
- model input data types, threat, and environment,
- parameter variations,
- the domain of applicability for the simulation,
- model outputs, MOEs, and intermediate results,
- designed and historical use in comparison with the intended use, and
- required accuracy of model performance.

A summary of the additional analysis and test requirements from these reviews is developed and the assessment team formulates a plan to accomplish the remainder of the assessment. Areas where the required model functionality is not supported by demonstrated capability receive particular attention during the assessment.

Application phase. The application phase entails the execution of the specific assessment plan laid out during the preparation phase. Attention is paid throughout to ensure that efforts and interim results are well documented.

The objectives of the application phase of a limited assessment are to

- apply assessment procedures, to the extent possible, to understand problem areas identified in the planning phase,
- document assessment findings, and
- prepare information for the evaluation phase.

The activities performed in this phase are described in detail later in this chapter.

Assessment procedures employed during this phase fall into three major categories:

- conceptual model validation,
- software verification, and
- operational validation.

Based on the specific requirements identified in the planning phase, selected assessment procedures within the new categories are applied to complete the assessment during this phase. (As discussed earlier, the other procedures, internal security verification and data validation are optional.) Detailed instructions for each assessment procedure are contained in Chapter 3.

Almost all of the simulations assessed will require application of some procedures if for no other reason than to verify the integrity of the developer's processes. Each of the assessment procedures selected are applied to the simulation as described in the assessment plan. The results of the application of specific procedures are compiled for later evaluation. Areas may be revisited several times during the analysis, either by design or in response to needs identified during earlier stages of the assessment.

Evaluation phase. During the evaluation phase, assessment results through the first three phases are compiled and evaluated. The objectives of the evaluation phase are to compile and analyze the results of the previous phases of the assessment. The details of the process used in the assessment, catalogues of the open risk areas for potential users, model characterization, and intended use characterization are documented. This phase involves three distinct steps. First the assessment team compiles the results from all of the previous phases of the assessment. Preliminary findings are discussed in findings meetings and then assigned to individual team members for development, consolidation, and grouping. These results are then evaluated and conclusions are formulated as to the effect on the intended use of the model. Lastly, the assessment report is drafted by the assessment team and submitted to management. These steps are summarized as follows.

- Review open problem areas and determine which are major and minor.
- Assess the impact of the open areas and their criticality to the intended use of the model.
- Form an assessment report.

At the conclusion of this phase, the risk areas, their impacts, and the model characterization are made available to management and/or the user. The activities performed in this phase are described in detail later in this chapter.

Reporting results. The final results and a description of the assessment can be compiled and summarized in a final report. The limited assessment final report contains the detailed assessment procedures followed, the results, and recommendations. All assessment information should be made available to internal experiment planners and future assessment teams. This will aid their efforts to find simulations for experiments and assess simulations for a particular experiment, or in further model development. The activities performed in this phase are described in detail later in this chapter.

As was recommended in Chapter 2, it is important to identify the needs, conditions, and criteria governing the final report. This effort should be made early in the assessment to avoid any ambiguities or unmet expectations. These issues include the following.

- Who will receive the final results? Who will have access to those results?
- Who is the final approving authority? Who determines the dissemination of results?
- What are the politics? What risks and stakes attend possible findings? Whose neck is on the line?
- What is the desired level of detail?
- How will the results and supporting data be archived? How will the information be secured?
- What degree of formality is required for presentation of findings?
- What format is preferred for presentation of the final results? Several options include a formal report with full documented substantiation, executive briefing, an executive summary for the read file, or memorandum for record.

Preparation phase activities

To a large extent, the activities conducted during the preparation phase of a limited assessment are identical to those provided for a formal assessment. It is difficult to limit the scope of effort in this early phase because the model has to be fully understood before the assessment plan can be drawn up for conducting the remaining phases of the assessment.

Establish assessment team and identify expertise. A simulation assessment team is established during the preparation phase. A team is required to perform the assessment because the specialized knowledge of the simulation and of its intended use need to be contained within the team for the assessment effort. The team is formed of the confidence assessment analysts and representatives from the developing and using agencies as appropriate. The team leader is normally selected from the assessment staff because of the staff's familiarity with the assessment process. This convention may be varied when specific technical knowledge is required to lead the assessment effort for a particular simulation.

The designated team leader then identifies assessment team members. Team members are selected from

- the confidence assessment group,
- management,
- affiliated personnel,
- developers,
- potential users,
- technical experts for the simulation, including hardware or software consultants, and
- technical experts in certain model specific areas.

Assessment requirements and the technical level of the model dictate the composition of the team and not all of these technical areas provide members for every assessment. However, maintaining access to the appropriate technical areas is essential to assure credibility of the assessment. These technical areas are consulted as necessary during the assessment process.

When possible, it is desirable to establish a working relationship with the model developer. The assessment team's relation with the developer defines and controls the tenor of the assessment. The assessment process is most effective when there is access to the necessary user feedback concerning the development process. The developer contributes to the assessment process by openly providing concerns about the model, the current areas of development and testing, testing results, undocumented assumptions and limitations, and insight into using the model. In addition, the developer responds to and verifies the assessment results through testing and analysis. The assessment resulting from a close relationship with the model developer provides for more model confidence and faith in the assessment process and for more efficient use of time and resources.

Equally important is the assessment team's relationship with the model user. The interface with the model user is essential for understanding the model's intended use. In particular, the user can assist the assessment team in defining the scope of the assessment by selecting algorithms or portions of the model that must be examined, identifying test cases, interpreting test results, and reviewing assessment findings. A close relationship with the model user during the assessment provides more information to the developer that can be used to make the model more responsive to the user requirements.

As soon as possible, a kickoff meeting is scheduled and chaired by the team leader. Other parties who require an overview of the direction to be taken during the analysis or who can provide unique inputs at the outset of the assessment are invited.

The agenda of the meeting includes

- a background brief containing top-level directional guidance and scope definition as well as a general description of the model to be assessed;
- setting initial milestones and target dates for the assessment including phase completion dates, procedure completion dates, and other required progress brief dates (see the sample schedule in Figure 8-1); and
- assigning general responsibilities to team members for all phases of the methodology implementation.

The meeting should also determine the desired venue of reporting results. Other issues of concern include who will receive results, who is the final approving authority, who disseminates assessment findings, what is the desired level of detail and formality of the presentation of those findings (a formal report or an executive brief), who will brief the results, who will draft the formal copy, and how will results be archived and preserved?

Compile simulation description. Some of the documents necessary for a limited assessment may not be available for a simulation or may still be under development, so the assessment team may need to compile or generate the necessary data. The following list is a subset of the documentation listed for the formal assessment that usually holds the information required to perform a limited assessment:

- *Specification and descriptive documents*
  - Requirements specification
  - Conceptual model description
  - Functional description
  - Algorithm references and justification
  - User's manual
  - Source code
  - Model specifications

- *Procedural documents*
  - Verification plans
  - Operational validation plans
  - Test plans, procedures, and results
- *Description of intended use*

This set provides the core data required to determine what the model is, what it is supposed to do, how to make it do it, and how it has been tested. This gives the assessment team some data from which to start deriving model capabilities and problem areas associated with using the model. Information contained in these documents can be derived from the code or other available data. However, derivation can be a very intensive, risky effort. Whenever possible more data should be collected to include

- the programmer's manual,
- a history of problems reported and how they were resolved,
- documentation on previous uses of the model (including inputs and results where possible), and
- algorithm references.

In addition to this data, the model version to be assessed must be specified. The model version to be assessed ties the assessment to the intended use. Models are often changing rapidly and the assessment must focus on one or, at most, two versions. Because of significant differences between model versions, an assessment of one model version may have limited bearing on another. A specific model version may be required to meet an intended use. The assessment team must work closely with management, model users, and model developers to ensure that technical direction, model version hosted, and intended use are consistent. It is sometimes advantageous to include two versions of a model in assessment. One of the versions would act as a *baseline* and be used as the primary focus for the assessment. A second version would be used as an excursion for the assessment. Only key algorithms and capabilities in the second version would be assessed. This option is most useful when the assessment effort is tied to development of a model version to meet a specific intended use.

Define assessment objectives. Assessment objectives establish the capability of the model or particular areas, and identify risks in using the model. These can be critical areas of the model design or important aspects of the intended use. Development of the assessment objectives is aided by the characterizations of the intended use and the model in the same terms.

Defining the assessment objectives focuses a model assessment. Within the general technical areas to be examined in a limited assessment, the identification of objectives narrows down the assessment to those specific issues that must be tested and closely examined. Some additional depth may be added to the assessment process to address the objective, but no additional scope is expected to address them.

Characterize the model's intended use. The intended use for the model should be summarized early in the preparation phase. This summary provides a textual description of the required model capability. All information required to complete this summary should be available from an initial review of the documented potential uses. Many of the people involved in the model's use are consulted in compilation of the intended use description. Items in the attributes list are used as a guide to assure complete characterization of the potential uses when consulting with these parties.

Characterize the model. The model attributes are also characterized using the attributes illustrated in Tables 5-1 and 5-2. Table 5-1 provides a textual descriptive summary of the developer's claims for model capability. This information is drawn from the functional description and the user's and programmer's manuals. Discussion with the developer can provide additional information to complete the characterization, particularly when the model is under development. This information is updated during the course of the assessment as capabilities are assessed and entries are made to the characterization matrix in Table 5-2. The list of attributes may have to change and evolve to meet model capabilities and system concepts.

A model description is compiled as part of the characterization. The model description is important to balance the tone of the assessment. All of the capabilities claimed by the model developer are contained in the description and characterization. While findings are noted in the model description, the intent of the description is to highlight the model capabilities in a balanced fashion. The description is compiled during the assessment and is an important part of the recommendations and final report.

```
(element - class 1)  Logistics                    (other components)  Marketing
        (type A)      - schedules                         (type A)     - sales
                        • (characteristics)                             • (characteristics)
                        •       "                                       •       "
                        •       "                                       •       "
        (type B)      - orders/deliveries                 (type B)     - advertising
                        • (characteristics)                             • (characteristics)
                        •       "                                       •       "
                        •       "                                       •       "
        (type C)      - protocols
                        • (characteristics)
                        •       "                  (other components)  Supplier/ Customer
                        •       "                          (type A)     - communications
        (type D)      - maintenance/repairs                             • (characteristics)
                        • (characteristics)                             •       "
                        •       "                          (type B)     - information processing
                        •       "                                       • (characteristics)
        ( etc...)                                                       •       "
                                                                        •       "

(element - class 2)  Facilities
        (type A)      - assembly plant
                        • (characteristics)        (other components)  Corporate Operations
                        •       "                          (type A)     - finance/comptroller
                        •       "                                       • (characteristics)
        (type B)      - warehouse                                      •       "
                        • (characteristics)                             •       "
                        •       "                          (type C)     - contracts
                        •       "                                       • (characteristics)
        (type C)      - shipping/receiving                             •       "
                        • (characteristics)                             •       "
                        •       "                          (type D)     - operations research
                        •       "                                       • (characteristics)
        (type D)      - office (admin/sales)                           •       "
                        • (characteristics)                             •       "
                        •       "
                        •       "
        ( etc...)                                  (other components)  Technical
                                                           (type A)     - scientific/engineering
(element - class 3)  Materiel                                          • (characteristics)
        (type A)      - raw materials                                  •       "
                        • (characteristics)                             •       "
                        •       "                          (type B)     - technical requirements
                        •       "                                       • (characteristics)
        (type B)      - equipment                                      •       "
                        • (characteristics)                             •       "
                        •       "                          (type C)     - R&D
                        •       "                                       • (characteristics)
        (type C)      - parts                                          •       "
                        • (characteristics)                             •       "
                        •       "
                        •       "                         ( etc...)
        ( etc...)


(element - class 4)  Personnel                    Simulation Attributes
        (type A)      - payroll                            - fidelity
                        • (characteristics)                - run-time
                        •       "                          - host computer
                        •       "                          - hardware/ software support
        (type B)      - training                           - code security
                        • (characteristics)                - language
                        •       "                          - modeling approach
                        •       "                          - maintainibility
        (type C)      - union/labor organization           - ease of use
                        • (characteristics)                - configuration management
                        •       "                          - pre-processors/ post-processors
                        •       "
        ( etc...)                                          ( etc...)
```

Table 5-1. Assembly plant simulation: sample characterization attributes.

The characterization attributes can be altered appropriately at this point in the assessment. A new set of characterization attributes, or a significant modification to the attributes listed in Tables 5-1 and 5-2, will be required to address some of those general intended uses. Changes may also be required as the system concepts and configurations evolve.

Functional Attributes / Assessment Actions	SUPPLIER/CUSTOMER (Communications, Information Processing etc...)	MARKETING (Sales, Advertising etc...)	MATERIEL (Equipment, Raw Materials, Parts)	FACILITIES: Office	FACILITIES: Shipping/Receiving	FACILITIES: Assembly Plant	FACILITIES: Warehouse	PERSONNEL (Payroll, Training, Labor Organizations etc...)	LOGISTICS (Schedules, Orders, Deliveries, Protocols, Maintenance/Repairs)
CONCEPTUAL MODEL VALIDATION									
SOFTWARE VERIFICATION									
OPERATIONAL VALIDATION TESTING									

Functional Attributes / Assessment Actions	CORPORATE OPERATIONS (Finance/Comptroller, Contracts, Operations Research etc...)	TECHNICAL (Natural Background, Manmade Background, R&D, Scientific/Engineering, Technical Requirements)	MIL CONSIDERATIONS (Decision Aids, Resource Control, Situation Assessment, Status Displays, Simulation Control, Simulation Configuration, Data Recording)	SIMULATION ATTRIBUTES (Fidelity, Runtime, Host Computer, Code Security Class., Language, Modeling Approach, Maintainability, Ease of Use, Configuration Man., Post-Processor, Pre-Processor)
CONCEPTUAL MODEL VALIDATION				
SOFTWARE VERIFICATION				
OPERATIONAL VALIDATION TESTING				

REFERENCES:

ARCHITECTURE STANDARD:

LEGEND:

–   Not Assessed/Not Modeled
□   No Problems Noted
▨   Minor Problems Noted
■   Major Problems Noted

Table 5-2. Assembly plant simulation: sample characterization matrix.

ASSEMBLY PLANT SIMULATION

        Performance and system design evaluation
        Costing analysis
        Productivity analysis

ELEMENT SIMULATION
        Engineering development model
        Personnel/ management
        Facilities design
        Scheduling/queueing

TEST SUPPORT

TECHNOLOGY SIMULATION
        Retool/product development
        Operations analysis

SIMULATION SUPPORT TOOL
        Shipping/receiving model
        Marketing/advertising model
        Machine design/scheduling model
        Logistics
        Maintenance
        Parts and equipment requisition
        Product demand model
        Warehousing model

TRAINING AND EDUCATION

Table 5-3. Model intended uses.

Characterization of the model and its intended use as described above identifies key areas of the model that must be emphasized during the assessment. These areas of emphasis are where the model performance is essential to meeting the study or experiment objectives. Key areas identified are considered in planning the assessment and selection of assessment procedures to be applied. Understanding the assessment objectives and their origin is essential for the assessment team to make proper judgments in selection of assessment procedures. The more specific this information is, the more concrete the assessment process can become.

The assessment objectives are derived from comparison of the model and intended use characterizations. These are listed as model capabilities that must be proven to meet the intended use. As assessment procedures are applied during the planning and application phases, additional knowledge becomes available that may update the characterizations and the list of objectives. Any updates represent changes in the focus for the assessment and can influence the selection of assessment procedures or direct additional effort into new areas.

Generate an initial assessment plan. Once the information on the simulation has been gathered, the intended use of the simulation has been defined, and the assessment objectives have been compiled, the initial assessment plan is created. The plan available at the completion of the preparation phase should include the following.
- *A model description.* This is a high-level description of the model capabilities. The text will be expanded in later phases to state the model capabilities in detail for the briefing and report.
- *An assessment approach.* The assessment approach contained in the plan highlights the areas of the model that are key to the assessment and procedures to be employed.

- *An initial schedule.* The relationship between assessment tasks is different for each assessment. Factors such as model size, complexity, classification, amount of supporting information, ease of use, intended model uses, and model runtime influence the schedule. Figure 8-1 in Chapter 8 shows a typical assessment schedule.
- *Identification of confidence assessment group functions and personnel.* This covers the assessment team composition and assignments. Of particular importance is the availability and tasking of system experts outside of the confidence assessment team including those people from other areas of assessing organization, appropriate Management personnel, consultants, technical experts, developer representatives, and potential users.
- *Compilation of simulation documentation and data, and additional data requirements.* This is a listing of available information for the assessment.
- *Statement of intended use of the simulation,* preferably in the context of the particular experiment or study to be conducted. The intended use of the simulation, along with the model description, serves as the basis for the assessment. This statement of the intended use of the model may be expanded during the assessment in cooperation with the model user.
- *Identification of hardware resources required.* Hardware resources are usually limited and their utilization must be planned and coordinated with other on-site users.

Planning phase activities

Determining the assessment requirements is a three-step procedure:
application of planning phase procedures that provide
  - a functional characterization of the model,
  - an evaluation of the development and testing efforts,
  - a review of the simulation's intended use, and
  - a comparison of the simulation's capabilities with the intended use;
compilation of procedure results and formulation of open problem areas that require additional assessment, and
identification of assessment procedures that can be applied during the application phase to understand the problem areas. In some cases, this step will include identification of additional information required to apply the procedures.

The compilation of problem areas found in review of the development and testing efforts and the capabilities of the simulation to meet the intended use forms an initial assessment of the model.

The planning phase effort requires that the assessment team operate in close coordination with the user and/or model development process. This allows for the most efficient use of resources and provides the most useful limited assessment results. The emphasis of the planning phase is for the assessment team to identify as many problem areas as possible, though there may not be time or resources available to understand all of them.

The procedures of this phase are designed to examine the conceptual model, provide a cursory review of the software, and develop an initial operational validation test plan. Table 5-4 shows the basic planning phase procedures of a limited assessment (compare this with Table 4-5). These procedures were described in detail in Chapter 3. Implementing these procedures results in the initial findings: input to the characterization matrix and a list of areas for which additional assessment action will be required in the application phase. Notice that internal security verification can be undertaken during this planning phase if time and resources permit, or if intended use of the model dictates this examination. (Data validation is best left as an option for the next phase to be discussed.)

The initial operational test plan developed during this phase is also modified here as a result of the findings. Additional tests are planned to examine critical areas where problems have been identified, and tests on the initial plan may be eliminated due to an indication from the planning phase procedures that the test is unnecessary.

A detailed review of the model as required by the planning phase procedures also allows further development of the detailed functional characterizations of the model started in the preparation phase. As the analysts apply the assessment procedures, the model documentation, intended use, and software are reviewed and the information is compared to the simulation attributes (such as those described in Chapter 2). The results of this comparison are used to revise the intended use and model characterization summaries.

In the event that a critical area in the model's intended use has been identified as a potential problem area and there are insufficient resources available to perform the necessary assessment action, the matter must be discussed with management (the user) to determine whether to leave the problem area open or to allow some level of additional assessment.

Conceptual model validation

Face validity analysis
Historical analysis
    Development history analysis
    Model derivative analysis
    Previous model Use analysis

Software verification

Software metrics analysis
    Process metrics analysis

Operational validation

Demonstration tests
    Limited standards testing

Internal security verification *

Configuration control analysis
    CM procedure analysis

Data validation *

    * Can be undertaken as time and resources permit

Table 5-4. Planning phase procedures (limited).

At the end of the planning phase, the following information should be available:
all information collected on the model and its intended use,
results of the preparation and planning phases,
an assessment plan to guide the application phase, including
- essential procedures,
- priorities for the problem areas,
- additional procedures to apply if resources are available, and
- a schedule. (See sample schedule in Chapter 8.)

Application phase activities

The plan developed during the planning phase provides the information required to accomplish this phase of the assessment. The results of the planning phase describe the open problem areas and assessment procedures to be applied to each. The application phase procedures emphasize detailed code analysis and operational validation testing due to the large amount of information gained in a short time frame. Table 5.5 specifies a minimum set of application phase procedures. (Instructions for application of each of the procedures are contained in Chapter 3.) The major areas of the formal assessment are conceptual model validation, software verification, operational validation, data validation, and internal security. Only the first three (conceptual model validation, software verification, operational validation) need be addressed during a limited assessment. A fourth additional area of data validation is worth undertaking, and should be considered if time and resources permit. (Internal security verification can be considered again at this point.)

```
Conceptual model validation
Model assumptions and fidelity analysis
        Modeling concepts analysis
        Input/output analysis
        Algorithm analysis

Software verification
Traceability analysis
Case and design methodology adherence analysis
Software metrics analysis
        Product metrics analysis
Internal software testing analysis
Code analysis

Operational validation
Demonstration tests
        Extreme-condition testing
        Limited standards testing
Analytical tests
        Sensitivity analysis testing

Internal security verification *

Data validation *
Data consistency analysis
        Imbedded data analysis
        Input data analysis
        Consistency analysis
Portrayal of constants analysis
        Dimensional and numerical verification analysis
Distributional form analysis
        Statistical analysis

* Can be undertaken as time and resources permit
```

Table 5-5. Application phase procedures (limited).

As assessment procedures are applied and more is learned about the model, additional problem areas may be uncovered. These new problem areas may be incorporated into the assessment. However, the team may decide to keep these new problem areas in the final assessment. The limited assessment findings sheet (Table 5-6) lists the problem areas identified.

Additional assessment actions that could lead to further understanding of the problem areas may have become apparent to the analysts during the assessment, but because of time and resource constraints, these procedures could not be applied. Documentation of assessment findings, therefore is crucial, and must include those areas where additional assessment could be fruitful, while identifying specific procedures that could be employed.

```
┌─────────────────────────────────────────────┐
│                                               │
│          Model assessment finding             │
│                                               │
│   Finding # :                                 │
│                                               │
│   Conceptual model validation:                │
│                                               │
│   Software verification:                      │
│                                               │
│   Operational validation:                     │
│                                               │
│   (Optional additional procedures)            │
│                                               │
│   Risk:                                       │
│                                               │
└─────────────────────────────────────────────┘
```

Table 5-6. Limited assessment findings.

Documenting results. The preceding discussion emphasized the role of thorough documentation of findings. A brief report should ensue each assessment procedure describing application of each procedure used, in order to document the assessment activity accomplished and form an audit trail describing the assessment. This level of information is very valuable to future assessments of the same model and to support assessment conclusions. These reports also contain the level of detail required to specify changes or enhancements to the model to better support the model's credibility and intended use. The reports are developed during the assessment process. The analysts involved in application of a procedure prepare the associated report as the procedure is applied. Related procedures may be documented in a single report.

A general report format is provided in Figure 5-2. Key elements of the report are the summary of the problem area, the purpose of the procedure application, a summary of expected results, a description of how the procedure was applied, findings and observations, and risk assessment. The purpose of applying the procedure describes what the procedure is intended to investigate in general terms and why the particular procedure has been selected. This is primarily a restatement of the problem area and procedure selection described in the plan. The analyst will have some familiarity with the simulation and will develop a summary of the expected findings. These findings describe particular areas of investigation and concentration the analyst will use to guide the assessment. Each of the steps used in applying the procedure will be documented to describe what was done in assessing the model. Description of the steps taken is important to document decisions made and intermediate results found during the assessment. A summary of the assessment procedure results will include any observations made by the analyst during the assessment. The results are compiled by the analyst to form conclusions that address the problem area being investigated. This level of evaluation may require discussion with other members of the assessment team and management.

```
┌─────────────────────────────────────────────────┐
│                                   Analyst:        │
│                 Title             Date:           │
│                                                   │
│   1. Purpose                                      │
│      1.1 Description of problem area              │
│      1.2 Procedures to be employed                │
│                                                   │
│   2. Expected results                             │
│                                                   │
│   3. Procedures                                   │
│         3.X Procedure Implemented                 │
│               3.X.1 Description of effort         │
│               3.X.2 Results                       │
│                                                   │
│   4. Summary of results                           │
│      4.1 Findings and limitations                 │
│      4.2 Open risk areas                          │
│      4.3 Further assessment action                │
│                                                   │
└─────────────────────────────────────────────────┘
```

Figure 5-2. Assessment procedure report outline

Assessment procedure results are also summarized according to the functional characterization developed in the planning phase. Procedure results are assessments of the correctness of the derivation and implementation of the model attributes described in the textual characterization of the model (such as those illustrated in Tables 5-1 and 5-2). Figure 5-2 is completed to document these results. Assessment results are placed in the appropriate row of the matrix based on the assessment area being covered (conceptual model validation, software verification, and operational validation). The possible categories of assessment results are: not assessed, no problems noted, minor problems noted, and major problems noted. References to the findings that correspond to each of the minor and major problem entries and the related procedure reports are added to the appropriate element of the textual characterization in Table 5-1.

Evaluation phase activities

The structure imposed during the assessment facilitates compilation of assessment results. Reporting mechanisms that are required during the application of the assessment procedures and the tables used to track and manage the assessment process provide much of the information required. Results of applying the assessment procedures are in terms of the risks involved in using the model. Each assessment procedure was applied to understand a problem area and the results of the effort are expressed in terms of remaining problem areas. Compiling these results produces a draft of the final assessment report as it is described in the next section. Most of the assessment results and associated documentation form the technical appendices of the document.

To determine the criticality of open problem areas on the model's operation and the extent of its effect on the simulation results, the assessment team reviews each area. Classification of a particular issue is not always a clear decision. Each issue is reviewed by all concerned to ensure that support for a classification is objectively based.

Guidance for the classification of problem areas is as follows.

- *Major problem area.* An individual area that impacts the model's credibility. These are problems that point to incorrect or dishonest model development and test practices or model implementations. These will be coded black on summary forms (such as Table 5-2). Existence of more than one of these is sufficient reason for limiting the potential uses of the model.
- *Minor problem area.* An area that points to weaknesses in model development, testing, or implementation and indicates possible modifications to the model that would improve its credibility. Identification of a reasonably small number of minor problem areas in the absence of more serious concerns is normally

acceptable. However the presence of an unusually large number of minor problems may itself become major. These will be coded gray on summary forms.

- *No problem area.* An area that does not seem to affect the simulation's results. These areas indicate correct model implementation, providing realistic results. These will be coded white on summary forms.

As each problem area is reviewed it is used to update the format shown in Table 5-2.

Reporting activities

Develop and review report. At the completion of the evaluation phase, a confidence assessment report and annotated brief are developed to document the assessment effort. (As mentioned in Chapter 2, the expectations for the content, format, and dissemination of the assessment results should be clearly stipulated early in the preparation phase). Results of the assessment are also stored in an available database or archived on tape for future use and further evaluation. Final coordination of the report and briefing content is conducted during the last meeting of the evaluation team. Figure 5-3 is a guide to the construction of the report.

Documentation at each step in the evaluation process, as has been emphasized throughout the guide, facilitates compilation of the report. Key elements are the introductory information for the assessment, a summary of the approach followed in each area of assessment (for example, conceptual model validation, software verification, operational validation), a list of assessment findings (Table 5-6), a summary of problem areas involved in using the model, and characterization of the model. The model characterization includes the model characterization matrix and the model description (for example, see Tables 5-1 and 5-2; for general form refer to Chapter 8). The intent of the model description is to highlight model functional characteristics, to identify sections of the model where problems were not found, and to address problem areas found during the assessment.

---

1. Preliminary

    1.1   Document purpose
    1.2   Organization of document

2. Assessment introduction

    2.1   Assessment background
    2.2   Model description
    2.3   Assessment scope
    2.4   Assessment team

3. Assessment approach

    3.1   Overview of assessment process
    3.2   Conceptual model validation approach
    3.3   Software verification approach
    3.4   Operational validation test approach
           1) Operational validation test concept
           2) Synopsis of operational validation test plan

4. Model characterization and description

5. Assessment findings

6. Summary of major risk areas

Appendices and enclosures:

    A. Operational validation test log
    B. Assessment procedure reports
    C. Model characterization back-up data
    D. Developer comments

Figure 5-3. Confidence assessment report outline.

The approach used to develop this report is to expand the text from the executive summary briefing, which is sometimes terse and not always self-evident. The appendices contain detailed test information, procedure reports, management reports, and the complete characterization data. In addition, an appendix is provided for the developer of the model to supply comments on the assessment and the assessment findings. These comments are added to the confidence assessment report in the form received from the developer.

In a typical assessment report, Appendix A is the assessment test log. The test plan and test results are included. Each test case is described in terms of purpose, scenario, and both expected and observed results including any anomalies in implementation. Cases are grouped functionally and results may additionally be depicted in summary form. Appendix B of the final report contains all assessment procedure reports. Each analyst participating in the assessment completes one or more procedure reports, structured in accordance with the guidance in the preceding sections.

Appendix C includes assessment characterization back-up data. Each line item on the model characterization attributes (Table 5-1) is expanded with the material presented in the order depicted on the characterization matrix. Brief notations on what specific references support each functional characterization area are included. Appendix D contains model characterization back-up data. Appendix E contains developer comments. The contents of this appendix are at developer discretion. Most model developers have chosen to address each assessment finding individually, in the order of presentation during the brief, with status notations from the developer's perspective.

Presentation of findings. The confidence assessment and recommendations package should be submitted to management. The package may then be distributed to developers and users, other than the host, for review and comment. Comments from users and developers can be consolidated and a memorandum prepared. The memorandum should contain a statement of approval or disapproval (with supporting rationale) of the use of the model.

Chapter 6

Man-in-the-Loop Models

> SPECIAL TOPICS - Guidance for assessing
> models involving human interface.
> Recommended for personnel involved with development
> and assessment of man-in-the-loop models.

In previous chapters, we have discussed the confidence assessment methodology. This chapter provides guidance for applying that methodology to models that involve human interface in the simulation process.

Man-in-the-loop models

Conceptually, simulations fall into two broad classes: batch and interactive. For a model operating in the batch mode, initial conditions are defined and key critical attributes and values are initialized. The objective of experimentation using simulations in this mode is to ascertain outcomes as produced by these initial conditions and parameter specifications. The actual uncertainties in the model arise in the fidelity of the algorithms and data, rather than in the process of execution. In other words, models operating dynamically in the batch mode either are subject to the random nature of certain components that the model attempts to define, or to the stochastic data on which those definitions rely or on which the model functions.

Interactive mode of operation. Models may also incorporate interactive capabilities. The human element of an interactive simulation is multifaceted and defined by three types of players.
- *Simulation controllers.* These are players tasked with selecting and defining the architecture of a scenario to be run. This role includes dynamic definition of environments, progression and development of events, and status of systems and elements being modeled. Players in this function define the simulation architecture (such as runtimes, initializations, and so on).
- *Decision makers.* These players enact the role of the human component being modeled. They respond to the dynamic situations being identified by the simulations controllers. These players fill the role of the actors who make the command decisions that drive the scenario dynamics. These actors can be amicable or hostile; their decisions can be based on predetermined policies or be made at random or ad hoc.
- *Operators.* These players are responsible for running the model, overseeing its execution, operating the hardware, and inputting the data.

Given the additional dimension of the human element, uncertainty in model operation and outcomes rises dramatically. This is especially true when the human element involves decision making, a capability essential, for example, in gaming simulations. The anomalies and errors resulting from operator/player interaction with a simulation tool (for example, manual data input, response format or content, or commands), represent another source of uncertainties.

The distinction of a man-in-the-loop (MIL) simulation is chiefly the man-machine interface (MMI) capability which it attempts to model. A MIL model will include algorithms to provide information to the human elements, accept information, and act on the information provided.

Coupled with these inherent difficulties in man-in-the-loop models is the consideration given to fidelity and scope: How much of a scenario does the model attempt to simulate, and to what level of detail?

Unique aspects of MIL models. MIL models have two intrinsic technical concerns.
- *Data generation and relay.* How does the model incorporate human interaction and data relay essential to its operation?
- *Event sequencing.* How does the model define certain decision-making capabilities and integrate them into the scenario dynamics?

The confidence assessment process, when applied to MIL simulations, needs to address several concepts pertinent to these two technical concerns.
- *Timing.* Providing realistic timing to operators.
- *Information display.* Providing appropriate information to the operators (this includes accommodating request for help menus or displays).
- *Information requests.* Accepting realistic commands and other information from the operators (which includes capability to screen input errors, contradictory or risky commands or responses, as well as identify response delays, and corrections).
- *Human input.* Supporting a wide variety of input as might be expected of the model in a realistic environment (recognizing, for example, variety that occurs in commands, response to query, formats for data input, units, and so on).
- *Operations.* Providing an operation mode as free as possible from unrealistic interruptions, data flows, and information requirements.
- *Simulation control.* Supporting appropriate start, stop, checkpoint, and restart of the model to facilitate human interaction.
- *Integration.* Providing thorough integration of inputs to support the interaction. This integration includes reliability of event sequencing to reflect scenario dynamics, as well as data integrity throughout the simulation.

Approach. The CA methodology can be modified to accommodate the technical areas peculiar to interactive simulations. By restricting a formal level of effort to concentrate on the procedures discussed for conceptual model validation, model implementation verification, and operational testing, one can perform a limited assessment (see Chapter 5) instead of a formal assessment.

MIL models. Some examples of MIL models are gaming models requiring human input for command decisions and models requiring dynamic human interface for some aspects of function and data definition. An illustration of such a simulation was provided in the Chapter 1 in the urban power plant gaming tool. This example covers only one application of MIL modeling and was intended to provide a flavor for the kinds of problems and modeling approaches expected. In this model, three components must be rigorously modeled.
- *Command function.* Integration of inputs from the decision makers into the simulation events.
- *Connectivity function.* Communications linkage between and among decision makers, as well as power linkage between the plant and its branches and customers.
- *Environments,* including time of day, weather conditions, electromagnetic or physical model of the power plant model, population distribution and urban design, urban and rural boundaries.

Another example is a disaster-planning simulation. Such a tool would model the actions of preparing for and responding to natural or environmental catastrophes. Simulations of this type would enable agencies and governments in regions subject to such disasters to train and plan for those eventualities. The measures that could be accounted for would range from prepositioning supplies, reserves, and emergency equipment to managing communications implementing public safety policies (specifically, provision of shelter, escape routes or evacuations, as well as medical operations and search and rescue). The strategies and time-critical decision and command functions could be rehearsed and the various options explored well in advance of the actual need.

Another example of a MIL model is the ubiquitous war-gaming simulation. War-gaming tools are provided in many venues, from recreational personal computer software to military applications in strategic defense planning. Such war-gaming models usually constitute a military contest between two hostile forces, one of which is the aggressor (the party who initiates an engagement of arms). The scenario of a war may involve the concomitant dangers of espionage (intelligence and counter-intelligence), sabotage, and terrorism. But often such broadly defined simulation would be too cumbersome or costly to develop. More likely a war-game analysis would concentrate on the more immediate features of battle so as to define strategic and tactical capabilities and options (usually of both sides) and to incorporate human interaction into the battle management functions of all involved contestants. The interactive human element would constitute the two opposing players representing the warring forces, and a third player, a referee to control the simulation flow, the definition of the battle scenario, and selected battle events.

Such military-oriented models could be characterized with respect to those functional areas critical to the model's intended uses. Consideration could be given particularly to implementation of the following major functional areas for both offensive and defensive forces.

- *Battle management, command, and control.* Simulates either a regional command architecture or an autonomous one. In addition it models the true outcome of engagements.
- *Communications.* Models communications including system connectivity and transmission delays.
- *Surveillance.* Models sensor assets including space-based and ground-based surveillance and tracking capabilities.
- *Weapons.* Models weapon assets including space-based and ground-based interceptors.
- *Environment.* Models natural contexts of the battle including season, time of day, weather, terrain, and environmental characteristics. Models may also want to consider the effects of *bright objects* for sensor purposes during the execution of the simulation. Man-made environments such as roads, bridges, population centers, urban and rural boundaries and design must be considered. This functional area also provides services to the other configuration items that return lists of object identifications or positions, velocities, and accelerations of offensive and defensive objects and troops.
- *Bases and facilities.* Models aspects of base operations and hangar and depot components not explicitly modeled in the command and control, communications, sensor of weapons functional areas. Included here may be some definition of physical security of personnel and assets to include sabotage, attrition of capabilities, and defense of C3 operations or troop and weapon deployment.
- *Populations.* Models both the military element and civilian populations. The military includes deployed and reserve troops, support personnel, POWs and casualties. The civilian population element includes location of daily activity centers as well as evacuation and provision of shelter for refugees.
- *MIL considerations.* Can simulate offensive and defensive team functions as well as a referee for simulation control.

Technical areas for formal assessment of MIL models

The Sargent Framework in Chapter 2 describes a general structure for simulation evaluation.[15] Figure 6-1 is a summary of that structure modified slightly to reflect MIL concepts. The structure highlights the products and processes that describe a model. Each element on this figure should be considered in model development and assessment. The inner triangle describes the model development process and the remainder of the figure shows the process of assuring that the model and its implementation are correct.

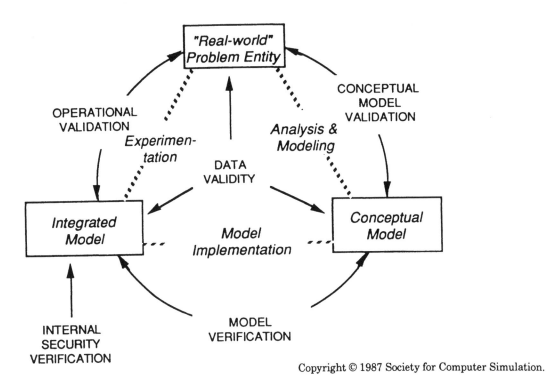

Figure 6-1. Structure for MIL simulation evaluation (formal).

The general content of the figure is the same for MIL models and the computer-based models considered in the main report. The words and concepts representing the model development and test process change to account for specific MIL considerations.

- *Real-world problem entity.* The problem entity is the system (real or proposed), idea, policy, or phenomena to be modeled. Problem entities to be assessed may be used for initial system concept studies, evaluation of options, and development or refinement of concepts or operations. In the case considered in this chapter, the real system will have human intervention required for its operation. Models to be considered may have human interaction required to reflect command decision processes, system operation, information relay, or other human-intensive systemic functions. The problem a given model is developed to formulate may not be the same as the intended use for which the model is being considered. In this event, the intended use will also be considered as part of the problem definition for the purposes of model assessment.

- *Analysis and modeling.* The model is developed from the problem entity through analysis and simulation. This process defines how the MIL considerations will be met in the model, specifically, the general capabilities to be allowed for interaction of man and model.

- *Conceptual model.* The conceptual model should be completely described to allow potential users the ability to understand what was modeled, why, and how. Description of the conceptual model must specify how the human is to interact with the model, specifying the information available to the human element and the information to be supplied by the human.

- *Conceptual model validity.* Validation of the conceptual model comprises justification of assumptions, algorithms, and modeling concepts. Conceptual model validation for MIL models must consider how the human is incorporated into the model as well as the assumptions, algorithms, and concepts used in the remainder of the model. Inherent in MIL models are assumptions concerning the adequacy and timing of information supplied to the human element and the capability of the model to handle the human response. The judgment of how valid the conceptual model is must be tempered in MIL models. These models are generally used to train decision makers or to examine widely varying hypothetical strategies. Thus the validity test may in fact be a reasonableness test.

- *Integrated model.* The integrated model is the suite of software, hardware, and humans that comprise the complete model. Software drives information flow and provides the background simulation activity. The hardware element of the model must be considered because the interfaces between the software and human elements are closely tied to the hardware capabilities available and the model is frequently tailored to the hardware. Human elements of the model are a key to the model. The operators have specific expertise, which is applied in the roles they must play in model operations. Adequate documentation of the capabilities, limitations, and applications are essential to the acceptance of the integrated model.

- *Model implementation.* As the developer implements the integrated model, many methods can be used to support model credibility. In addition to the elements of software development, operational testing of the complete integrated model and model configuration control are key elements in assessing the model development. Operational testing of the model should fully exercise the model capability. Configuration control of the integrated model is important because of the close ties commonly found between the software, hardware, and human elements of the model.

- *Model implementation verification.* Verification of model implementation must include verification of the ability of the human to interact with the model in the manner specified by the conceptual model. In addition to the common software verification tests, the range of MIL inputs available, information available to the human element, and the time element of human response must be considered.

- *Experimentation.* How the model was used, acceptance of results, and problems noted in the application contribute to the overall assessment of model credibility.

- *Operational test.* Operational test emphasizes demonstrated consistency with the real-world problem entity which includes demonstration of the human interaction with the model. The operational test program must consider operation of the complete model, including human elements, in the target hardware environment and must consider the range of human actions allowed by the model. Part of the testing effort requires scripts to be used in testing the model. The scripts define the scenario the model was to represent and the kinds of interaction or decisions the human is expected to provide in the simulation.

- *Data validation.* Assessing the validity of the data used in development and operation of the model.

- *Internal security verification.* Determining if the integrated model is currently free of any tampering devices that would affect its operation or results.

Technical areas for limited or maintenance assessment of MIL models

The preceding section explored the significant impacts of an MIL capability present in a model on the conduct of a formal assessment of that model. The same discussion can be suitably applied to the limited or maintenance assessment of MIL models, but it is sufficient to simply emphasize the following considerations. An assessment of MIL models needs to clearly identify the model's intended scope and level of fidelity. For example, in assessing a war-gaming tool, the CA analysts would need to determine whether it was intended to be an end-to-end engagement simulation (from war start to final outcome), versus a discrete-event or weapon-specific model.

The initial characterization of the model (introduced in Chapter 2) will be developed from those functional areas important to the model's intended use. This characterization can be refined and detailed throughout the application of the assessment procedures.

Briefly, the three areas of a limited/maintenance assessment to concentrate on are conceptual model validation, model implementation verification, and operational validation testing. These processes can be applied to MIL models in the effort to identify model capabilities as well as areas of risk for a potential user.

Assessment considerations in *conceptual model validation* would concentrate on validation of all those conceptual model components that are part of the intended use. This includes examination of the models for degree of restrictiveness, inappropriate modeling approach, and inconsistent levels of detail. In particular, how each model contributes to the information provided to the operator, in addition to the algorithms defining that information, as well as its timeliness and completeness, should be examined. Examination of the conceptual model also includes those portions of the model that interface with the operators such as those modeling communication of information provided to and received from the operators. The conceptual models governing these interfaces define the limitations placed on the operator's actions.

Verifying the model implementation is a means of examining whether the conceptual model was correctly implemented. Detailed examination of the model software is accomplished using automated code analysis tools and manual review of the code. The review includes examination of the components in the computer model and of the software and hardware defining the operator interface. In the same manner as conceptual model validation, the software is examined to determine the flow of information to the operators, and the receipt of responses from the operator to the software, as well as the timeliness of that transmitted information.

Operational validation testing would examine the model performance over the range of model inputs expected for the intended use. A test plan is developed based on the intended use description. Key elements of the test plan would examine the performance of model components, the man-machine interface, and the ability of the model to handle the scenarios planned. Examination of component performance can be accomplished by comparing the model results with expected system results. The comparison may be at a relatively high level, examining such items as elapsed time and ranges of critical parametric results versus the probability of such values. Component testing can be accomplished using the batch mode of model operation, in order to isolate specific functionality of those components. The man-machine interface is examined by assessing

- the adequacy of information provided to the operators to make the decisions required,
- the timeliness of the information provided to make the decisions within an appropriate time frame, and
- the ability of the model to accept the responses desired.

The man-machine interface testing is accomplished by the confidence assessment staff augmented by knowledgeable analysts, and by participation (either as an observer or a data collector) in the preparation for a simulation run. The complete operational validation testing plan should be designed to cover the scope of scenarios as defined or implied in the intended use. Again, internal security verification and data validation activities can be undertaken as optional areas of evaluation.

Assessment procedures for MIL models

Modifications to the procedures previously defined for computer-based model assessment must be considered for MIL model assessments. This section describes the modifications to the assessment procedures. The format of the section imitates that of Chapter 3, which describes the assessment procedures. Material presented here relies on that description, and expands or modifies where appropriate. Procedure references to appropriate sections are included to facilitate use of this chapter in conjunction with the previous material.

Conceptual model validation. Some additions are required as part of conceptual model validation for an MIL model assessment. The following paragraphs outline modifications to procedures discussed in Chapter 3 under conceptual model validation.

Development history analysis: interface standards and documents. Chapter 3 covers the procedure for detecting interfaces used in the model that cannot be easily integrated into the user's environment. The first section of that chapter describes how generic interfaces between software units and other software or hardware can be evaluated. There are several potential new man-machine interfaces that must be evaluated as part of the assessment of MIL models. Some of the interfaces that should be included are software to operator terminal, operator to terminal, and participant to operator.

The objective of this portion of the assessment is to determine if the interfaces are reasonable, that is, that the interface will allow the model to meet the intended use. There are many facets that need to be examined including the performance measures taken during the operational test: information availability, timeliness of information, and ability to input appropriate information. There are many other factors commonly addressed concerning the man-machine interface. These additional performance measures are usually associated with a particular study or have been assessed in previous experiments whose intent is to examine how well humans can interact with and control the system under study. For this reason, the more complex human factors measures and testing may not be accomplished as part of the confidence assessment of a model. Instead, a review of results from a previous application of the model can assist the assessors in their reasonableness testing (specifically, did the model support the man-machine interface? Was it responsive?). Over time and repeated application, the user may develop standards that he expects the model to meet. As the user develops these standards for the interfaces, the assessment should consider them to assure that the model meets those standards.

Algorithm analysis. The procedure for detecting incompatible, inappropriate, or restrictive definitions embedded in the algorithms is covered in Chapter 3, which details the assessment of algorithms for elements and functions that do not involve human interaction. A MIL model will include algorithms to provide information to the human elements, accept information, and act on the information provided. These algorithms must be assessed to assure that the model actions are appropriate. Issues that must be included in the assessment are include the following.

- *Adequacy and completeness of information provided to the operator.* All information must be provided for the operator to make appropriate decisions.
- *Timeliness of information.* The information provided must be the best information that would be available at that point in the battle. The information provided should be neither too stale, nor from a future event.
- *Allowable operator actions.* Actions allowed for the operator must be sufficient for the model to meet its intended use.

Model implementation verification. The procedure for tracing the computerized model back to the conceptual model and the intended use is covered under software verification in Chapter 3.

Traceability analysis. The traceability of the conceptual model to the intended-use definition and problem definition for an MIL model may not be as specific as for computer-based models. The intended use for an MIL model includes many aspects that include human in the simulation process. Some examples of intended uses for this type of model are to train potential users in the model operations, to test a new or revised concept of operations, and to investigate system sensitivity to alternate criterion or scenarios. Particular aspects of incorporating the human element will depend extensively on the specific use. The description of the intended use, as defined in Table 4-3 (also Table 5-3) should be modified to reflect the characteristics of how humans will contribute to the simulation process. The specific areas where, and the extent to which, human interaction is allowed should be included in the characterization. The remainder of the characterization description, as contained in Tables 4-1 and 4-2 (or Tables 5-1 and 5-2) should be followed and modified to meet the specific capabilities of the model to reflect the system attributes considered.

The resulting characterization will be a textual description of the model's potential use based on these model attributes. An equivalent characterization will be completed of the capabilities noted in the conceptual model. The two characterizations are compared to assure that the conceptual model capabilities cover those required by the intended use and to identify areas where the model capabilities are not directly traceable to the intended use.

Internal software testing analysis. The procedure for internal software testing at the module, unit, and integration level is covered in Chapter 3 under software verification. A MIL model adds human and hardware considerations to developer and assessment team testing. All of these considerations may not be able to be module, unit, and integration tested in the same sense as computer-based models. Both the human and hardware elements can be separately tested, but the complete integration tests may require test resources similar to the intended experiment. The human elements of the model could be tested stand-alone and could be tested as units. Hardware could be unit tested in conjunction with surrogate operators using the software in a combined test effort.

The integration of the human, hardware, and software components is very important for a MIL model. The nature of a MIL model, with its reliance on the handling of data, necessitates that the action of one component results in the appropriate reaction in the other components. If the operator enters a command, other displays and the other terminals should reflect the command, if a requirement, and the software should use the command correctly. Without a thorough integration testing program, either by the developer or the confidence assessment team, that extensively exercises the data-handling capabilities of the model, there would be a high level of risk in undertaking operational validation testing. Problems would be encountered not only with the ability to run operational tests, but questions would also arise concerning the validity of the results.

Operational validation. The procedure for assuring the adequacy of modeling-perceived reality is covered in Chapter 3 under Data validation. Operational validation testing of computer simulation models concentrates on comparison of the model results to some standard derived from real-world test, another model, physics principles, or internal model consistency. Operational validation for a MIL model may not be as concerned about overall comparison with a standard. The emphasis should be more on the reasonableness of the model response to the input scenario and operator action. The depth of operational validation testing is closely tied to the model's intended use. For example, a model to be used in analysis of high-level command decision processes may not require that the algorithms used for physical models (such as power plant output or projectile dynamics) be rigorously tested against real-world, experimental performance data. The testing requirement for the element models might be to assure that reasonable time, sequence of events, component interaction, and status updates are reflected to the operator. MIL model operational validation testing emphasizes the areas of model performance in support of the human element of the model. The performance measures of adequacy, completeness, and timeliness of information, ability to input appropriate actions or commands to the model, and the actions the model makes based on user input are the core of the assessment.

Operational validation testing for MIL models becomes more complex than for computer-based models due to the addition of human and hardware into the testing process. To adequately test a MIL model as it would be used, a complete set of qualified operators and related support personnel would be required. Also, the suite of hardware hosting the integrated model would have to be used for all testing. (For example, in a war-gaming run, it might be extremely difficult if not impossible to assemble appropriate people to represent offensive, defensive, and referee team members for confidence assessment testing. Thus, a mock team will likely be assembled for confidence assessment testing. This injects a risk into the testing process: the mock team may not have the experience necessary in all cases to judge the adequacy of the implementation. This risk can be mitigated by having the mock team review training manuals, take actual training, and participate in actual gaming situations.)

Because of the difficulties in developing a complete operational test program for a MIL model, extensive use will be made of data from other experiments. Data from an experiment can include review or participation in training conducted before the start of the experiment, review of the actual experiment or data recordings, sharing data collection during the experiment, and by debriefing participants. Information from the actual experiment is the most reliable data available for assessing the appropriateness of information presented to the operator and the operator's ability to input the required information into the model.

Chapter 7

Hardware-in-the-Loop Models

SPECIAL TOPICS - Guidance for assessing models
that interact with hardware.
Recommended for personnel involved with development
and assessment of hardware-in-the-loop models.

This chapter provides guidance for applying the confidence assessment methodology, as described in Chapters 1-5, to models that interface with hardware in the simulation process. Under the term hardware-in-the-loop (HWIL) simulations, we include models that incorporate hardware interfaces with software or with operators, and models that integrate a conceptual machine interface into the model's functional definition.

Hardware-in-the-loop models

There is a wide array of HWIL models. In this chapter, we discuss those involving hardware components emulating some portion of the system being modeled. However, this is only representative of the HWIL class. Some examples of the HWIL models under consideration in this chapter include:
- machine emulators (for example, those emulators driven by software-controlled scene generators),
- real hardware (such as those providing real-time information to the model, for example, communications units with message traffic provided by the model), and
- integrated portions of the system being modeled using real hardware components or emulators as part of final system integration tests.

These are only a few examples of the various HWIL models that may need to be considered in an assessment. The CA methodology is flexible enough to assess almost any model, but the depth and breadth of the assessment may change with each type of model or with the model's intended use.

Unique aspects. The technical considerations unique to hardware-in-the-loop simulations include the following.
- *Timing.* Provide realistic timing to hardware elements.
- *Software-to-hardware information relay.* Provide appropriate information to the hardware.
- *Hardware-to-software information relay.* Accept realistic information from the hardware.
- *Data definition flexibility.* Support a wide variety of input/output as might be expected of the model in a realistic environment.
- *Operations.* Provide a mode of operation as free as possible from unrealistic interruptions, data sequences, and task requirements.
- *Integration.* Provide thorough integration of inputs to support the interaction. This integration includes reliability of event-sequencing to reflect scenario dynamics, as well as data integrity throughout the simulation. Integration is one of the most critical issues to be addressed by HWIL models.

Approach. The integrated HWIL model can be assessed using the current confidence assessment methodology, but it must be modified to give consideration to the above technical considerations. Here we discuss the procedures for assessing HWIL models in the context of a formal assessment (see Chapter 4). We pay attention chiefly to modifications required of that formal process to meet the needs of HWIL assessment. By restricting a formal level of effort to concentrate on the procedures discussed for conceptual model validation, model implementation verification, and operational testing, one can appropriately perform a limited assessment instead (refer to Chapter 5).

Example of HWIL model. The urban power plant simulation, first presented in Chapter 1, is an example of an HWIL model. The power plant example represents only one type of model from that broad class, but provides a flavor for the kinds of problems and modeling approaches expected.

The power distribution problem could be described by an HWIL model using generator emulators to produce electrical power data to the model and employing real *prototype* emulators of the generator component. Data provided from this source would be integrated into the simulation, along with the other various hardware and software components. The integrated system-level simulation can serve as a test bed for the management of power at an urban plant, using real-time software to evaluate system failures and distribution trade-offs. The model's objectives could be to evaluate software, develop policy, develop algorithms, analyze performance, and generate procedure and training scenarios. The model could provide gaming command and control, man-in-the-loop, data communications, data fusion, correlation, and relay. The complex command connectivities and power links could be studied, and optimal output capacities could be selected.

Technical areas for formal assessment of HWIL models

Chapter 2 describes a general structure for simulation evaluation based on the Sargent Framework. Figure 7-1 depicts a slight modification of that structure to reflect HWIL concepts. The structure highlights the products and processes that describe a model. Each element in this figure should be considered in model development and assessment. The inner triangle describes the model development process and the remainder of the figure shows the process of assuring that the model and its implementation are correct.

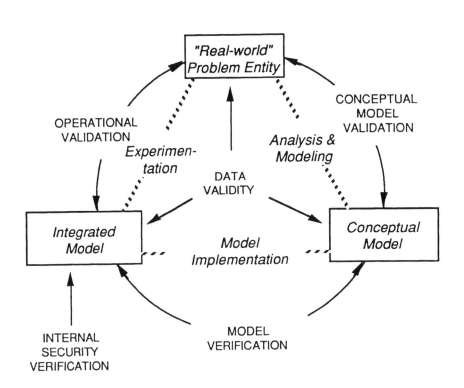

Figure 7-1. Structure for HWIL simulation evaluation (formal).

The general content of the figure is the same for HWIL models and the computer-based models considered in the main report. The words and concepts representing the model development and test process change to account for specific HWIL considerations. The following elements of the figure address HWIL issues.

- *Real-world problem entity.* The problem entity is the system (real or proposed), idea, policy, or phenomena to be modeled. Problem entities to be assessed address the system and may be used for element system development, concept demonstration, and system or subsystem integration testing. For example, this could be a functioning system comprised of all required hardware and software components. Tests for the system concepts would likely be done in a step-wise fashion with some elements for the real system replaced by hardware or software emulators. Most HWIL models are being considered for the same intended use they were developed for. However, in models where this is not the case, the intended use will also be considered as part of the problem definition for the purposes of model assessment.

- *Analysis and modeling.* The model is developed from the problem entity through analysis and simulation. This process defines how the HWIL considerations will be met in the model - the general capabilities to be allowed for interaction of hardware and model.

- *Conceptual model.* The conceptual model should be completely described to allow potential users the ability to understand what was modeled, why, and how. The conceptual model's description must specify how hardware should interact with the model, indicating the information available to the hardware element and the information to be supplied by the hardware. The conceptual model will outline the requirements of the hardware or emulators.

- *Conceptual model validity.* Validation of the conceptual model comprises justification of assumptions, algorithms, and modeling concepts. Conceptual model validation for HWIL models must consider how the hardware is incorporated into the model as well as the assumptions, algorithms, and concepts used in the remainder of the model. Inherent in HWIL models are assumptions concerning the adequacy and timing of information supplied to the hardware element and the capability of the model to act on the hardware response. The judgment of the conceptual model's validity must be tempered in HWIL models.

- *Integrated model.* The integrated model is the suite of software and hardware that comprise the complete model. Software drives the information flow and provides the background simulation activity. The hardware element of the model must be considered because the interfaces between the software and hardware elements are closely tied to the hardware capabilities available, and the model is frequently tailored to the hardware. Adequate documentation of the capabilities, limitations, and applications are essential to the acceptance of the integrated model.

- *Model implementation.* As the developer implements the integrated model, many methods support model credibility. In addition to the elements of software development, operational testing of the complete integrated model, if possible, and model configuration control are key elements in assessing the model development. Operational testing of the model should fully exercise the model capability. Configuration control of the integrated model is important because of the close ties commonly found between the software and hardware.

- *Model implementation verification.* Verification of model implementation must include verification of the ability of the hardware to interact with the model in the manner specified by the conceptual model. In addition to the common software verification tests, we must consider the range of HWIL inputs available, information available to the hardware element, and the time element of the hardware.

- *Experimentation.* How the model was used, acceptance of results, and problems noted in the application contribute to the overall assessment of model credibility.

- *Operational test.* Operational test emphasizes demonstrated consistency with the real-world problem entity, which includes demonstration of the hardware interaction with the model. The operational test program must consider operation of the complete model, including hardware elements, and consider the range of hardware actions allowed by the model.

- *Data validation.* Assessing the validity of the data used in development and operation of the model.

- *Internal security verification.* Determining if the integrated model is currently free of any tampering devices that would effect its operation or results.

Technical areas for limited or maintenance assessment of HWIL models

The preceding section explored a formal assessment of an HWIL model. The same discussion can be applied to the limited or maintenance assessment of HWIL models, but we should emphasize the following considerations. An assessment of HWIL models needs to clearly identify the model's intended scope and level of fidelity. For example, in assessing a gaming tool, the CA analysts would need to determine whether it was intended to be an *end-to-end* gaming simulation (that is, from some start to final outcome), versus a discrete-event or component-specific model.

The initial characterization of the model (as was introduced in Chapter 2) will be developed from those functional areas important to the model's intended use. This characterization can be refined and detailed throughout the application of the assessment procedures.

Limited and maintenance assessments (Chapter 5) concentrate on three areas:

* conceptual model validation,
* model implementation verification, and
* operational validation testing.

These processes can be applied to HWIL models in the effort to identify model capabilities as well as areas of risk for a potential user.

During conceptual model validation, the assessment should consider the many interfaces between hardware elements, and between hardware and the controlling simulation. Among the interfaces to examine are those between the customer power receptacle and the power plant generator; the customer and the power plant service center; plant engineering, the service center, and dispatch repair staff; city and county officials and the power plant management; plant engineering and plant management; and the communications interfaces. Each of the interfaces should be examined to assure that the interfaces are adequate to meet the needs of the experiment in terms of data available at each node, the quality of the data, and the timeliness of information provided. The conceptual models for other system components used should also be examined to assure that they are accurate representations of the system capabilities.

The model implementation verification process should concentrate on examining the developer testing program. The software contained in the model and controlling the interfaces should be examined in detail using standard code analysis techniques. Module, unit, and integration testing could be accomplished by the assessment team to some extent, but the bulk of the software and complete integration testing should be accomplished by the developer in final system readiness reviews. Some areas in which developer testing should be reviewed are data controllers, merging of multisource data, and data recording.

For operational validation, the primary source of test results should be the experiment itself and the integration tests and readiness reviews accomplished by the developer. The geographic dispersion of the system components and the large number of people and agencies involved in the experiment preclude specific confidence assessment operational testing. Some specific test parameters might be gained to support confidence assessment of the model during all pretest and experiment test programs. Again, internal security verification and data validation activities can be undertaken as optional areas of evaluation.

Assessment procedures for HWIL models

Modifications to the procedures previously defined for computer-based model assessment must be considered for HWIL model assessments. This section describes the modifications to the assessment procedures. The format of the section imitates that of Chapter 3, which describes the assessment procedures. Material presented here relies on that description and expands or modifies where appropriate. Procedure references to appropriate sections are included to facilitate use of this chapter in conjunction with the previous material.

Conceptual model validation. Some additions are required to the procedures discussed in Chapter 3 to perform a conceptual model validation for a hardware-in-the-loop model assessment.

Development history analysis: interface standards and documents. The section on conceptual model validation in Chapter 3 describes how to evaluate generic interfaces between software units and other software or hardware. Assessing HWIL models may require evaluating several other interfaces, including hardware to hardware, model software to test hardware, and inclusion of any special interconnecting hardware. The standards for these interfaces and their documentation must be followed for test and development of the host-specific hardware. Not all standards apply to every situation and each model and experiment must be examined to determine which, if any, of the standards apply.

In the absence of standards, the interfaces will be examined in detail and exercised during operational testing of the model. The objective of this portion of the assessment is to determine if the interfaces are reasonable and will allow the model to meet the intended use. There are many facets that need to be examined including the performance measures taken during operational test, such as the hardware function, availability of information to the hardware, receipt of appropriate information from the hardware, and timing of messages and other information passing to and from the hardware. As standards are developed within the user's organization or found to be applicable for these interfaces, the assessment will consider them to assure that the model meets the standards.

Development history analysis: test plans, procedures, and results. The procedure for developer testing analysis is covered in Chapter 3, in the section on conceptual model validation. The assessment team will probably not be able to test most HWIL models themselves. Therefore, the only way for the assessment team to verify the model implementation is to review the developer's testing documentation. Test plans, test procedures, and test results should be reviewed to ensure that all aspects of the model, both hardware and software, were tested adequately. Special attention should be given to configuration management for hardware and software.

Algorithm analysis. The procedures for detecting incompatible, inappropriate, or restrictive assumptions imbedded in the algorithms is also covered in the section on conceptual model validation in Chapter 3. Those procedures cover assessment of algorithms for the given system elements and other capabilities that do not involve the hardware model components. An HWIL model will include algorithms to provide information to the hardware, accept information, and act on the information provided. These algorithms must be assessed to ensure that the model actions are appropriate. Issues that must be included in the assessment include the following.

- *Adequacy and completeness of information provided to the hardware.* Information details may include the types, destinations and uses.
- *Timeliness of information.* The information provided must be the best available at that point. The information provided should be neither too stale nor from a future event.
- *Hardware responses.* Responses allowed for the hardware must be sufficient for the model to meet its intended use.

Model implementation verification. Additions are also required to perform a model implementation verification for an HWIL model assessment. The following paragraphs outline modifications to the internal software testing at the module, unit, and integration level covered under software verification in Chapter 3.

An HWIL model adds hardware considerations to developer and assessment testing. These models may not be able to be module, unit, and integration tested in the same sense as computer-based models. The hardware components may or may not be available to the assessment team for testing. If available for testing, the hardware and software should be unit tested.

Integration of the hardware and software considerations is very important for an HWIL model. The nature of an HWIL model, with its emphasis on the handling of data, necessitates that the action of hardware causes the appropriate reaction in the software. In addition to integrating hardware and software, there may be several software components or several hardware components that must be integrated first before the hardware can be integrated with the software. Without a thorough integration-testing program, either by the developer or the confidence assessment team that extensively exercises the data-handling capabilities of the model, there would be a high level of risk in undertaking operational-validation testing. Not only could problems be encountered with the ability to run operational tests, but also questions could arise as to the validity of the results.

Operational validation. The procedure for assuring the adequacy of modeling perceived reality is covered in Chapter 3, in the section on data validation. HWIL model operational validation testing emphasizes model performance in support of the hardware element of the model. The core of the assessment is made up of

- performance measures of adequacy, completeness, and timeliness of information, and
- the actions the model makes based on hardware actions.

Operational validation testing of an HWIL model as part of an assessment effort may be difficult if not impossible. Assembling the entire configured system may not be feasible. For some HWIL models, hardware and software components may be geographically dispersed or contain elements that can be linked only intermittently. The experiment team personnel, data collection and reduction systems, and the hardware and software components are all necessary. The cost and time commitment required to perform many of these tests would be very large and perhaps prohibitive. Most testing of these models as part of a confidence assessment will be as part of the development tests or as part of the actual experiment.

Because of the difficulties in developing a complete operational test program for an HWIL model, extensive use should be made of any available data from an experiment. Data from an experiment can include

- review or participation in experiment planning,
- review of the actual experiment or data recordings,
- sharing data collection during the experiment, and
- debriefing participants.

Information from the actual experiment is the most reliable data available for assessing the appropriateness of information presented to the hardware and the ability of the hardware to input the required information into the model. The assessment team should be augmented by representatives of the user organizations.

Chapter 8

Assessment Aids

> **SPECIAL TOPICS - Tools to assist in planning, organizing, and conducting an assessment effort.**
> **Recommended for assessment team leadership; useful to managers concerned with the scope of assessment effort.**

A formal assessment may appear to be a formidable task. Simulation tools can be very complex and the customer requesting or sponsoring a confidence assessment may want a detailed examination of each model function. This chapter contains the tools to assist in planning, organizing, and conducting a systematic assessment. Assessment aids include a method of identifying the simulation class, a question list for formal assessments, a characterization matrix, a typical assessment schedule, as well as forms and formats for recording results derived during the planning and application phases.

The assembly plant example. Here we will again use the example of the assembly plant problem, introduced in Chapter 4, to illustrate how to apply the tools provided here to the methodology described in the preceding chapters of this book. To introduce all the available tools, a hypothetical assessment of the assembly plant simulation will be described at the level of a formal assessment, described in Chapter 4. (The formal assessment process is summarized in Figure 4-1.)

The discrete-event simulation, PLANT, was developed to model an assembly plant for the production of widgets by the manufacturing company Clangen, Banger & Associates. The CEO, R.U. Clangen, asked his industrial engineering division to study their operations under certain product demand scenarios. Because the PLANT simulation is 10 years old, Clangen also hired the consulting firm of Goodbytes Corporation to validate the simulation. Goodbytes held a meeting with Clangen and his industrial engineers. From this initial conference the scope and level of detail that could be committed to the effort was identified. A second significant result of this meeting was that they agreed on the intended use for the simulation: PLANT would be used to evaluate the cost-effectiveness trade-offs of various production schedules given specific product demand conditions. Goodbytes then listed PLANT's attributes (Table 4-1) and formulated the shell of a model characterization matrix (Table 4-2), and modified the characterization of the model's intended use (compiled in Table 4-3). Both of these were given to the industrial engineers for their review and comment. The ground work for the assessment was laid, and the formal assessment process could now be implemented.

Simulation characterization

As illustrated by the assembly plant example, determining a model's intended use is essential to conducting a simulation assessment. Equipped with this understanding at the outset, we can characterize the model. This characterization is one of the earliest activities of the preparation phase, and from it we can determine the best approach to undertaking the other phases of the assessment.

Simulation classes. Simulations can be characterized by many attributes and qualities. In addition to the development of a concise functional description of model capabilities, these include a characterization of model intended use and key implementation and design issues.

We provided a detailed breakdown of simulation classes in Chapter 2. These classes help identify and distinguish model types appropriate for various uses in research, industry, or government. Whether simulating manufacturing systems or military operations – for use in a particular operational mode or to a specified accuracy in performance – this classification of attributes may be used as an indicator for potential users in their evaluation of whether a given simulation is appropriate or adequate for their needs.

The attributes of models within a class are listed in a characterization matrix as an overview of the model's capabilities. The attributes are standardized to the extent possible. These characterization attributes may need modification to address different intended uses or reflect changes as system concepts and configurations evolve.

Several design attributes unique to a given simulation may affect a potential user's ability or desire to use a given simulation. Attributes considered to be important are: fidelity, runtime, host computer, language, modeling approach, maintainability, ease of use, configuration management (CM), code security classification, post-processor, and preprocessor. These attributes are important to all simulations and are therefore included as part of all characterization matrices regardless of the model's intended use. These attributes were discussed in Chapter 2.

The wide range of functional attributes and scope of intended use which characterizes models can be most useful in determining the approach needed to conduct an assessment of a given simulation. The scope and detail of a model classify it as one of the following types:

- system level,
- integrated system level,
- tier or segment level,
- component or element level,
- subsystem level, or
- technology level.

Model's intended use. As noted in Chapter 4, the model's intended use is summarized by a short statement in coordination and agreement with the assessment team, the users, and the developers. An especially important objective at this point is establishing the model's required accuracy. A ballpark figure calls for a different level of assessment effort than does pinpoint accuracy. Judging the relative importance and potential consequences of decisions that may be based on simulation results helps establish these accuracy requirements. (See Table 4-3.)

Characterization matrix. After the intended use is identified, the model can be summarized by listing its attributes and creating a characterization matrix (refer to Tables 4-1 and 4-2). These summaries provide textual, tabular descriptions of the required model capability. The characterization of model attributes will be altered as needed at this point in the assessment. An example of the general intended uses foreseen for various models include those shown in Table 4-3. A new set of characterization attributes, or a significant modification to the attributes suggested in Tables 4-1 and 4-2, will be required to address some of these general intended uses. Changes may also be required as the fundamental concepts and system configuration evolve.

The model capabilities are also characterized using the attributes illustrated in Table 4-1 and in the characterization matrix, as provided in the sample Table 4-2. This summary provides a textual description of the developer's claims for model capability. This information is drawn from such documents as the functional description, user's manual, and programmer's manual. The developer can provide additional information to complete the characterization, particularly when the model is under development. This information is updated during the course of the assessment as capabilities are assessed and entries are made to the characterization matrix. These attributes are oriented towards a specific end-to-end simulation model, to be used only for illustration. As described for the attributes used to characterize intended uses, the list of attributes may have to change and evolve to meet model capabilities and system concepts. Justifications and back-up data for the assessment values are provided as supporting data to the final assessment report (see the section on reporting activities in Chapter 4).

Define assessment objectives. Assessment objectives are the evaluation of particular areas of the model or its capability. These can be critical areas of the model design or important aspects of the intended use. Development of the assessment objectives is aided by characterization of the intended use and model in the same terms.

Defining the assessment objectives focuses a model assessment. Whereas the questions and assessment procedures define the general areas to be examined in a formal assessment, the assessment objectives define those specific issues that must be tested and closely examined for the given model. Some additional depth may be added to the assessment process to address the objective, but no additional scope is expected to address them.

Characterization of the model and its intended use as described above identifies key areas of the model that must be emphasized during the assessment. These areas of emphasis are where model performance is essential to meeting the study or experiment objectives. Key areas identified are considered in planning the assessment and in selection of assessment procedures to be applied. Understanding the assessment objectives and their origin is essential for the assessment team to make proper judgments in selection of assessment procedures. The more specific this information is, the more concrete the assessment process can become.

The assessment objectives are derived from comparison of the model and intended use characterizations. These are listed as model capabilities that must be proven to meet the intended use. As assessment procedures are applied during the planning and application phases, additional knowledge becomes available that may update the characterizations and the list of objectives. Any updates represent changes in the focus for the assessment and can influence selection of assessment procedures or direct additional effort into new areas.

Assessment schedule

An initial schedule can be drafted during the preparation phase. Development of this schedule depends on the approach to be taken for the assessment procedures, and by the best understanding of the model as summarized in Tables 4-1, 4-2, and 4-3. This is because the relationship between the tasks and activities is different for each application of the methodology and will be dictated by the scope of the assessment and level of effort, as well as by model attributes. The schedule will need to reflect both management's and the assessment team's appreciation of those issues. Figure 8-1 shows a typical schedule.

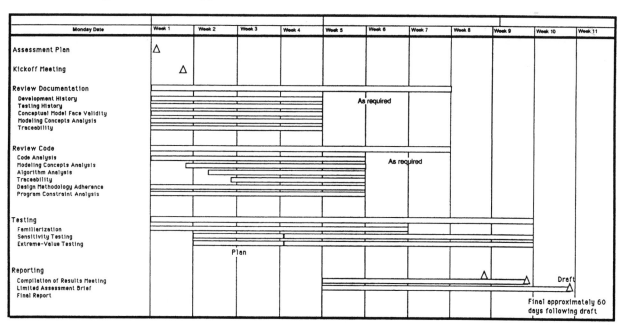

Figure 8-1. Assessment schedule.

Formal assessment question list

The questions provided in detail on the next few pages are designed to guide the assessment process and aid in the determination of assessment procedures to apply during the application phase. The issues addressed by this formal assessment inquiry are summarized as follows.

1. Review of intended use

2. Review of simulation developer's effort

- Problem entity

- Conceptual model derivation

- Conceptual model structure

- Conceptual model validation

- Software development

- Computerized model

- Software verification

- Historical use

- Operational validation

- Data validation

- Internal security validation

- Configuration management/quality assurance

- Other

3. Comparison of simulation capability to intended use

- Problem entity versus intended use

- Conceptual model versus intended use

- Computerized model versus intended use

1. Review of intended use

- Is the intended use to be supported documented?
- Are the elements needing to be modeled documented?
- Is the level of detail and fidelity needed for each entity documented?
- Are the outputs and measures of effectiveness (MOEs) needed documented?
- Are the required key inputs documented?
- Are the ranges of values necessary for the key inputs documented?
- Were special requirements to be levied on the model documented?

2. Review of simulation developer's effort

Problem entity
- Was the original intended use to be supported documented?
- Were the elements needing to be modeled documented?
- Was the level of detail and fidelity needed for each entity documented?
- Were the outputs and MOEs needed documented?
- Were the required key inputs documented?
- Were the ranges of values necessary for the key inputs documented?

Conceptual model derivation
- Was a plan developed for deriving the conceptual model?
- Does the conceptual model provide the level of detail and fidelity for each element that was required for the problem entity?
- Does the conceptual model provide the outputs and MOEs needed for the problem entity?
- Does the conceptual model provide the key inputs that the problem entity required?
- Does the conceptual model provide the range of values for key inputs required by the problem entity?
- Were the assumptions made and theories used during the derivation of the conceptual model documented?
- Were the assumptions made and theories used during the derivation of the conceptual model supported?

Conceptual model structure
- Does the conceptual model contain the elements required by the problem entity?
- Are the limitations and restrictions of the conceptual model documented?
- Are the limitations and restrictions of the conceptual model supported?

Conceptual model validation
- Was there a plan developed for validating the conceptual model?
- Were credible methods used for validating the conceptual model?
- Did the validation of the conceptual model include:
    - validation of the assumptions made?
    - validation of the theories used?
    - validation of the range of inputs expected?
    - validation of the data used?
    - validation of the outputs?

Software development
- Was a plan created for developing the software?
- Was a software development methodology employed?

- Were design standards employed during the development cycle?
- Were coding standards employed during the development cycle?
- Was CASE (computer-aided software engineering) technology employed?
- Was a plan developed for testing the software during the development?
- Were credible methods used for testing the software during the development?
- Did the testing of the software during the development cycle include testing at the following levels:
  - module level?
  - unit level?
  - integration level?
- Were the following aspects of software tested:
  - interfaces?
  - assumptions?
  - inputs?
  - error cases?
  - paths?
  - theories?
- Were external interfaces documented?
- Were internal interfaces documented?

Computerized model
- Were the following aspects of the model documented:
  - elements modeled?
  - level of detail and fidelity of the elements?
  - outputs and MOEs?
  - ranges of values for outputs and MOEs?
  - inputs?
  - ranges of values for inputs?
  - assumptions made during development?
  - theories used in the software?
  - restrictions and limitations of the software?
  - changes made since the code was baselined?
- Do the following aspects of the model match the conceptual model:
  - elements modeled?
  - level of detail and fidelity of the elements?
  - outputs and MOEs?
  - ranges of values for the outputs and MOEs?
  - inputs?
  - ranges of values for inputs?
  - assumptions made during development?
  - theories used in the software?
  - restrictions and limitations of the software?
- Were assumptions made and theories used in the software supported?
- Were the restrictions and limitations in the software supported?
- Does the software documentation include the following:
  - complete user-level information?
  - complete programmer-level information?
  - complete design specification information?
  - complete requirements information?

- Does the code contain the following attributes to make it more maintainable:
    - amplifying comments?
    - organized structure?
    - module-level input/output specification?

Software verification
- Was there a plan developed for verification of the software?
- Were credible methods used during the verification of the software?
- Did the verification of the software include verification of the following:
    - modules?
    - module-level interfaces?
    - assumptions?
    - limitations?
    - restrictions?
    - paths?
    - equations?
    - global data use?

Historical use
- Was a plan developed for the previous use of the model?
- Was the model configuration for that use clearly defined?
- Is that model configuration similar to that proposed for the intended use?
- Are the inputs, outputs, and MOEs from the previous use relevant to the intended use of the model?
- Was the previous use of the model accepted by that user of the model?
- Was the previous use of the model assessed by this confidence assessment team?

Operational validation
- Was there a plan developed for the operational validation of the model?
- Were credible methods used for operational validation of the software?
- Did the operational validation of the software include validation of the following:
    - input-output relationships?
    - event ordering?
    - event occurrence?
    - extreme conditions?
    - stochastic variability?
    - sensitivity to key parameters?

Data validation
- Was a plan developed for collection of data from external sources?
- Were the data collected from external sources supported?
- Were the data collected from external sources checked for the following:
    - consistency?
    - units?
    - range of values?
- Was a plan developed for the generation of data not collected from external sources?
- Were the generated data supported?
- Were the generated data checked for the following:
    - consistency?
    - units?
    - range of values?

Internal security validation
- Was there a plan developed for the validation of internal security?
- Were credible methods employed during the internal security validation effort?
- Did the internal security validation effort include validation of the following:
  - code-locking techniques?
  - configuration management (CM) procedures?
  - possible inputs and outputs?
  - code constructs used?
  - nonexistence of viruses?

Configuration management/quality assurance (CM/QA)
- Were CM/QA controls provided during the following phases of the model's development and use:
  - conceptual model derivation?
  - conceptual model validation?
  - software development?
  - development cycle software testing?
  - software verification?
  - each instance of previous use?
  - operational validation?
  - external data collection?
  - data generation?
  - internal security validation?
- Did these CM/QA controls provide the following for each phase:
  - Was there a CM/QA plan produced for each phase?
  - Were there procedures for verifying compliance with CM/QA controls?
  - Were there procedures for the controlled incorporation of the results of various analyses and testing back into the design and code of the simulation?
  - Were there procedures for controlling changes to interfaces?

Other
- Were any external reviews or audits (such as independent verification and validation), conducted on this simulation?

(Repeat relevant portions of the above question list for each review)

3. Comparison of simulation capability to intended use

Problem entity versus intended use
- Do the elements needing to be modeled for the intended use match the entities that were needed for the problem entity?
- Does the level of detail and fidelity required for the problem entity match the level of detail and fidelity required for the intended use of the model?
- Do the outputs and MOEs required for the intended use match the outputs and/or MOEs needed for the problem entity?
- Do the key inputs required for the problem entity match the key inputs required for the intended use of the model?
- Do the ranges of values for key inputs into the problem entity match those required for the intended use of the model?
- Does the problem entity support the special requirements of the intended use?

Conceptual model versus intended use
- Does the conceptual model contain the elements needed for the intended use of the model?
- Does the conceptual model contain the level of detail and fidelity necessary for the intended use of the model?
- Does the conceptual model provide the outputs and MOEs required for the intended use?
- Does the conceptual model provide the key inputs needed for the intended use?
- Does the conceptual model provide the range of values on input needed for the intended use?
- Do the assumptions made or theories used by the conceptual model conflict with the intended use?
- Do the limitations or restrictions of the conceptual model conflict with the intended use?
- Does the conceptual model support the special requirements of the intended use?

Computerized model versus intended use
- Are the elements needed for the intended use developed in the software?
- Is the level of detail and fidelity of the elements modeled in the software sufficient for the intended use of the model?
- Are the outputs and MOEs needed for the intended use provided by the software?
- Are the key inputs needed for the intended use provided by the software?
- Is the range of values for the input needed for the intended use provided by the software?
- Are the assumptions made during the development compatible with the model's intended use?
- Are the theories implemented during the development compatible with the model's intended use?
- Do any limitations or restrictions of the computerized model conflict with the model's intended use?
- Does the computerized model support the special requirements of the intended use?
- Were interface standards used during the development?

Aids for planning and application phases

This section contains the guiding matrices and blank forms used to plan, organize, and conduct the formal assessment. They help determine what procedures apply to answer the questions above, and what procedures the answers to those questions imply. In addition, these matrices and forms are needed for planning and scheduling the application phase, and for tracking and reporting the findings of the assessment process.

Tables 8-1 and 8-2 aid in planning the assessment by identifying issues addressed by the formal question list and responses to those questions as potential problem areas. The matrix in Table 8-1 maps these questions into applicable planning phase procedures. Procedures are listed by a shortened form of the procedure name; for a quick reference, check the schematic on the fly leaf. There are two extra columns in this matrix that do not map into Chapter 3. The first, *Other*, is designed to be a place holder for two types of procedures. These include any future procedures that may be developed and any assessment-specific procedures that the assessment team may create. The second extra column, *Basic Requirement*, is mapped to questions related to the existence of various pieces of data versus the quality of the data. As such, no specific, detailed procedures are required to answer these questions. Notice that some procedures answer a large number of questions, and some may be of limited value.

The matrix in Table 8-2 maps the responses to these questions into application phase procedures. To get a better feel for areas of focus of the assessment, this table is filled in to note anticipated problem areas, as identified during the planning phase. The extra column in this matrix is for specialized procedures not covered in Chapter 3. It is labeled *Other, More Data Req.* and is meant as both a place holder for future assessment-specific procedures and to show where a lack of data to answer a question impacts the analysis.

In the actual performance of the application phase procedures, considerable data is assembled. For example, compiled data includes information of configuration management, information on model design, model documentation, and past applications. Table 8-3 pairs a complete list of data items with the related application phase procedures. This is used to help assemble information to support the application phase. Information requirements are listed as *essential* or *useful* depending upon whether they are mandatory for the application of the procedure. The data items on this matrix can be further decomposed into several other bits of data. Detailed data descriptions can be found in Appendix B, Table B-1. The descriptions of the procedures are also necessary for a complete understanding of the information needs of a given procedure.

Table 8-4 breaks out the application phase procedures by how much time they take to apply. This is not given as a numerical value but rather as a relative weighting between the various procedures. This is done because the actual time requirements will be based on the size, complexity, and data availability of a given model.

After all preparations have been completed, Table 8-5 serves as the blank worksheet for the execution of the application phase. It is filled in by the assessment team during the assessment, with the guidance provided by Table 8-2. The items are filled in to document problems as they are observed. (A complete description of the mechanics of this process may be found in Chapter 4).

QUESTION	#	FACE VALIDITY	DEVELOPMENT HISTORY	IV&V SUPPORT	MODEL DERIVATIVE	PREVIOUS MODEL USE	CRITICALITY	SYSTEM	MODELING CONCEPT	INPUT/OUTPUT	COMP. TO CONCEPT. TRACE	COMP. TO USE TRACE	CASE/DESIGN METHODOLOGY	PROCESS METRICS	PRODUCT METRICS	DELPHI TESTS	TURING TESTS	I/O RELATIONSHIP	EVENT SEQUENCING	LIMITED STANDARDS	CM PROCEDURE	CM TOOL	CODE LOCKING TECH.	OTHER BASIC REQUIREMENT
INTENDED USE	1						●	●																
	2						●	●																
	3						●	●																
	4						●	●																
	5						●	●																
	6						●	●																
	7						●	●																
PROBLEM ENTITY	1																							●
	2																							●
	3																							●
	4																							●
	5																							●
	6																							●
CONCEPTUAL DERIVATION	1		●																					
	2	●								●	●													
	3	●								●	●													
	4	●								●	●													
	5	●								●	●													
	6																							
	7	●																						●
CONCEPTUAL STRUCTURE	1	●								●														
	2																							●
	3	●																						
CONCEPTUAL VALIDATION	1		●																					
	2	●	●																					
	3		●																					
S/W DEVELOPMENT	1		●											●										
	2		●											●										
	3		●																					
	4		●																					
	5		●										●											
	6		●											●										
	7	●	●											●										
	8		●											●										
	9		●											●										
	10		●											●										
	11		●											●										
COMPUTER MODEL	1																							
	2																							●
	3	●								●														
	4	●																						
	5		●																					●
	6																							●
S/W VERIFICATION	1	●	●											●										
	2		●											●										
	3		●											●										

Table 8-1. Questions to planning phase procedures.

QUESTION		FACE VALIDITY	DEVELOPMENT HISTORY	IV&V SUPPORT	MODEL DERIVATIVE	PREVIOUS MODEL USE	CRITICALITY	SYSTEM	MODELING CONCEPT	INPUT/OUTPUT	COMP. TO CONCEPT. TRACE	COMP. TO USE TRACE	CASE/DESIGN METHODOLOGY	PROCESS METRICS	PRODUCT METRICS	DELPHI TESTS	TURING TESTS	I/O RELATIONSHIP	EVENT SEQUENCING	LIMITED STANDARDS	CM PROCEDURE	CM TOOL	CODE LOCKING TECH.	OTHER BASIC REQUIREMENT
HISTORICAL USE	1					●																		
	2					●																		
	3					●																		
	4					●																		
	5					●																		
	6					●																		
OPERATIONAL VALIDATION	1		●																					
	2	●	●																					
	3		●																					
DATA VALIDATION	1		●																					
	2	●	●																					
	3		●																					
	4		●																					
	5	●	●																					
	6		●																					
SECURITY VALIDATION	1		●																		●	●	●	
	2	●	●												●						●	●	●	
	3		●												●									
CM/QA	1		●											●										
	2		●											●										
OTHER	1			●	●																			
PROBLEM vs. USE	1																							●
	2																							●
	3																							●
	4																							●
	5																							●
	6																							●
CONCEPT vs. USE	1	●									●													
	2	●									●													
	3	●									●													
	4	●									●													
	5	●									●													
	6	●									●													
	7	●									●													
	8	●									●													
COMPUTER vs. USE	1	●										●			●	●	●		●	●				
	2	●										●			●	●	●	●	●	●				
	3	●										●			●	●	●	●	●	●				
	4	●										●			●	●	●	●	●	●				
	5	●										●			●	●	●	●	●	●				
	6	●										●												
	7	●										●												
	8	●										●												
	9	●														●	●	●	●	●				
	10		●												●									

Table 8-1. Questions to planning phase procedures (concluded).

QUESTION	#	DEVELOPMENT HISTORY	MODELING CONCEPT	INPUT/OUTPUT	ALGORITHM	LOGIC TRACE	COMP. TO CONCEPT. TRACE	COMP. TO USE TRACE	CASE/DESIGN METHODOLOGY	PRODUCT METRICS	INTERNAL S/W TESTING	CODE ANALYSIS	CORRECTNESS PROOFS	I/O RELATIONSHIP	EVENT SEQUENCING	ANIMATION TESTS	FIXED VALUE TESTS	SIMPLIFIED ASSUMPTION	PREDICTIVE VALID. TESTING	INTERNAL VALIDITY	EXTREME-CONDITION	N-VERSION	LIMITED STANDARDS	PREDICTIVE VALIDATION	COMPARISON TO TEST DATA	SENSITIVITY	FEEDBACK LOOP	EMBEDDED DATA	INPUT DATA	CONSISTENCY	DIM. & NUM. VERIFICATION	LOC. & RET. VERIFICATION	GRAPHICAL ANALYSIS	STATISTICAL ANALYSIS	UNDOCUMENTED INPUTS	VIRUS	OTHER, MORE DATA REQ.
INTENDED USE	1																																				
	2																																				◎
	3																																				◎
	4																																				◎
	5																																				◎
	6																																				◎
	7																																				◎
PROBLEM ENTITY	1																																				
	2																																				●
	3																																				●
	4																																				●
	5																																				●
	6																																				●
CONCEPTUAL DERIVATION	1		◎	●	●	●	○		○	○											○																
	2		○	◎	●	●			○	○											○																
	3			◎	●	●	○																														
	4			◎	●	●	○																														
	5			◎	●	●	○																														
	6		○	○	◎	●																															
	7		○	○	○	●																															●
CONCEPTUAL STRUCTURE	1		◎	●	●																																
	2		○	◎	●	●																															●
	3		○	◎	●	●																															
CONCEPTUAL VALIDATION	1		○	◎	●	●	○																														
	2		○	◎	●	●																															
	3	◎	○	◎	●	●																						●	●	●	●	●	●	●			

○ NO PROBLEMS NOTED   ◎ MINOR PROBLEMS NOTED   ● MAJOR PROBLEMS NOTED

Table 8-2. Question responses to application phase procedures.

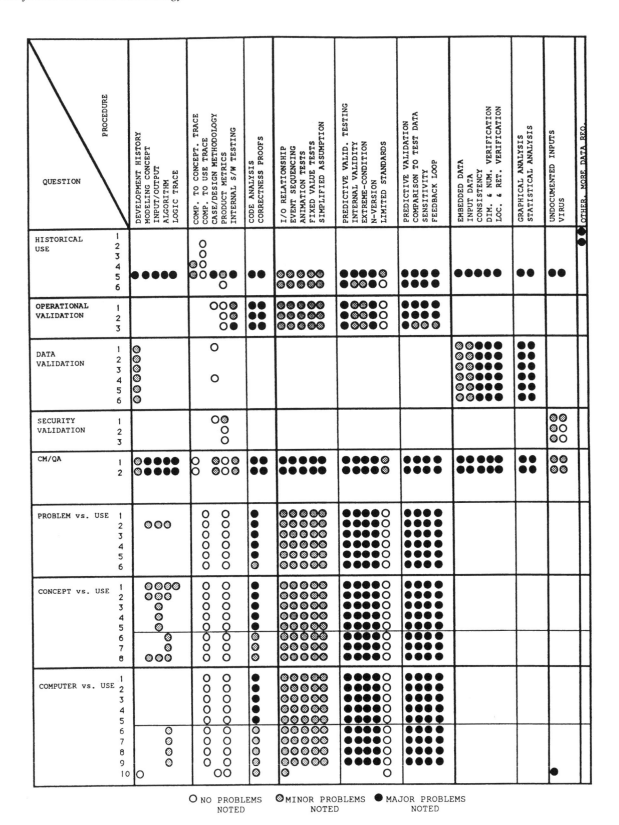

Table 8-2. Question responses to application phase procedures (concluded).

Column headers (PROCEDURES):
DEVELOPMENT HISTORY · MODELING CONCEPT · INPUT/OUTPUT · ALGORITHM · LOGIC TRACE · COMP. TO CONCEPT. TRACE · COMP. TO USE TRACE · CASE/DESIGN METHODOLOGY · PRODUCT METRICS · INTERNAL S/W TESTING · CODE ANALYSIS · CORRECTNESS PROOFS · I/O RELATIONSHIP · EVENT SEQUENCING · ANIMATION TESTS · FIXED VALUE TESTS · SIMPLIFIED ASSUMPTION · PREDICITIVE VALID. TESTING · INTERNAL VALIDITY · EXTREME-CONDITION · N-VERSION · LIMITED STANDARDS · PREDICTIVE VALIDATION · COMPARISON TO TEST DATA · SENSITIVITY · FEEDBACK LOOP · EMBEDDED DATA · INPUT DATA · CONSISTENCY · DIM. & NUM. VERIFICATION · LOC. & RET. VERIFICATION · GRAPHICAL ANALYSIS · STATISTICAL ANALYSIS · UNDOCUMENTED INPUTS · VIRUS · PLANNING PHASE ONLY

DATA ITEMS (FROM APPENDIX B):

Data Item	Marks
ALGORITM REFERENCES	O (Modeling Concept); ● (CASE/Design Methodology); O (Code Analysis)
CASE TOOLS	● (CASE/Design Methodology)
CASE TOOLS GENERATED INFORMATION	O O ● (Comp. to Use Trace / CASE/Design Methodology)
CM PROCEDURES	
CM TOOLS	X (Planning Phase Only)
CM TOOLS DOCUMENTATION	X (Planning Phase Only)
CODE LOCKING DATA	X X (Planning Phase Only)
COMPILERS/ASSEMBLERS	O (Product Metrics); O (Code Analysis)
COMPUTER RESOURCE UTILIZATION STATISTICS	● (Product Metrics)
CONCEPTUAL MODEL DESCRIPTION	● ● ● ● (Dev History ... Algorithm); ● (Comp. to Concept Trace); O (I/O Relationship)
CONCEPTUAL MODEL (VALIDATED)	O (Comp. to Concept Trace); O (Code Analysis)
CONSTANTS DOCUMENTATION	
CONSTANTS MEMORY MAP	O O (Graphical Analysis)
DATA FLOW DIAGRAMS	O O (Dev History/Modeling Concept); O (Statistical Analysis)
DATA SUPPORT DOCUMENTATION	● ● ● (Sensitivity / Feedback Loop)
DESIGN DOCUMENTATION	
DESIGN METHODOLOGY	● ● (Comp. to Use Trace / CASE/Design Methodology); O (Code Analysis)
DEVELOPMENT CYCLE DOCUMENTATION	● (Dev History)
DEVELOPMENT TEST REPORTS	
DIFFERENCES BETWEEN CURRENT MODEL AND PREVIOUS MODEL	X (Planning Phase Only)
DOCUMENTATION SUPPORTING ADHERENCE/ NON-ADHERENCE TO PLANS AND STANDARDS	X (Planning Phase Only)
EXPECTED BEHAVIORS OF ENTITIES	● (Modeling Concept); X (Planning Phase Only)
FEEDBACK LOOP INFORMATION	
GRAPHICAL TOOLS	● (I/O Relationship); ● (Feedback Loop)
INFORMATION ON ENTITIES OF INTEREST	● (Modeling Concept)
INPUT/OUTPUT SPECIFICATIONS	
INPUTS/OUTPUTS OF OTHER ACCEPTED MODELS/REAL SYSTEM	● ● (Event Sequencing / Animation Tests); ● ● ● (Predicitive Valid. / Internal Validity / Extreme-Condition); ● (Undocumented Inputs)
INTENDED USE DESCRIPTION	● ● ● (Dev History/Modeling Concept/Input-Output); ● (Comp. to Concept Trace)
IV & V DOCUMENTATION	
KNOWN/ACCEPTED SCENARIO DESCRIPTION	X (Planning Phase Only)
MODEL DOCUMENTATION	X (Planning Phase Only)
MODEL EXECUTABLE CODE	● (CASE/Design Methodology); O O (Animation Tests)
MODEL INPUT DATA	● ● ● ● (I/O Relationship ... Fixed Value); ● ● ● ● ● (Simplified Assumption ... Extreme-Condition); ● ● ● ● (N-Version ... Predictive Validation)
MODEL INTERFACE DOCUMENTS	● ● (Dev History/Modeling Concept); ● ● (Dim. & Num. / Loc. & Ret. Verification)
MODEL REQUIREMENTS SPECIFICATION	● (Comp. to Use Trace); ● (Internal S/W Testing)
MODEL RUN INPUTS/OUTPUTS	
MODEL SOURCE CODE	O O O O (Dev History ... Logic Trace); ● ● (Comp. to Concept/Use Trace); ● ● (Product Metrics/Internal S/W Testing); ● ● (Code Analysis/Correctness Proofs); ● ● (I/O Relationship/Event Sequencing); ● (Fixed Value); ● (Predicitive Valid.); ● (Feedback Loop); ● (Embedded Data); ● ● ● (Consistency/Dim.&Num./Loc.&Ret.); ● ● (Graphical/Statistical); ● ● (Undocumented Inputs/Virus)
MODULE TEST DOCUMENTATION	O (Dev History); X (Planning Phase Only)
NTB INTERFACE STANDARDS	
OTHER VERSIONS OF THE MODEL	● (Predicitive Valid.)
PHYSICAL EXPERIMENT DATA	O (Modeling Concept)
PREVIOUS MODEL DOCUMENTATION	O O (Graphical Analysis); X (Planning Phase Only)
PREVIOUS USE DOCUMENTATION	O (Comp. to Concept Trace)
SYSTEM BEHAVIOR INFORMATION	● ● (Event Sequencing/Animation Tests)
STATISTICAL ITEM INFORMATION	● (Predicitive Valid.)
TARGET COMPUTER/LANGUAGE REFERENCES	O O (Graphical Analysis)
TEST TOOLS	● (Comp. to Concept Trace); O (Code Analysis)
TRADE-OFF STUDIES	O (Modeling Concept)
UNIT TEST DOCUMENTATION	
"UNIQUE" CONSTRUCTS INFORMATION	O (Virus); X (Planning Phase Only)
USER'S MANUAL	O (Code Analysis)

O USEFUL   ● ESSENTIAL

Table 8-3. Application phase procedure information requirements.

8 - 15

Low time-consumption procedures
    Animation tests
    Development history analysis
    Dimensional and numerical verification analysis
    Extreme-condition testing
    Predictive-validation testing
    Simplified-assumption testing
    Product metrics analysis
    Traceability of computerized model to conceptual model analysis
        (May be in low or medium categories, depending on data available)

Medium time-consumption procedures
    Case and design methodology adherence analysis
    Comparison to test data
    Consistency analysis
    Embedded data analysis
    Event sequencing
    Fixed-value tests
    Input data analysis
    Input-output relationship testing
    Internal software testing analysis
    Internal validity testing
    Location and retrieval verification analysis
    Modeling concepts analysis
    Traceability of computerized model to intended use analysis

High time-consumption procedures
    Algorithm analysis
    Code analysis
    Correctness proofs
    Feedback loop analysis
    Graphical analysis
    Input/output analysis
    Logic trace analysis
    N-version testing
    Predictive validation
    Sensitivity analysis
    Statistical analysis
    Undocumented inputs analysis
    Virus analysis

Table 8-4. Relative time requirements for application phase procedures.

QUESTION \ PROCEDURE		QUESTION RESPONSE	DEVELOPMENT HISTORY MODELING CONCEPT INPUT/OUTPUT ALGORITHM LOGIC TRACE	COMP. TO CONCEPT. TRACE COMP. TO USE TRACE CASE/DESIGN METHODOLOGY PRODUCT METRICS INTERNAL S/W TESTING	CODE ANALYSIS CORRECTNESS PROOFS	I/O RELATIONSHIP EVENT SEQUENCING ANIMATION TESTS FIXED VALUE TESTS SIMPLIFIED ASSUMPTION	PREDICITIVE VALID. TESTING INTERNAL VALIDITY EXTREME-CONDITION N-VERSION LIMITED STANDARDS	PREDICTIVE VALIDATION COMPARISON TO TEST DATA SENSITIVITY FEEDBACK LOOP	EMBEDDED DATA INPUT DATA CONSISTENCY DIM. & NUM. VERIFICATION LOC. & RET. VERIFICATION	GRAPHICAL ANALYSIS STATISTICAL ANALYSIS	UNDOCUMENTED INPUTS VIRUS	OTHER, MORE DATA REQ.
INTENDED USE	1 2 3 4 5 6 7											
PROBLEM ENTITY	1 2 3 4 5 6											
CONCEPTUAL DERIVATION	1 2 3 4 5 6 7											
CONCEPTUAL STRUCTURE	1 2 3											
CONCEPTUAL VALIDATION	1 2 3											
S/W DEVELOPMENT	1 2 3 4 5 6 7 8 9 10 11											
COMPUTER MODEL	1 2 3 4 5 6											
S/W VERIFICATION	1 2 3											
PRIORITY												

Table 8-5. Application phase planning table.

QUESTION / PROCEDURE	QUESTION RESPONSE	DEVELOPMENT HISTORY / MODELING CONCEPT / INPUT/OUTPUT / ALGORITHM / LOGIC TRACE	COMP. TO CONCEPT. TRACE / COMP. TO USE TRACE / CASE/DESIGN METHODOLOGY / PRODUCT METRICS / INTERNAL S/W TESTING	CODE ANALYSIS / CORRECTNESS PROOFS	I/O RELATIONSHIP / EVENT SEQUENCING / ANIMATION TESTS / FIXED VALUE TESTS / SIMPLIFIED ASSUMPTION	PREDICITIVE VALID. TESTING / INTERNAL VALIDITY / EXTREME-CONDITION / N-VERSION / LIMITED STANDARDS	PREDICTIVE VALIDATION / COMPARISON TO TEST DATA / SENSITIVITY / FEEDBACK LOOP	EMBEDDED DATA / INPUT DATA / CONSISTENCY / DIM. & NUM. VERIFICATION / LOC. & RET. VERIFICATION	GRAPHICAL ANALYSIS / STATISTICAL ANALYSIS	UNDOCUMENTED INPUTS / VIRUS	OTHER, MORE DATA REQ.
HISTORICAL USE 1 2 3 4 5 6											
OPERATIONAL VALIDATION 1 2 3											
DATA VALIDATION 1 2 3 4 5 6											
SECURITY VALIDATION 1 2 3											
CM/QA 1 2											
PROBLEM vs. USE 1 2 3 4 5 6											
CONCEPT vs. USE 1 2 3 4 5 6 7 8											
COMPUTER vs. USE 1 2 3 4 5 6 7 8 9 10											
PRIORITY											

Table 8-5. Application phase planning table (concluded).

Formats for reports

Assessment procedure reports. Key elements of the assessment procedure reports are
- the summary of the problem area (either from application of planning phase procedures or from statement of the assessment questions being answered),
- the purpose of the procedure application and why the procedure was chosen,
- the summary of expected results,
- a description of how the procedure was applied,
- findings and observations, and
- a risk assessment.

The description of the procedure's purpose also describes why the particular procedure was selected. This is primarily a restatement of the problem area and procedure selection described in the plan. The analyst will have some familiarity with the simulation and can develop a summary of the expected findings. These findings describe particular areas of investigation and concentration the analyst can use to guide the assessment. Each of the steps used in applying the procedure should be documented to describe what was done in assessing the model. Description of the steps taken is important to document decisions made and intermediate results found during the assessment. A summary of the assessment procedure results should include any observations made by the analyst during the assessment. The results should be compiled by the analyst to form conclusions that address the problem area being investigated. This level of evaluation may require discussion with other members of the assessment team and the customer.

Confidence assessment report outline. As described in Chapter 4, at the completion of the model evaluation a confidence assessment report can be constructed by documenting the assessment effort. Results of the assessment should be stored in a database for future use and further evaluation. Final coordination of the report and briefing content is best conducted during the last meeting of the evaluation team. Documentation at each step in the evaluation process, as has been emphasized throughout the guide, facilitates compilation of the report. Key elements of the report are
- introductory information for the assessment,
- a summary of the approach followed in each area of the assessment (such as conceptual model validation and software verification),
- a list of assessment findings,
- a summary of problem areas involved in using the model, and
- characterization of the model.

The model characterization includes the model characterization matrix and the model description. The intent of the model description is to highlight model functional characteristics, to identify sections of the model where problems were not found, and to address problem areas found during the assessment. Figure 4-4 is a guide to the construction of the report.

Appendix A

Glossary and Acronyms

Glossary

Application phase	The third step in the assessment methodology, defined by applying assessment procedures based on requirements identified in the planning phase.
Characterization	Specification of the key model or intended use functional attributes as determined during an assessment.
Computerized model	An operational computer program which implements a conceptual model.
Conceptual model	Verbal description, equations, functional relationships, or *natural* laws that attempt to define the problem entity.
Conceptual model validation	Determination of the adequacy of the conceptual model to provide a reasonable description of the real world problem for the intended application.
Confidence assessment	The process of assessing the credibility of a simulation by means of the methodology as described in this book.
Configuration management	Procedures for technical and administrative direction and supervision to • identify and document the functional and physical characteristics of an component or system, • control any changes to such characteristics, and • record or report the change, process, and implementation status.
Credibility	The establishment of confidence in the validity of the model.
Data validation	Substantiation that the data used in model development and operation are adequate and correct, or that its source is dependable.
Domain of applicability	Prescribed conditions for which the computerized model has been tested, compared against the problem entity to the extent possible, and judged suitable for use.
Evaluation phase	The last step in the assessment methodology defined by evaluating the information procured from the previous phases to form a recommendation concerning the use of the candidate simulation.
External documentation	Model documentation including manuals, guides, test logs and records, standards and specs, and configuration management.
Formal assessment	The process of thoroughly investigating all aspects of a simulation, in detail. Formal assessment is the most rigorous application of the CA methodology.

Intended use	The application, experiment, or study for which the model has been proposed or chosen as a tool.
Internal documentation	Internal coded comment lines, descriptive text, and headers.
Internal security	Assurance that the model development and subsequent configuration control are adequate to minimize the possibility of external tampering.
Limited assessment	A subset of the formal assessment methodology that is intended to provide a characterization of the simulation and an indication of the risks involved in using the simulation.
Maintenance assessment	An application of the assessment methodology performed on a model which has been previously assessed.
Major problem area	A risk area that individually impacts model credibility. These areas point to incorrect, incomplete, or unsupported model development, test, or implementation practices.
Methodology	A collection of procedures used for evaluation of a simulation.
Minor problem area	A risk area that is not essential to operation of the model and does not seem to affect the simulation's results. These areas point to weaknesses in model development, testing, or implementation and indicate possible improvements to the model that could increase its credibility.
Model	An abstract entity consisting outwardly of a problem entity, conceptual model, and computerized model and also encompassing the processes by which each of the components were created.
Planning phase	The second step in the assessment methodology defined by: • reviewing the simulation, its development, testing, documentation, and the intended use to form an initial determination that the simulation can meet the intended use, • performing limited independent testing of the simulation to demonstrate key performance capabilities, and • planning the remainder of the assessment based on open risk areas identified in this phase.
Preparation phase	The first step in the assessment methodology defined by • compiling the required information about the simulation and its intended use, and • confirming that the assessment can be accomplished with the information available and meet the requirements of the assessment itself.
Problem entity	An entity, situation, or system selected for analysis.
Procedure	A systematic process for performing an evaluation task of a model.
Prototyping	Successive model releases that reflect incremental levels of fidelity.

Quality assurance	A planned and systematic application of procedures necessary to provide confidence that adequate technical requirements are established, that the model and documentation conform to those technical requirements, and that satisfactory performance is achieved.
Range of accuracy	Demonstrated agreement between the computerized model and problem entity within a specified domain of applicability.
Risk	A measurable probability of consequence associated with a set of conditions or actions.
Simulation	Modeling of systems and their operations using various means of representation.
Validation	Substantiation that a computer model, within its domain of applicability, possesses a satisfactory range of accuracy consistent with the intended application of the model (also called operational validation).
Verification	Substantiation that the computer program implementation of a model is correct and performs as intended (also called software verification).

Acronyms

ANOVA	Analysis of variance
CA	Confidence assessment
C3	Command, control and communications
CASE	Computer-aided software engineering
CM	Configuration management
DFD	Data flow diagram
DOF	Degrees of freedom
DR	Discrepancy report
HWIL	Hardware-in-the-loop
I/O	Input/output
IV&V	Independent verification and validation
MIL	Man-in-the-loop
MMI	Man-machine interface
MOE	Measure of effectiveness
QA	Quality assurance
QP	Quantile-percentile
TEMP	Test and evaluation master plan
TQM	Total quality management

Appendix B

Data descriptions

Table B-1 is the Data item descriptions table, provided to aid in review and use of the procedures. This table provides amplified descriptions of each of the data items referenced in the procedures and the suggested source for each of those items.

Data item	Description of contents	Source
Algorithm references	Descriptions of algorithms	Developer
	Journal references	Developer
	Papers	Developer
Case tools	Names of case tools used	Developer
	Capability descriptions	Developer
Case tools - Generated information	Documentation	Developer
	Traceability	Developer
	CM accounting	Developer
	Specification model	Developer
	Design model	Developer
	Code	Developer
CM procedures	Checklists	Developer
	Reports	Developer
CM tools	Source and executable	Developer
CM tools documentation	User's manual	Developer
	Program guide	Developer
	Vendor's manual	Developer
Code locking data	Procedures used	Developer
	Physical controls	Developer
	Software controls	Developer
Compilers/ assemblers	(as stated)	Vendors
Computer resource utilization statistics	(as stated)	Developer

Table B-1. Data item descriptions.

Data item	Description of contents	Source
Conceptual model description	Elements modeled	Developer
	Fidelity of elements modeled	Developer
	Inputs and range of values	Developer
	Outputs and MOEs	Developer
Conceptual model (validated)	System elements modeled	Developer
	Fidelity of elements modeled	Developer
	Inputs and range of values	Developer
	Outputs and MOEs	Developer
Constants documentation	Location of constants	Developer
	Description of constants	Developer
	Value of constants	Developer
	Use of constants	Developer
	Development of constants	Developer
Data item	Description of contents	Source
Constants memory map	Location of constants	Developer
	Use of constants	Developer
Data flow diagrams	(as stated)	Developer
Data support documentation	Paper studies	Developer
	Statistical analysis	Developer
	Validation reports	Developer
Design documentation	Design specifications	Developer
	Design trade-off decisions	Developer
	Guidance to designers	Developer
	Data structure attributes	Developer
Design methodology	Modeling language description	Developer
	Methodology description	Developer

Table B-1. Data item descriptions (continued).

Data item	Description of contents	Source
Development cycle documentation	Analytical studies	Developer
	Test results	Developer
	Problem reports/DR history	Developer
	Requirements specifications	Developer
	Design specifications	Developer
	Interface documents	Developer
	Interface standards	
	- Interface descriptions	
	- Memoranda of agreement with	
	External agencies	
	- User interface Information	
	- Guide for designers	Developer
	Development plans	
	- Schedules	
	- Standards to use	
	- Management controls to use	
	- Walk-through process description	
	- Description of development team	
	- Automated tools to use	Developer
	Validation plans	
	- Schedules	
	- Standards to use	
	- Management controls to use	
	- Walk-through process description	
	- Types of testing to do	
	- Depth of testing to do	
	- Description of test team	
	- Automated tools to use	Developer
	QA/CM plans	
	- Review process to use	
	- Walk-throughs to attend	
	- Depth of review to do	
	- Breadth of review to do	
	- Description of QA/CM team	
	- Automated controls to use	
	- Automated tools to use	
	- Checklists to employ	Developer
	Design standards	
	- Guidance to designers	Developer
	Coding standards	
	- Programmer's guide	Developer

**Table B-1. Data item descriptions
(continued).**

Data item	Description of contents	Source
Development cycle documentation (continued)	Validation plans - Schedules - Standards to use - Management controls to use - Walk-through process to use - Types of verification to do - Depth of verification to do - Automated tools to use	Developer
	Testing plans/procedures - Schedules - Standards to use - Management controls to use - Walk-through process description - Types of testing to do - Depth of testing to do - Automated tools to use - Test descriptions - Test procedures - Test results - Problems uncovered/DRs written - Description of test team	Developer
	Data collection plan - Source for data - Collection technique description - Descriptions of data needed - Validation checks to perform on Data - Automated tools to use	Developer
	Data generation plan - Generation technique description - Descriptions of data needed - Validation checks to perform on Data - Sources for information to derive Data from - Description of data - Generation team - Automated tools to use	Developer
	Data validation plan - Standards to use - Management controls to use - Walk-through process description - Types of validation to do - Depth of validation to do - Description of validation team - Automated tools to use	Developer

Table B-1. Data item descriptions (continued).

Data item	Description of contents	Source
Development cycle documentation (continued)	Internal security plans - Management controls to use - Walk-through process description - Types of verification to use - Depth of verification to use - Automated tools to use	Developer
Development test reports	Test description	Developer
	Test procedures	Developer
	Test results	Developer
	Problems uncovered/ DRs written	Developer
	Description of test team	Developer
	Test coverage metrics	Developer
	Test sufficiency metrics	Developer
Differences between current model and previous model	(as stated)	Developer
Documentation supporting adherence/ non-adherence to plans and standards	Completed checklists	Developer
	Completed walk-through forms	Developer
	Problem reports/DRs	Developer
	Test reports	Developer
	Process metrics	Developer
		Developer
Expected behavior of entities	(as stated)	User
Data item	Description of contents	Source
Feedback loop information	Real-system feedback process description	Developer
	Descriptions of feedback loops in model	Developer
Graphical tools	Real-time sampling tools	Vendors
	Post-processing data reduction tools	Vendors
	Device map tools	Vendors
	Graphing utilities	Vendors

**Table B-1. Data item descriptions
(continued).**

Data item	Description of contents	Source
Information on entities of interest	(as stated)	User
Input/output specification	Model input description	Developer
	Model output description	Developer
	Range of value information	Developer
	Range of value limitation information	Developer
	User interface information	Developer
Inputs/outputs of other accepted models/ real system	(as stated)	Community experts
Intended use description	Study to support	User
	Ranges of inputs to apply	User
	Needed system elements	User
	Needed MOEs	User
	Special requirements	User
IV&V documentation	Analytical studies	IV&V agency
	Test results	IV&V agency
	Problem reports/DR history	IV&V agency
	Design analysis reports	IV&V agency
	Code analysis reports	IV&V agency
	Requirements analysis reports	IV&V agency
Known/accepted scenario description	Inputs and ranges of values	User
	MOEs	User
	elements	User
Model documentation	Requirements specifications	Developer
	Design specifications	Developer
	Conceptual model description	Developer
	Interface descriptions	Developer
	Functional specification	Developer
	Technical reference	Developer
Model executable code	(as stated)	Developer

Table B-1. Data item descriptions (continued).

Data item	Description of contents	Source
Model input data	Input descriptions	Developer
	Data specifications	Developer
Model interface documents	Interface standards	Developer
	Internal interface descriptions	Developer
Model requirements specification	(as stated)	Developer
Model run inputs /outputs	(as stated)	Developer/ Previous users
Model source code	(as stated)	Developer
Module test documentation	Test descriptions	Developer
	Test procedures	Developer
	Test results	Developer
	Problems uncovered/DRs written	Developer
	Test tool description	Developer
System interface standards	Interface descriptions for relevant models	Developer
Other versions of the model	(as stated)	Developer
Physical experiment data	Sampling data	Varies
Previous model documentation	Analytical studies	Previous dev.
	Test results	Previous dev.
	Problem reports/DR history	Previous dev.
	Problem entity description	Previous dev.
Previous use documentation	Study description	Previous user
	Test results	Previous user
	Software failure documentation	Previous user

Table B-1. Data item descriptions (continued).

Data item	Description of contents	Source
Data item	Description of contents	Source
System behavior information	Variability information Anomalous behaviors noted Performance envelope Characteristics	System developer. System developer System developer System developer
Statistical item information	Distributional forms used Justification for forms used	Developer Developer
Target computer/ language references	User's manuals Programmer references	Vendor Vendor
Test tools	Drivers Stubs	Developer Developer
Trade-off studies	Analytical comparisons Statistical comparisons Functionality comparisons	Developer Developer Developer
Unit test documentation	Test descriptions Test procedures Test results Problems uncovered/DRs written Test tool description	Developer Developer Developer Developer Developer

Unique constructs information	Descriptions of unusual
	  solutions to problems
	Descriptions of "macro"
	  solutions to problems
		
		Developer
		
		Developer

User's manual	(as stated)	Developer

Table B-1. Data item descriptions (concluded).

References

1. R.G. Gados, *Guidelines for Evaluating Simulation Models of the Strategic Defense System*, MITRE Tech. Report 9463, Apr. 1989.
2. Simulation Evaluation Methodology Technical Group (SEMTG), *Guidelines for Evaluation of SDS Simulation Models Used at the National Test Bed*, National Test Bed Joint Program Office, Falcon Air Force Base, Colo., 1988.
3. National Test Bed, *Confidence Methodology Guide*, NTB-237-022-06-02, SDIO, Washington, D.C.
4. U.S. General Accounting Office, *DOD Simulations: Improved Assessment Procedures Would Increase Credibility of Results*, GAO/PEMD-88-3, Washington, D.C., 1987.
5. Computer Professionals for Social Responsibility, Inc., *The SDI's National Test Bed, An Appraisal*, CPSR No. WS-100-5, CPSR, Inc., Palo Alto, Calif., 1988.
6. L. Lee, *The Day the Phones Stopped*, Donald I. Fine, Inc., 1991.
7. O. Balci and R.G. Sargent, "A Bibliography on the Credibility Assessment and Validation of Simulation and Mathematical Models," *Simuletter*, Vol. 15, 1984, pp. 15-27.
8. A.M. Law and D. Kelton, *Simulation Modeling and Analysis,* 2nd ed., McGraw-Hill, New York, 1991.
9. Society for Computer Simulation (SCS) Technical Committee on Model Credibility,"Terminology of Model Credibility," Report of SCS Technical Committee, Simulation, Mar. 1979, pp. 103-104.
10. R.W. Conway, B.M. Johnson, and W.L. Maxwell, "Some Problems of Digital Systems Simulation," *Management Science*, Vol. 6, 1959, pp. 92-110.
11. R.W. Conway, "Some Tactical Problems in Digital Simulation," *Management Science*, Vol. 10, No. 1, 1963, pp. 47-61.
12. T.H. Naylor and J. M. Finger, "Verification of Computer Simulation Models," *Management Science*, Vol. 14, No. 2, Feb. 1967.
13. T.H. Naylor, *Computer Simulation Experiments with Models of Economic Systems*, Wiley, New York, 1971.
14. R.G. Sargent, "A Tutorial on Verification and Validation of Simulation Models," *Proc. 1984 Winter Simulation Conf.*, Society for Computer Simulation.
15. R.G. Sargent, "An Expository on Verification and Validation of Simulation Models," *Proc. 1985 Winter Simulation Conf.*, Society for Computer Simulation.
16. R.G. Sargent, "An Overview of Verification and Validation of Simulation Models," *Proc. 1987 Winter Simulation Conf.*, Society for Computer Simulation.
17. R.G. Sargent, "A Tutorial on Verification and Validation of Simulation Models," *Proc. 1988 Winter Simulation Conf.*, Society for Computer Simulation.
18. R.G. Sargent, "Simulation Model Verification and Validation," *Proc. 1991 Winter Simulation Conf.*, Society for Computer Simulation.
19. S.I. Gass, "Validation and Assessment Issues of Energy Models," *Proc. of a Workshop*, National Bureau of Standards Special Publication 569, U.S. Government Printing Office, Washington, D.C., 1980.
20. S.I. Gass, ed., *Validation and Assessment of Energy Models*, National Bureau of Standards Special Publication 616, U.S. Government Printing Office, Washington, D.C., 1981.
21. S.I. Gass, "Decision-Aiding Models: Validation, Assessment, and Related Issues for Policy Analysis," *Operations Research*, Vol. 21, No. 4, July-Aug. 1983.
22. S.I. Gass, "Decision-Aiding Models: Validation, Assessment, and Related Issues for Policy Analysis," *Operations Research*, Vol. 31, 1983, pp. 603-631.
23. S.I. Gass and B. W. Thompson, "Guidelines for Model Evaluation: An Abridged Version of the U.S. General Accounting Office Exposure Draft," *Operations Research*, Vol. 28, 1980, pp. 431-439.
24. C.A. Fossett et al., "An Assessment Procedure for Simulation Models: A Case Study," *Operations Research*, Vol. 39. No. 5, 1991, pp. 710-723.
25. G. Labovitz, *Total Quality Improvement System*, Organizational Dynamics, Inc., Burlington, Mass., 1989.
26. B. Boehm, "A Spiral Model of Software Development and Enhancement," *Computer*, May 1988, pp. 61-72.

27. L. Schruben, *SIGMA: A Graphical Simulation System*, The Scientific Press, 1991.
28. A.A.B. Pritsker, *Introduction to Simulation and SLAM II,* 3rd ed., Halsted Press, New York, 1986.
29. C.D. Pegden, R.P. Sadowski, and R.E. Shannon, *Introduction to Simulation Using SIMAN*, Systems Modeling Corp., Sewickley, Pa., 1990.
30. CACI Products Company, *COMNET II.5 User's Manual*, La Jolla, Calif., 1988.
31. CACI Products Company, *LANNET II.5 User's Manual*, La Jolla, Calif., 1990.
32. CACI Products Company, *SIMFACTORY II.5 User's Manual*, La Jolla, Calif., 1990.
33. *Gandalf*, Logicon Corporation, San Pedro, Calif.
34. *ANALYZE*, CSTI System Technology Group, Columbia, Md.
35. *LOGISCOPE*, Verilog USA, Alexandria, Va.
36. *McCabe*, McCabe & Associates, Columbia, Md.
37. *ADAMat*, Dynamics Research Corp., Andover, Mass.
38. National Bureau of Standards, "Structure Testing: A Software Methodology Using Cyclomatic Complexity Metric," National Bureau of Standards Special Publication, U.S. Government Printing Office, Washington, D.C.
39. *SQMS*, Software Quality Tools Corp., Westborough, Mass.
40. V. Basili, Tutorial on Models and Metrics for Software Management and Engineering, IEEE Computer Society Press, Los Alamitos, Calif., 1980.
41. Logicon, *A Guidebook to Independent Verification and Validation*, Logicon Corporation, San Pedro, Calif., 1981.
42. MITRE Corporation, *Software Reporting Metrics*, ESD-TR-85-145, MTR 9650, Rev. 2, 1985.
43. Rome Air Development Center, *Specification of Software Quality Attributes*, RADC-TR-85-37, 1985.

Other readings

D.K. Pace, "A Perspective on Simulation Validation," *Proc. 1986 Summer Computer Simulation Conf.*, Society for Computer Simulation.
R.E. Shannon, "Tests for the Verification and Validation of Computer Simulation Models," *Proc. 1981 Winter Simulation Conference*, Society for Computer Simulation.
Aviation Week & Space Technology, "Report Doubts Simulation's Value in Testing SDI System," May 23, 1988, pp. 24.
O. Balci, "Credibility Assessment of Simulation Results: The State of the Art," *Proc. Conf. on Methodology and Validation*, Society for Computer Simulation, 1987, pp.19-25.
J. Banks, D. Gerstein, and S. Searles, "Modeling Processes, Validation, and Verification of Complex Simulations: A Survey," *Proc. Conf. on Methodology and Validation*, Society for Computer Simulation.
S.V. Hoover, .and R.F. Perry, "Validation of Simulation Models: The Weak/Missing Link," *Proc. 1984 Winter Simulation Conf.*, Society for Computer Simulation.
R.L. Van Horn, "Validation," in *The Design of Computer Simulation Experiments*, T.H. Naylor, ed., Duke University Press, N.C., Jan. 1971.
N.A. Kheir et al., "Credibility of Models" (panel discussion), *Simulation*, August 1985.

About the Authors

Peter L. Knepell is a senior scientist for Logicon R&D Associates (RDA) with specialized experience in computer-based prediction models, intelligent systems technology, and technical education. He draws on that experience as a consultant and teacher of process quality improvement tools and techniques. He is particularly interested in improving processes involving development of software, application of simulation tools, automation of factories, and growth of employee skills.

He held positions as the National Test Bed's (NTB) technical director for simulation confidence assessment and manager for studies and analysis. The NTB was established to support simulations and experiments for the Strategic Defense Initiative (SDI). He directed the NTB's first study of strategic defense system design alternatives using a large-scale, event-driven simulation. He later worked on the confidence assessment of several large-scale SDI simulation tools. Those tools ranged from system simulations to interactive gaming tools. Since the simulation tools were being used to support decisions on national defense systems, those assessments received a great deal of attention. His desire to share his experiences in the complex process of directing and conducting a thorough assessment inspired him to co-author this book.

A graduate of the US Air Force Academy, he received his PhD in operations research from Cornell University. As a tenured professor at the Air Force Academy, he directed a vanguard effort to implement microcomputers as instructional aids for teaching mathematics. This included the use of simulations to inspire innovative thinking and group problem solving. He is currently an adjunct professor for the George Washington University and Colorado Technical College. He is world-known for his computer-based courses and workshops in simulation, neural networks, and process quality improvement. His practical approach appeals to a broad audience including academia, industry, government agencies, and professional societies.

Deborah C. Arangno was employed as a senior systems analyst/mathematician for Geodynamics Corporation. She worked at the National Test Bed in the definition, design, development, and implementation of Strategic Defense Initiative concepts. She conducted system design studies, involving both proposed and current simulations. This work required the definition of requirements and the modeling of space system elements and strategies. After that experience, she participated in the assessment of several large-scale simulations. She is well-versed in the many complex assessment techniques applied to gain confidence in a simulation tool.

She previously worked as a mathematician for the Directorate of Astrodynamics in the North American Aerospace Defense Command (NORAD) and the US Space Command. While there, she modeled the dynamics of artificial earth satellites. This included the study of lunar/solar perturbation, and catastrophic decay of satellite orbits. She also assisted in the automation of a large-scale test bed for the NORAD command complex. Prior to that, she served as the project specialist and subject matter expert for the undergraduate space training program for the US Air Force.

She is currently pursuing a PhD in mathematics. She holds an MS in pure mathematics from Emory University and was a magna cum laude graduate of Mercer University with majors in mathematics, physics and Latin. As an honoraria faculty member, she has taught mathematics for the University of Colorado since 1982. She published *A Calculus Roadmap* in 1985 and is currently working on *Modern Algebra — A Handbook of Rudiments*.

Phases and Activities
for the
Confidence Assessment of a Simulation

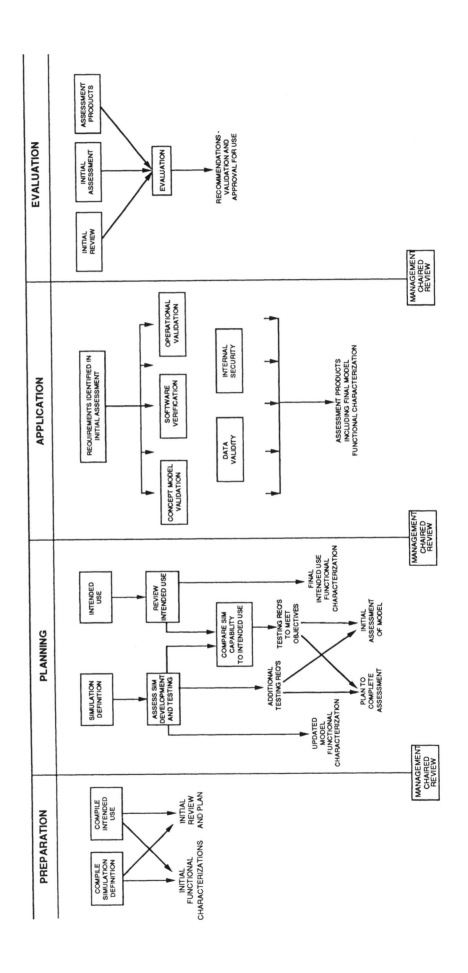

Assessment Activities

SOFTWARE VERIFICATION (left box, upper)

FACE VALIDITY ANALYSIS

HISTORICAL ANALYSIS
- Development History Analysis
  - Requirements
  - Interface Standards
  - Development Plans
  - Verification & Validation Plans
  - QA/CM Plans
  - Design Standards/Specifications
  - Coding Standards
  - Test Plans, Procedures, Results
  - Data Collection Plan & Procedures
  - Data Generation Plan & Procedures
  - Data Validation Plan & Procedures
  - Internal Security Verification Plans
  - Problem Reports/ Discrepancy Report History
  - Studies & Analysis
- IV&V Support Analysis
- Model Derivative Analysis
- Previous Model Use Analysis

INTENDED USE & REQUIREMENTS ANALYSIS
- Criticality Analysis
  - Definition of Criticality Classes
  - Classification of Requirements
  - Definition of Assessment Levels
  - Correlation of Assessment Levels with Criticality Classes
  - Assignment of Assessment Levels to Requirements
- System Analysis
  - Derivation of Submodel Requirements
  - Comparison of Submodel Requirements to Similar Models
  - Traceability Analysis

MODEL CONCEPTS & FIDELITY ANALYSIS
- Modeling Concepts Analysis
- Input/Output Analysis
- Algorithm Analysis

LOGIC TRACE ANALYSIS

(left box, lower)

INSPECTION TESTS
- Delphi Tests
- Turing Tests
- Input/Output Relationship Tests
  - Static Analysis
  - Dynamic Approach
- Event Sequencing Tests
  - Static Analysis
  - Dynamic Approach

DEMONSTRATION TESTS
  - Animation Tests
  - Fixed-Value Tests
  - Simplified Tests
  - Predictive Validation Tests
  - Internal Validity Tests
  - Extreme-Condition Tests
  - N-Version Tests
  - Limited Standards Tests

ANALYTICAL TESTS
  - Predictive Validation
  - Comparison to Test Data
  - Sensitivity Analysis
  - Feed-Back Loop Analysis

SOFTWARE VERIFICATION (right box)

COMPUTERIZED MODEL TRACEABILITY ANALYSIS

CASE AND DESIGN METHODOLGY ADHERENCE ANALYSIS

SOFTWARE METRICS ANALYSIS
- Process Metrics Analysis
  - Development Progress Metrics
  - Testing Progress Metrics
  - Fault Density Metrics
  - Test Coverage Metrics
  - Test Sufficiency Metrics
- Product Metrics Analysis
  - Efficiency Metrics
  - Security Metrics
  - Reliabilty Metrics
  - Correctness Metrics
  - Maintainability Metrics
  - Verifiability Metrics
  - Interoperability Metrics

INTERNAL SOFTWARE TESTING ANALYSIS
- McCabe's Complexity Metric

CODE ANALYSIS
- Program Logic Analysis
  - "Super"-Compiler
  - Automated Flow-Charter
  - Call-Structure Generator
  - Interruptability Analyzer
  - Symbolic Executor
- Program Data Analysis
  - Data Structure Analysis
  - Dimensional Analysis
  - Data Usage Analysis
  - Data Flow Analysis
- Program Interface Analysis
  - Subroutine Calls/Parameter Passing Analysis
  - Global Data Usage Analysis
  - External Interface Analysis
- Program Constraint Analysis
  - Timing Analysis
  - Sizing Analysis

CORRECTNESS PROOFS

DATA VALIDATION

DATA CONSISTENCY ANALYSIS
- Embedded Data Analysis
- Input Data Analysis
- Consistency Analysis

REPRESENTATION OF CONSTANTS ANALYSIS
- Dimensional & Numerical Verification Analysis
- Location & Retrieval Verification Analysis

DISTRIBUTIONAL FORM ANALYSIS
- Graphical Analysis
- Statistical Analysis

INTERNAL SECURITY VERIFICATION

CONFIGURATION CONTROL ANALYSIS
- CM Procedure Analysis
- CM Tool Analysis
- Code Locking Technique Analysis

SECURITY CODE ANALYSIS
- Undocumented Inputs Analysis
- Virus Analysis